Adrian Hamilton

£ $ ¥ £ $ ¥ £ $ ¥ £ $ ¥ £

THE
FINANCIAL
REVOLUTION

The Big Bang Worldwide

VIKING

VIKING

Penguin Books Ltd, Harmondsworth, Middlesex, England
Viking Penguin Inc., 40 West 23rd Street, New York, New York 10010, U.S.A.
Penguin Books Australia Ltd, Ringwood, Victoria, Australia
Penguin Books Canada Limited, 2801 John Street, Markham, Ontario, Canada L3R 1B4
Penguin Books (N.Z.) Ltd, 182–190 Wairau Road, Auckland 10, New Zealand

First published 1986
Copyright © Adrian Hamilton, 1986

Filmset in Monophoto Plantin Light
Printed in Great Britain by
Richard Clay (The Chaucer Press) Ltd,
Bungay, Suffolk

British Library Cataloguing in Publication Data

For my family

CONTENTS

—

PREFACE AND
ACKNOWLEDGEMENTS

———

Money has always been regarded as special: too valuable to be left to the tender mercies of speculators and con men, too important to the wealth of a nation to be left free to run its own course, untrammelled by control. Until today, that is.

The last few years have seen the start of a revolution in finance. There is now a revolution in the way that money is raised by companies, traded on the market and gathered from the saver, a revolution in the way that technology is undermining old market manners and creating new ones in their place and a revolution in the structure of the finance industry itself. Money is ceasing to be a medium of exchange, the direct link between saver and borrower. It has become a commodity in its own right, to be traded across the world over the green screens of dealers as currency, as bonds and as equity. Deregulation is becoming the order of the day. Like the airlines and the oil industry, the steel companies and the computer concerns, the industry that serves finance – the investment and commercial banks, the brokers and the insurance companies – is being forced by deregulation, battered by competition and threatened by technical change into the greatest shake-out in a century or more.

Only money isn't the same as any other commodity, nor is the financial community like any other industry. An effective, and a publicly reliable, system of finance remains the cornerstone of any economy and the means to growth. The balance between effective competition and public responsibility has always been seen differently for finance than for automobiles and supermarkets. The balance may change over time. But balance there must be if the saver is to be encouraged to save, the investor to invest and the borrower to borrow in confidence of the future. Finance is proving to be one of the last areas of activity to be deregulated. It may yet prove the most dangerous, the area where competition becomes most destructive and technology reaches most rapidly beyond the capacity of the practitioners to cope with it.

Any effort to draw such diverse strands together and to touch, however lighly, on the issues concerned, must by its nature be restricted in its depth. In covering so broad an area one is made continuously aware just how limited is one's knowledge and how quickly the pace of change may overtake judgement and description.

One is also made aware of just how much one owes to the time, patience and perceptions of those who do know – the financiers and their supervisors. In a series of visits to research this book in Tokyo, New York, Washington, Singapore and Hong Kong and the financial centres of Europe, I met little but openness, debate and a genuine concern that the forces behind change be understood.

Attempting to acknowledge one's debts is like drawing up the guest list for a wedding – you either invite only a best man or you end up inviting everyone. In my case the best men must include Bernard Asher of the Hongkong and Shanghai Bank, Yoh Kurosawa of the Industrial Bank of Japan, 'Pen' Kent of the Bank of England, Walter Wriston of Citicorp, 'Gus' Ciechanowski of Morgan Guaranty, Ray Richardson of the London School of Economics, Christopher Johnson of Lloyds Bank, Peter Readman of Abercromby, Richard Aspinwall of Chase Manhattan, the staff of the Bank of Japan and Nomura in London and Tokyo, my colleague William Keegan, the *Observer*'s editor, Donald Trelford and, not least, my own bank, Coutts, which financed Charles James Fox's gambling debts, Wilberforce's anti-slavery campaign and now myself through this book. The full guest list should include many dozens more. They won't all agree with what is written: just the opposite, in some cases. They certainly aren't responsible for the mistakes. But they, and the many banks and institutions that opened their doors to me, helped to make the research fascinating and fulfilling.

A. H.
December 1985

PART ONE

£ $ ¥ £ $ ¥ £ $ ¥ £ $ ¥ £

THE REVOLUTION

ONE

THE REVOLUTION

In Japan they call it *zaiteku*, the high technology of finance, the new expertise that the Japanese are determined to master just as they have mastered the high technology of electronics. In the City of London they talk of the 'Big Bang', the moment in autumn 1986 when all the old rules of market trading will be abolished and a new world of financial dealing will be ushered in. In America financiers refer to 'securitization', 'disintermediation' and 'globalization' to summarize a process that is forcing all the major banks to re-examine fundamentally their role in finance and their chances of survival.

'During the last two or three years,' Christopher 'Kit' McMahon, then Deputy Governor of the Bank of England and the man who organized the $8 billion transfer of funds to free the American hostages in Iran, told an audience of high-flying bankers in Switzerland in September 1985, 'international banking – and indeed financial activity more generally – has embarked on changes which are probably as far-reaching as any in its long history. The rapid development of the euromarkets in the 1960s and the subsequent emergence during the 1970s of international banking as we know it are the most recent examples of significant change. But these will, I think, be outstripped in the breadth of their impact, both on financial institutions and on the range of instruments available to borrowers and lenders, by what is going on now.' *

Central bankers do not exaggerate. Their words are taken too seriously by the markets. What is going on now is a revolution: a revolution in the way finance is organized, a revolution in the structure of banks and financial institutions and a revolution in the speed and manner in which money flows around the world.

Wall Street is no longer a 'partnership of partnerships'. Three-quarters of the old firms are gone. Most of the best-known names are now merged with quite different institutions. Salomons, the biggest name in bulk share and bond dealing, is now part of the Phibro commodities group. Lehman Brothers, until recently the oldest

* Speech to the MIMEDE Banking Management Conference, Lausanne, 17 September 1985.

partnership in Wall Street, has recently been merged with Shearson to become part of the giant American Express credit card, travel and insurance conglomerate. Bache has been bought by the Prudential Insurance Company. Dean Witter has been taken over by Sears Roebuck, the world's biggest retail stores concern.

The great money-centre banks of New York, Chicago and San Francisco are struggling to find a different future. Citicorp now aims to be one of the biggest dealers in the world of bonds and paper – and equities as well if U S law will allow. Bankers Trust has now abandoned its retail branch network altogether and plans to turn all its loans into saleable paper. Chase Manhattan is buying out stricken thrifts across America in a bid to become a national bank serving nearly all the major states.

In London the closing of the old rule book of the Stock Exchange has set off the greatest rush to merge, to sell out and to find new partnerships that the City has seen in its three-hundred-year-old history. The merchant banks, which had financed American industry in the last century, have in this century lent to the U S Treasury experts to start new paper markets. Having once prided themselves on their small size and select associations, they have banded with traders and brokers: Warburg is combining with jobbers Akroyd and Smithers and brokers Rowe and Pitman and Mullens; Hambros has taken a stake in Strauss Turnbull; Kleinwort Benson has chosen Grieveson Grant; and Samuel Montagu has picked W. Greenwell. L. Messel, one of the oldest and most prestigious brokers in the City of London, is selling itself out to American Express. Quilter Goodison, the brokers whose senior partner, Sir Nicholas Goodison, is chairman of the Stock Exchange, sold out a holding to the Swedes only to find the share being handed on to the French. Other brokers have gone to Hong Kong, Canada, New Zealand and Austria to find new owners.

In Japan, once the most protected, conservative and nationalistic country of all, American and European securities houses are being allowed to trade in Japanese government debt, to invest pension-fund money and to take seats on the Tokyo Stock Exchange. A market in futures and options, instruments of which no Japanese financial group had any experience a few years ago, has actually been started in Tokyo. An off-shore banking facility, which was universally opposed by the whole government when first mooted five years ago, has now been approved in principle and could start by 1987–8.

Wherever you now go in the industrialized world, and in many parts of the world that are only just beginning to industrialize, the story is the same: the barriers are coming down, both within markets and between them.

For generations (centuries in the case of many of the great financial capitals of the world) the principles guiding the financial markets have been specialization and national control. The Chicago commodity markets concentrated on futures in pork bellies and other local produce, just as the Sydney Exchange dealt mainly with 'greasy wool' and the Baltic Exchange in London developed the market for freight rates by sea. Local co-operative banks in Japan and Europe collected local savings; building societies in the UK and savings and loans in the US specialized in home loans; US retail banks made the mainstay of their business local lending; the big commercial banks, especially in the USA, went in for business lending; and the investment banks and merchant banks made their money from advising clients on fund-raising and from underwriting their debt. Markets for short-term, medium-term and long-term funds were separated, and the whole structure was traditionally buttressed by central authorities that controlled interest rates and currency movements to manage the economy better, keep a hold on the domestic money supply and ensure stability and solidity in the most crucial and most vulnerable area of the economy.

Now all this is changing, and changing far faster than anyone would have thought conceivable even a few years ago. Exchange controls are almost everywhere being dismantled because they were becoming a less and less effective means of controlling the value of a currency and the direction of investment funds. The Treasuries and central banks of the USA and Europe – and those of Japan will soon – no longer directly control interest rates or tell the thrifts and banks what they can charge. Gyrating exchange rates, unpredictable inflation and unbalanced trade have caused investors to seek, and the financial industry to provide, more and more flexible instruments of savings, from interest-bearing chequing (current) accounts and variable-interest-rate mortgages to the whole panoply of options, futures and bonds. There is less and less distinction between types of borrowing and lending, between short-term and long-term, between national and international. There are fewer and fewer means, therefore, for governments or central banks to preserve the old separations between them. And, as the barriers come down, so the brokerage houses, the banks and the investment houses are pushing voraciously into each other's territories and out into the newly liberalized markets around the globe.

The Chicago markets are now doing infinitely more business by trading futures on financial instruments such as Treasury bills, shares, price indices and currencies than ever they did on agricultural commodities. Technology is making it possible for a customer to deal in stocks and shares and to draw out money from his account with the aid of a home computer and without ever going near a bank. It is also making it increasingly possible for traders to deal along wires totally divorced from the old exchange floors and for the exchanges themselves to link up together to allow dealing to follow the sun around the globe. Already the Chicago Mercantile Exchange has joined with Singapore in a single twenty-four-hour dealing day. Already the fastest growing exchange in the world is not an exchange in the old-fashioned sense at all. It is an electronic network of dealing on screens in the USA: NASDAQ, the National Association of Securities Dealers Automated Quotations, the third largest stock market in the world.

The groups at the head of this revolution are ceasing to talk of national markets and local conditions. Instead they are talking of international markets, of round-the-clock dealing and the issuing of global equity and debt. The old divisions between particular institutions charged with special tasks and particular markets for the varying types of financial instruments are collapsing under pressure from high-technology communication and global money flows. The new world is, according to the vision of its proponents, a world of 'financial supermarkets' able to provide their customers with everything from a house and insurance to a portfolio of shares; and of 'capital-market' groups able to deal with anything from options on the future level of the stock-exchange index to commercial paper borrowings that can be converted from debt to equity and from currency to currency and even swapped entirely with the borrowings of an unrelated company on the other side of the world at the push of a computer button.

Walter Wriston, the former chairman of Citicorp, talks of a 'quantum leap in the efficient channelling of capital', a change that is making everything before it redundant. John Gutfreund, the gritty trader who heads Salomon, Inc., has declared, 'We find ourselves torn asunder from a past it is useless to yearn for,' and talks of an age of 'total relativity', in which all markets in every part of the globe respond instantly to each other. Charles Sanford, the youthful radical who is president of Bankers Trust, no longer talks of 'banks' and 'bonds' and 'notes' and 'loans' but of financial agents and simple 'IOUs'. And he has proved the force of his words by packaging all the loans made by the bank into groups of paper that can be marked like any other bond or security.

By the end of the 1980s, perhaps much earlier, the most active banks and dealers foresee a world centred on the three great financial centres of New York, London and Tokyo, in which national barriers do not exist and in which the major financial houses conduct a twenty-four-hour operation, handing on their 'books' from centre to centre continuously with the sun. Investors and borrowers will decide to buy or to borrow in their domestic market or in Asia or Europe simply on the basis of which offers the highest yield. There will no longer be clear dividing lines between raising money for corporations through commercial paper or through share issues, through long-term or through short-term instruments, depending on regulation and requirement. Instead debt will become interchangeable, an endless stream flowing through a whole range of instruments that can be converted from one currency to another and from one type of paper to another without difficulty. No longer will you have to go to a bank to deposit your money, a building society (in Britain) to buy your house or a broker to invest your savings. In their stead will be a two-decked structure. At the bottom will be innumerable small boutiques. At the top will be international financial groupings, virtually indistinguishable in their structures and in their nationalities, that will handle wholesale funds for corporations and for the very rich and a mass of small boutiques charging fees to handle the smaller customer. The world of finance will have become one, an international capital market dominated by a few dozen big players, swamping any national effort to confine it.

It is a vision that appals some, who fear that a world of international money revolving at ever greater velocity will become ever more volatile and more dangerous. After all, whatever the faults of control and regulation, they have seemed essential where money has been concerned. And they have proved effective only when the flows of people's savings and borrowings can be kept within national markets and channelled through distinct and separate institutions. As long as savings and loans in the USA or building societies in Britain knew that their job was to lend long-term on housing and borrow short-term on safe savings, and as long as the investment houses supporting share issues were separate from those advising clients on which shares to buy, and as long as banks were concerned with lending money put on deposit by savers and not with speculative dealing in markets, then the chances that the system would go awry were that much less.

There is a good deal of concern too about the breakdown of barriers between different financial markets. While there was some separation between long- and short-term lending, between equity and debt, there was some chance of preventing the damage in any one sector from spreading to the financial system as a whole. That was, after all, a primary aim in preserving the divisions. In today's extraordinary world of new products, in which short-term borrowing can be automatically rolled over to become medium-term financing, in which bonds can be readily converted to equity and in which interest can be separated from principal – the world, in other words, of options, swaps, convertibles, revolving underwriting facilities and hybrids – no one can be quite certain how to assess risk and where to place it.

Nor is the dream of finance without barriers by any means accepted even by those within the financial institutions that are most directly benefiting from it. There is many a partner in merchant banks and brokerage houses who regrets the passing of the old ways, not just out of nostalgia but out of the profound belief that specialist institutions served the client's needs best and best insured the probity with which his needs were met. Whatever the faults of traditional banking and financial markets, they did rest on the direct relationship between the client and the institution. A local bank lent to the farmer in Ohio or to the oil driller in Texas because the bank manager knew him and could size up the risk. A money-centre bank lent to companies whose problems it knew because it also managed the company's cash balances and cleared its cheques. Companies went to investment houses to issue shares because they knew that they would get a specialist service. A small saver might go to a thrift in the USA, a co-operative in Japan or a 'landbank' in Europe because it was a local enterprise and he could feel part of it.

A new era in which money is no longer an obvious means of saving and lending but a commodity in its own right, dealt with on international exchanges and speculated in by international financial giants, is all very dramatic, but in the end it cannot replace those relationships. After today's froth is over, say the conservatives, it will be the small that is beautiful in finance, just as in other service industries.

The trouble is that the changes now under way in the financial field are happening quickly and on a broad scale, Although the general trend towards deregulation and internationalization can be traced back to the 1970s – to the development of the eurocurrency markets in Europe, the ending of brokerage commissions on Wall Street on

'May Day' 1975, and the dismantling of foreign-exchange controls in the U S A in the mid-1970s – the acceleration of change and its spread to other countries is only just beginning. Government-imposed ceilings on interest rates ended formally in the U S A only as late as January 1983, while the first major regulatory breaches of the rules governing the ability of financial institutions to start diversifying into other fields arrived only with the Garn–St Germain Depository Institutions Act of 1982 and the Supreme Court decision on regional banking in 1985.

The 'Big Bang' in London, when set commission rates on bond and share transactions will be abolished, the old distinctions between jobbers and brokers discarded and the Stock Exchange opened up to full ownership of member firms by outside institutions, will not occur, in principle, until the autumn of 1986. All the shuffling to find new partners, the mergers and take-overs, the movement of complete teams of specialists and the astonishing payments made to buy out partnerships that have had London agog in the two years up to 1986 – all these have developed in anticipation of the moment. What the new world will mean, who will survive and who will fail, which markets will grow in international interest and which will falter: these questions will be answered only from experience.

Similarly, Japanese deregulation under the U S–Japanese Yen–Dollar Committee did not start until the summer of 1984. Most of the basic measures – the liberalization of domestic interest rates, the establishment of short-term money markets, the encouragement of yen-denominated international loans and commercial paper – are not due to take real effect until 1986–8. It is still an open question how far the Japanese authorities really intend to take liberalization and how sincere they are in their promises, since actual experience is yet to come.

For other countries, such as Sweden, Germany, Australia and even Switzerland, changes to the stock market, the introduction of new futures and options exchanges and the ending of traditional underwriting cartels on local currency issues are only just starting in 1986. Scandinavia and Australia made the first moves towards opening up their local banking markets to foreign banks as late as 1985 (indeed, it was only then that the U K allowed the first foreign bank, Citicorp, to join the select group of clearing banks). It would be a foolish banker who thought that most nations were ready to see really open competition on their home turf of retail banking. It would be equally naïve to believe that financial authorities are yet ready to give open licence to their pension funds and insurance companies to invest freely abroad. Exchange controls have gone, or are going, in almost every major industrial nation with the exception of France. But controls over the proportion of funds that can be invested abroad, under either direct rules or informal guidance, will persist in most countries for a long time.

The sudden enthusiasm for financial liberalization has not come about merely as an act of the political will of finance ministers. The history of financial controls has tended to be one of late reaction. Governments have usually abolished them when events have made them obsolete in any case and have introduced them (as in the recession years of the 1920s and 1930s) when scandals and collapses have made the retrospective need for bolting the stable door apparent to all. Current deregulation around the globe is no exception. The Garn–St Germain Financial Institutions Act of 1982 was finally passed in the USA because competition, interest-rate movements and technology made it impossible to observe the old conventions concerning what thrifts and others could or could not do. Exchange control has been abolished in most countries because when a currency did come under pressure, as it did for the dollar and sterling at different times during the 1970s, it became increasingly difficult to stop the money pouring out, with or without controls.

The cause and effect of financial regulation is the subject of endless debate. Which is the chicken and which the egg in international or domestic money flows? The biggest single factor in finance may well be taxation rather than regulation. It is the tax structure that has pushed such an overbalanced proportion of US investment into real estate, encouraged the remorseless growth of institutional saving through pensions and insurances in Europe and America, conserved the unique position of the Post Office in the Japanese banking system and effectively promoted, as a means of tax avoidance, the growth of off-shore banking centres in London, Luxembourg, the Cayman Islands and Singapore. Without regulations in the USA to control domestic interest rates (Regulation Q) and to force banks to hold non-interest-bearing reserves in the USA, the market in eurodollars (the market for dollar deposits and loans outside the USA) might never have taken off. Without the imposition in 1963 of the Interest Equalization Tax (IET) on foreign issues in America, it would certainly never have exploded in the way that it did in Europe. 'I was sitting in my office,' says one of London's biggest commercial lawyers, 'when somebody stuck his head round the door and asked me if I knew anything about Interest Equalization Tax. The next thing I knew, a proposed issue for the City of Oslo landed on my desk, already half-prepared for the American market, complete with huge maps of Europe and a large arrow showing where Oslo was.'

As it turned out, the eurodollar market was the perhaps the most important international financial development of the 1960s, growing, within a decade, from a market worth a few hundred million dollars and handling issues of between $2 million and $5 million each in the mid-1960s to a market worth several hundred billion dollars a year and handling issues of between $200 million and $500 million a time. Now it is worth $300 billion a year, and it is a market whose development can be charted very much in terms of reaction to regulation within the domestic financial systems of the USA, Europe and Japan.

In those terms finance is just part, if perhaps the most important part, of the process of deregulation going on throughout Western economies. Airlines, the gas and oil industries, even agriculture, have all been the subject of deregulation in the mid-1980s and, for similar reasons, technology, the restructuring of traditional manufacturing industry, the reaction against what is regarded as the excessive role of government and the mounting size of public debt in the major industrial nations. The world has become smaller as technology has speeded up communications and forced the internationalization of companies. But it has also become more uncertain, more volatile in its shifts and searches for a return to sustained growth. Just as the electronic or chemical industries now refer to the world as divided into regions – America, Europe and Asia – so finance is now tending in the same direction. Just as even the newer microchip industries are going through a phase of shake-out and restructuring, so are the banks and financial institutions.

Only finance is not like any other industry. Because it so directly affects both the savings and well-being of individuals and confidence in the commercial system as a whole, it has always been regulated in a special way. Because it lies at the heart of economic management – control over financial flows, so the belief goes, assists control of inflation, growth and the direction of the economy – it has always been treated as a special field of government interest and public concern. In one sense, it has always been relatively free, and that is on the international side. The requirements of trade finance have long produced specialist financial institutions, the merchant banks of Europe and the metals, shipping, fur and commodities markets of the major trading cities. But side by side with these have been domestic markets and institutions, tightly controlled because they have been charged with the security of people's savings, given national or local protection because the flow of funds in the economy and the raising of public-sector debt have been too important to be allowed to fall into the hands of foreigners and subject to a pendulum swing of regulation as economic growth has brought with it freer markets and recession has brought with it scandal and collapses.

During the first couple of decades after the war the domestic financial structure of most countries remained surprisingly similar to the pre-war pattern. The changes occurred on the international side of the picture as American finance and American trade came to dominate the globe. The story of the first generation in international finance after the war was, indeed, largely the story of the dollar as American companies, followed by American banks, expanded internationally and as American aid and funds financed post-war reconstruction. The effect of this in making the dollar an international trade and speculative currency was not one that the USA particularly liked. But efforts to control the use of the dollar led only to an accelerated development of both the eurocurrency markets outside the domestic system and an increasingly sophisticated market for long-term, fixed-interest debt, based in London and dominated by a steadily rising and broadening group of investment houses and banks. It is doubtful, however, whether the development of the eurocurrency markets profoundly affected methods of carrying out financial business at home. All but a limited number of international companies continued to raise money on the stock exchanges of their home country if they wanted equity finance and either fixed-rate bonds or, in Europe, bank borrowing if they wanted debt finance. Customers continued to go to thrifts or building societies for housing finance and to deposit most of their money at local banks for their general financial needs.

The first major shock to the old system came with the related combination of the oil crisis of 1973, the move from fixed- to floating-rate currencies at the same time and the emergence during the 1970s of progressively more volatile rates of inflation in the Western world. The oil shock produced a dramatic shift in wealth between the major consuming countries of the industrialized world and the major oil-producing countries of the Middle East. As Walter Wriston likes to record, he was called in by John Connally, the US Treasurer, to be asked the blunt question, 'Can the financial system manage?' Wriston answered yes, the banks could effectively manage a rebalancing of financial flows. And he proved right.

He proved right, however, only because the oil producers, being relatively unsophisticated in finance, preferred to use the banks as the natural channel for their surplus funds. The first result of this 'intermediation', as it is called, was the explosion in international banking and syndicated loans (or lending by groups of banks) of the 1970s. The subsequent debt crisis among Third World borrowers has been in the headlines ever since. But, whatever the eventual problems it threw up, this 'recycling' did provide a remarkably effective short-term answer to the problem of a quadrupling of oil prices that each year transferred an extra $150 billion to the coffers of the Organization of Petroleum Exporting Countries (OPEC) from 1974 onwards.

It also forced the development of a truly international banking industry. Before the energy crisis international banks were largely specialist banks or branches dealing in trade, or American, British, Japanese or other banks serving their domestic customers abroad. The bountiful pool of recycled OPEC funds now attracted banks from every part of the globe that wished to participate in borrowing and lending outside their home ground. Through the 1970s the proportion of loans and borrowing by banks in the Organization for Economic Co-operation and Development (OECD) area undertaken abroad doubled, from around 12 per cent to nearly 25 per cent. In the case of individual countries such as Switzerland, Belgium and the UK foreign business climbed to well over half of all their loans or 'assets', as they are described on bank-balance sheets. In the case of the USA the proportion of foreign assets went up even faster, from 2.5 per cent to over 15 per cent within that decade, with the money-centre banks of New York recording figures nearer 50 per cent. International banking had arrived with what has since proved to be a bang.

At the same time the style of both domestic and international finance was profoundly altered by the surge in inflation rates in industrial countries during the second half of the 1970s. Abruptly the traditions of fixed-interest borrowing and bonds that had served the financial markets for centuries were overthrown; financial institutions at home and abroad looked to fund long-term debt through short-term variable-rate borrowing and, as far as possible, to lend at rates that would move with general interest rates.

Floating-rate notes (FRNs) were developed on the euromarkets; syndicated loans switched from fixed-rate terms to interest rates based on the moving London interbank offered rate (LIBOR); banks themselves turned more of their attention to the way in which they funded their business, the 'liability' side of their balance sheet, and issued their own short-term paper as Certificates of Deposit (CDs), which could be traded in the markets. Thrifts, building societies and banks tried to lend more on variable-rate interest for housing. Securities houses, followed by the banks, developed funds based on the money markets. And the whole process was both intensified and made more volatile by the abolition of exchange controls in the major countries, making it progressively more difficult to isolate interest-rate developments abroad from the deposit-rate structure at home.

The revolution now under way is both an extension of these trends of the 1970s and a departure from them. It is a departure in the sense that the great boom in syndicated international lending has now ended – many think for a generation at least – caught in the mire of the sovereign debt crisis of Latin America. The flows of money are no longer being recycled from rich to poor and from the developed to the developing world. They are being kept within the Western system by the reluctance of banks to increase their exposure to further lending to the Third World. Sovereign debt as such has not stopped, but it is the industrial countries that are borrowing, not the Third World.

Nor is the present flow passing through the banks or from the oil producers. The fall in oil prices as a result of the surpluses of the 1980s has turned a number of key oil creditors into major debtors, most notably Venezuela, Mexico and Nigeria. Even Saudi Arabia, once the biggest and richest oil exporter of them all, was by 1985 having to recall some of the $120 billion in foreign reserves that it had built up during the heady days of the 1970s. The oil that fuelled the internationalization of banks in the 1970s has become a drag that is pulling them down in the 1980s.

In place of flow of funds from oil producer to Third World by way of the banks has come a quite different flow, the flow of investment funds from Japan to America. The USA, which for two generations after the war was the creditor of the world, just as Britain had been in the nineteenth century, is now fast becoming the biggest debtor of them all. By the end of 1985 the USA had turned from a net exporter of capital to a net importer of capital with a balance-of-payments deficit running at $100 billion a year and a budget deficit that was headed for $200 billion, a debt that, unchecked, would make it the largest sovereign borrower in the world by the 1990s.

Financing this debt are European investors, American banks bringing funds invested abroad back to the USA and, above all,

Japan, which in 1985 was buying over $30 billion of dollar bonds annually and owned some $40 billion of US government debt. This development is not merely changing the balance of financial power in the world; it is also altering the way in which money flows. The oil exporters deposited their money in banks. The Japanese institutional investors are investing directly in US Treasury bonds as well as in the commercial bond market and international equities. Japanese banks, securities houses and financial institutions, from being background participants in syndicated eurocurrency loans, are emerging as giant players in their own right. And they are helping a financial world move from traditional syndicated loans to growing global markets for bonds and for equities, fundamentally altering the nature of the international financial game.*

At the same time, what is developing internationally is also switching rapidly back to the domestic markets. Money, as regulators have ruefully learned, not only talks; it acts. Given the glimmer of gain, it can move, like water, through the smallest crack and become a flood. Once one part of the regulatory framework is dismantled, therefore, it becomes almost impossible to maintain the other parts.

When the leading industrial nations eased exchange controls, they also made it impossible to sustain domestic controls on interest rates for long, still less when inflation was causing investors to become increasingly careful in their approach to savings. If they did not get a good enough rate of return at home, then they would send their money abroad. And once controls on interest rates had to be eased in the domestic markets, as they were most classically in the USA in the early 1980s, then it became impossible to maintain rules about what each individual institution in the market could do. Also once the banks and financial institutions moved into each other's territory in an effort to keep the depositors' custom, then the whole structure of the industry began to disintegrate. The blurring of distinctions between banks, securities houses and other financial institutions, the displacement of banks as the main conduit for depositing and borrowing money (the process of 'disintermediation', as it is inelegantly termed), the erosion of the distinction between debt and equity

* Some idea of the growing importance of the Japanese in international finance can be seen from a study of the interbank market by the Bank of International Settlements (BIS), published in the summer of 1985. The study showed that in 1984 the Japanese provided nearly as many funds to non-banks as the USA, at $154 billion; the next largest group was the British banks, providing less than half that at $63 billion. As net suppliers of funds to non-banks (loans minus deposits made with them by non-banks) the Japanese banks were actually four times as large as those of the USA at $113 billion. Other analyses suggest that as much as half the interbank market in London is now supplied by Japanese banks.

through the development of tradeable paper ('securitization', as it is termed), the 'globalization' of markets – all these trends are becoming as real in the domestic marketplace as they are in the international sphere. For centuries banking and finance have been pursued at a local level with scant regard to changes or movements in the world scene. The problems of a falling currency, foreign interest rates and big-bank trends in automation could all be ignored as beyond the concern of the ordinary investor, the ordinary company with a loan or the householder with a mortgage. No longer.

The most immediate impact of this revolution is clearly on the industry itself, the players in the market. For them this has so far been a story largely of competitive forces and opportunities for growth. The mergers and failures that followed the ending of commission scales in Wall Street on May Day 1975, the regrouping of brokers, jobbers and merchant banks that has been preceding the removal of the commission structure in London towards the end of 1986, the readjustment of the position of long-term credit banks and of the commercial and regional banks that is following the ending of interest-rate controls in Japan, the stream of failures and mergers among American thrifts in 1984–6: these are the eruptions of financial change gathering pace. And, inevitably, they are the major focus of attention within the industry itself.

Banks are being forced to decide how far to become dealers in the wholesale paper markets of the world and how far to concentrate on their traditional strengths as retailers collecting and lending money in a domestic market. At one end they must compete with the investment banks and the brokerage houses, which have always been salesmen and dealers. At the other end they must compete with department stores and even automobile companies with an eager interest in developing the consumer-credit side of their business. Even – most of all, some would argue – their corporate clients are deserting them as they find it cheaper to borrow by issuing their own paper in the market than by going to a bank and more effective to invest their cash surpluses directly on the money markets rather than placing them on deposit with a bank.

Equally, investment houses and brokers have now to decide how far to challenge the world as global players in international markets and how far to stick to offering specialist services to clients on an advisory basis. For British merchant banks and brokers, perhaps more than for any other institutions in the world, it is now a question of independence and survival. Either they form larger groups, or even sell themselves out altogether, in order to gain the capital base that will enable them to continue playing in the much higher-stake game that is the global market today or they remain small and specialist, and risk irrelevance. The formation and reformation of new groupings in the City of London, the obscene sums being paid to individuals and sometimes whole teams to desert their firm for another, sometimes within months of a previous change, the despair of traditionalists in London at new standards and new aggressions: these are not just reflections of a sudden seizure of collective greed. They have the tinge of life-or-death decisions, the tension of the move that must be right, for the moment comes only once in a lifetime.

When economists and consultants talk dramatically of 40 per cent of the U S A's thrifts disappearing by the end of the decade, of only half the numbers of new groups in London surviving beyond the end of the decade, of the numbers of building societies in Britain or the local co-operatives in Japan being cut by a third or more, they are not making alarmist prophecies. They are talking of logical directions in trends that are already apparent. To the stock exchange in New York or London, to the bank in Chicago or Geneva, these questions are what matter: Is it my institution that survives or the next one? Does the business come through my market or another's? If some two hundred banks and other institutions can claim international size and competitiveness and perhaps only thirty to fifty can truly thrive in the top league, that is still an abstraction. The real issue is whether the Bank of America can succeed in turning itself round, whether Warburg of London has made a disastrous error or anticipated a strategic triumph in going for the big time in a new group, whether it is the Industrial Bank of Japan or the Long-Term Credit Bank that comes out on top in the diversification of the long-term credit banks in Japan.

Just as it is with institutions, so, on a far grander geopolitical scale, is it a competition of who wins among markets and among financial centres. When the eurocurrency markets started in the 1960s there was at least a chance that they could have been centred on Paris rather than London. It was the French inability to refrain from regulation as much as the talents of the British banks that finally ensured that London came out on top. So, when the Stock Exchange in London first approached the question of ending commissions in 1982, uppermost in the minds of officials and some of the merchant banks was the very real issue of whether the City could maintain its position as the natural financial capital of Europe against the bigger investment pools and greater economic muscle of Germany or even Switzerland.

When Hong Kong's role as the Asian international banking centre seemed to be slipping during the uncertainties of the negotiations with China in 1982–3 Singapore and Sydney were quick to stake their claims as substitutes. When the Chicago Mercantile Exchange teamed up with Singapore in 1984 to provide round-the-globe trading in financial futures the move was aimed as much at stealing a march on the Chicago Board of Trade as at seeking international links for their own sake.

Even if the financial centres of the industrial world are not vying for premier position in international trading, they are now finding it increasingly difficult not to fall into line with the general trend of liberalization, if only for fear of losing their attractiveness to capital – their own or others'. Centres from Stockholm to Sydney that would never have dreamed of opening their doors to foreign banks in the early 1980s are embracing change with fervour in the mid-1980s. If capital is free to move about the world at will, it does not pay to keep obstacles in its way on your landing patch. This revolution seems irresistible.

What people in the industry, and their supervisors, have asked themselves less often is what benefits the revolution is bringing to the final user. Comment and criticism have inevitably concentrated on the safety aspect of this wild new game of international dealing, in which new products are introduced by the day, the stakes are growing higher by the month and the major players seem determined to keep in the game whatever the cost. It is bound to end in tears for some, possibly for many. It is bound to end in scandal. And it contains the seeds of a rapidly spreading crisis when boom will give way to bust, as it inevitably does in the economic cycle. These are supervisory problems, and very real ones. They are also ethical problems in a world in which many quite genuinely believe that the end of tradition means the end of standards in the City of London, Tokyo, Frankfurt and Geneva.

The benefits are there. Many of the changes in the markets have been at the direct behest of the large users of finance: the big corporations, the pension funds and the insurance companies. And these have seen results in cheaper borrowing for corporations and higher and more flexible rates of return for institutional investment than would otherwise have occurred. Competition and deregulation have undoubtedly made finance more efficient and cheaper, even for the small depositor. The electronics that make possible the automatic transfer of funds and withdrawal facilities of modern banking are also the electronics that help to make it possible for depositors to gain a far more realistic rate of return on their money held in the bank. Money-management accounts, high-interest deposit accounts and credit-card facilities are already revolutionizing retail banking. Competition will ensure that they continue to improve. There is no technical reason why individuals or small companies, using home computers, cannot manage their funds, or have them managed, as easily as a large corporation. It is already happening in Scandinavia, led by the Finns and the Swedes. The U S A has perhaps been slower to start but is already catching up.

The question now is whether the new world is safer than the old and whether it is as conducive to economic welfare. The old structures directed funds from savings into employment and housing remarkably effectively, whatever the shortcomings in efficiency of old-style compartmentalized finance. The new world of finance is efficient. It has brought considerable advantages to the investor and the investing institution. What we have still to see is whether it will help to create jobs, to create growth and to develop trade.

TWO

THE TECHNOLOGY

'The information standard has replaced the gold standard as the basis of world finance,' declares Walter Wriston. And in a series of speeches in recent years he has gone on to paint his vision of a new world without barriers.

'The iron laws of the gold standard,' he said in one, 'and later the gold exchange standard have been replaced by new laws which are just as inflexible, but have attracted considerably less attention. The twenty-first-century scientists working with the seventeenth-century economists and twentieth-century politicians have created a world that the American Wendell Wilkie wrote about in the 1940s but never lived to see. These new laws are not made by economists and politicians but flow out of the expansion of the electromagnetic spectrum up to 300 gigahertz. In its simplest terms, this scientific advance in the art of communication has created trouble for governments on all the world's continents.

'It is also fair to say it has created an entirely new system of world finance based on the incredibly rapid flow of information round the world. I would argue that what one might call the information standard has replaced the gold standard and indeed even the system invented at Bretton Woods.'

In place of these systems based on government-established rules, communications now enable and ensure that money moves any-where around the globe in answer to the latest information or mis-information. Governments can no longer get away with debasing the coinage or controlling the flow of capital. There now exists a 'new order, a global marketplace for ideas, money, goods and services that knows no national boundaries'.

As the architect of Citicorp's rise to become *the* global and universal bank, as the best-known international banker of the last decade and the man who led the internationalization of banking through sover-eign loans on the argument that 'countries would never go broke', Walter Wriston is the financier who has always seen change in its grandest terms and has proved it in what he has done at his own bank. Citicorp owns its own satellite transmitter-receivers, is one of the few banks in the world to run on its own a system of automatic teller machines (A T Ms) and the only one to have organized an entire section of its business around the sale and management of information.

Walter Wriston was one of the first to redefine the role of the bank as that of the 'financial services company'. From early on in his fourteen-year reign as chairman of Citicorp (1970–84) he defined his competition as American Express, Merrill Lynch and Sears Roebuck. After a difficult start, when he attempted to introduce to the corporation a matrix system of management under which managers reported both to regional bosses and to international heads of particular business streams, he reorganized Citicorp in the late 1970s around three basic worldwide businesses, the 'three Is'. These were, and are, the 'institution bank', handling relations around the world with governments, other banks and large corporations; the 'individual bank', taking care of consumer accounts on a worldwide basis; and the 'investment bank', the capital markets group organized on the lines of a merchant bank.

In this plan technology became not just the symbol of a changing marketplace but also the means of effecting growth in the retail banking area. Contrary to his public reputation largely as the promoter of international lending, Wriston's contribution to Citicorp was most emphatic in its drive to become a major provider of consumer finance within the U S A. Handicapped by the 1927 McFadden Act prohibiting interstate banking, and aware that he needed a cost advantage to give Citicorp a competitive edge in an overbanked market, Wriston saw technology as the vehicle for bringing a full range of services to consumers across the U S A at low cost and without breaching the law. In the mid- to late 1970s, using as the manager John Reed, his protégé and now his successor as chairman, Wriston and the bank poured tens of millions of dollars into developing its own A T M network, investing in central computing facilities to process information and going out to the customer by post, by credit card and by telephone. 'Bricks and mortar didn't interest me, communications did,' he recalls. During his time as chairman there was virtually no aspect of communications and processing technology in which Citicorp did not become involved, and very few that it did not attempt to develop on its own, in the drive to make Citicorp America's premier retail bank.

As a strategy it had its limitations. Wriston's insistence that the bank be first in the field and do things itself rather than contract out its technology brought large losses and a number of false starts in the early years. At one point the bank's whole cheque-processing capacity was brought to a halt for a week, and it was only the determination of the top that saved Reed and what one employee called 'an experi- menter's playpen'. A project to produce Citicorp's own personal computer had to be abandoned. Its insistence on using its own proprietary ATM system limited its growth because of its incompatibility with other systems where Citicorp was not so well represented.

However, over the years Wriston not only kept up with the strategy but continually developed it. In the 1980s he added two new 'Is' to the corporation, 'insurance' and 'information', and he added three new names to the bank's major competitors for the 1990s: Reuters, AT&T and IBM. 'Information about money has become almost as important as money itself,' he declares. 'The competitive advantage of the banks used to be that they knew more about their customers than anyone else. Now, with the explosion of technology, that know- ledge can be had at the push of a button. The guy with the competitive advantage is the one with the best technology – Reuters with their dealing screens or IBM with their computers. Information is a busi- ness in itself.

'It's also something that has made control impossible. Kings and princes can no longer hide what they're doing, nor can you get customers to accept prices in one place when they know there's a better deal elsewhere. It's a whole new world. When Lincoln made his Gettysburg Address, it was heard by two hundred people. Now it would be heard by 60 million.'*

Wriston's vision of a world of unfettered movement of capital and ideas is not one that is shared throughout the industry. There are many who doubt that the 'all-singing, all-dancing' bank is what the customer wants, however good the technology of delivery. There are a number who fear precisely the lack of control and the volatility of markets that Wriston sometimes seems to welcome and who point to sovereign debt as the classic example of what goes wrong when banks

---

* Remarks in an interview with the author, November 1985. See also Wriston's speeches on his retirement, 'The City of Tomorrow – Today', a speech to financial analysts in New York in March 1984, and at the City of London in June 1984. Wriston, who has always hung in his office a contemporary portrait of Sir Thomas Gresham, the Elizabethan financier who founded the Royal Exchange in London, helped to finance the early settlements in North America and coined Gresham's Law (that bad money drives out good), emphasized his own belief in the future importance of information by becoming a director of Reuters in 1984.

and other financial concerns are left free to seek growth without restraint.

But on one point all would agree: the world of finance has been fundamentally changed by technology. More than in any other area of activity, the growth of international communications, the development of the data-processing capability of the big computer and the personal desk-top facility and the arrival of the day of the wired society have revolutionized the way in which finance is transacted.

For the man on the other side of the bank counter it has been a matter of substituting computer printout for paper and the automatic teller in the wall for the bank clerk facing him behind a grille. Indeed, this is largely how the banks saw it in the beginning. Bought on an increasing scale by banks around the world in the early 1960s, mainframe computers were used principally in head offices to ease the paperwork load, keeping the accounts of clients, calculating interest rates and charges and providing a central services to branches. Like retail groups, insurance companies, oil companies and the utilities, banks saw computing as a means of improving the efficiency of accounting and, in the case of the relatively underbanked European nations, a means of expanding demand.

Electronic banking, in the sense that the ordinary user of bank services could understand it, did not come until the 1970s, when the larger bank groups started to install machines in their branches. At first limited simply to giving out a set sum on production of a card with a magnetic tape whose number could be checked by the machine, cash dispensers (CDs), as they were called, began to give way through the 1970s and early 1980s to the more sophisticated ATMs.

In retail banking terms, the first half of the 1980s has been dominated by investment in ATMs, and in the central computing facilities to back them, by banks and other financial institutions. By 1985 banks, thrifts, building societies and retail groups around the world were estimated to have spent well over $2 billion on ATMs. In the USA, where the greatest investments have been made, the total number of ATMs had reached 90,000 by the end of 1985; in the UK 6,700 had been installed by the same time, a doubling in three years; in France, where the nationalized banks had been encouraged by government to develop the technology, there were a similar number; while in Europe as a whole there were over 20,000, and Japan has nearly double that figure.

At their simplest, these are machines in the wall or in the bank lobby offering customers a round-the-clock service: they enable customers to withdraw money, and they respond to basic requests such as the transfer of funds, the ordering of a new cheque book or a printed statement of a current balance. At their more sophisticated, however, the machines are capable of dealing with most financial transactions, from moving money between accounts to automatically billing an account for purchases in stores, organizing foreign-exchange needs and buying stocks and shares. Technology already enables the transactions to be carried out (to borrow computer jargon) either 'on-line' or in 'real time' – that is, implementing the instructions while the terminal is in direct communication with the centre – or 'off-line', in which case the messages are stored and the debiting of the account or the transfer of funds is effected later by centralized computer. The choice in consumer banking is as much a question of the availability of good communications as of consumer need. Countries with advanced internal communications, such as the USA, Canada and Japan, have tended to develop more on-line power than European countries without.

The central thrust of development in the industrial nations is now towards both home banking, to take advantage of the exploding purchase of home computers and televisions able to display two-way transactions, and the installation in stores of point-of-sale terminals or EFTPOS (Electronic Funds Transfer at Point of Sale), as they are termed. Side by side with this is experimentation with the 'smart card', the plastic card containing its own intelligence and memory chips, which can automatically revise the state of the holder's account as the card is used.

Intriguingly, it is Scandinavia, and Finland in particular, that has led the way to home banking, as much as anything because of the high cost of labour in Scandinavia and the isolation of the rural population, spread over large distances in small communities. And it has been the French as much as anyone else, at least in Europe, who, with forceful government encouragement to develop key areas of future technology, have helped to lead the way in point-of-sale systems.

In the Finnish system, developed by the Union Bank of Finland, the customer simply has to key his or her personal identification number (PIN) into the ordinary telephone system, follow it with a changing security number and then proceed with instructions, using a home or office computer, to transfer money, pay bills or find out the state of an account. The system even speaks to the caller via a voice-synthesis system that decides to use Finnish or Swedish depending on the PIN. Sweden, Germany, Japan, Canada and the USA are all experimenting with equivalent services with varying degrees of success in the light of customer resistance or enthusiasm.

Meanwhile the development of point-of-sale systems has been hampered by, as much as anything, the need to standardize account systems, if they are really to work, and to develop central communications systems so that the marketplace can be linked effectively and fully. Many is the country – the UK in 1980, for example – that has dreamed up ambitious plans for nationwide systems based on central computers and covering retail stores throughout the country only to find they have come to naught because neither the banks nor the main retail chains can agree on whose system should be standard. Scandinavia has advanced because its banking procedures and cheque-numbering formats are standardized. France proved to be one of the first countries to develop an EFTPOS scheme (that of Saint-Etienne introduced by Société Générale, the country's third largest bank) in 1983, thanks partly to government enthusiasm. The USA has been driven to some extent by the ambition of the banks to cross interstate lines in the development of business, while in Canada efforts have been propelled largely by the early interest in computerization of the Bank of Montreal.

'By the end of the century we shall be a totally cashless society,' said the head of retailing banking of one of the largest US banks at a conference. Perhaps, but probably not to the extent imagined. The vision of a host of devoted bank customers organizing their accounts on a home computer each evening always owed more to the banker's wish than to human needs. Experiments with home banking, although they are still going on, have come across marked resistance on the part of customers, even quite rich ones, who have not displayed the devotion to maximizing their financial assets that has sometimes been ascribed to them.

The cost, the essential communications, the uniformity of codes, the need for security from fraud and prying eyes and the counter-rise of the cash or 'black' economy have all made the development of a plastic world a great deal more difficult than was initially thought. The USA, because of its traditional regionalism and its sheer size, has led most other countries in the development of the necessary infrastructure. Credit cards were introduced in the USA a full decade before they were introduced into Europe or Asia. The Federal wire system for the settlement of interbank transfers of funds in the same day was a generation ahead of anything in Europe. The Clearing House Interbank Payments System (CHIPS), founded by the New York Clearing House Association in 1970 by the major money-centre banks in New York, became fully automated in the early 1970s. Its nearest equivalent outside the USA, the Bankers' Automated Clearing Service (BACS), was founded in 1968 by the members of Britain's clearing banks and declares itself to be the biggest individual automated clearing house in the world. Although it is fully electronic, receiving most of its data via the telecommunications network, it is intended to handle standardized payment instructions, such as standing orders for regular payments to insurance, mortgages and other items, and automated credits such as salaries and pensions. Until 1984 the actual clearing of cheques between banks was achieved by bringing the cheques, orders and instructions to a central clearing hall in London, where they were redistributed to the desks of the clearing banks and the Bank of England. It is only since 1984, and then only for cheques of over £10,000 drawn on a town branch of a bank, that this system has been replaced by an automated one, named, in a very British way, CHAPS (the Clearing House Automated Payments System). CHAPS was originally called, apparently, the Financial Institutional Settlement House (FISH), designed to go with the American CHIPS.

It is not the technology that is holding up development of a wired and cashless world – the technology is already there. So-called smart cards are coming off the drawing board into test production. The development of communications technology in digital exchanges and package-switching (through which messages are broken up into constituent impulses and then reassembled at the other end) enable almost limitless amounts of information to be transmitted and processed on-line around the globe. Security, while a constant worry to banks and a nagging doubt among customers, is not insoluble, particularly with the development of smart cards and laser or memory cards, which can store detailed and easily checkable facts about the card holder.

The problem is that, if the next stage of centralized and costly development is to bring the average financial transaction (from buying clothes to receiving social security payments) into the electronic ambit, the financial institutions themselves must agree a common system or be brought together by another party. And the communications and ancillary facilities must be in place.

The prize is the biggest advance in retail finance in a century. In all the discussion about high technology in finance people often forget just how cash-based and underbanked most of even the industrialized world is. The U S A has long been in advance of most other countries in the degree to which cheques and credit cards are used for payment. But throughout most of Europe between 80 and 90 per cent of all financial transactions are still done in cash. In Japan the proportion is even higher. In Britain, despite the strength of its banking system, a quarter of the working population is still without bank accounts, and a dominating proportion is still paid weekly in cash. Despite having some of the technically most highly developed systems of interbank and back-room automated settlement anywhere, the Japanese have remained extraordinarily inefficient and slow on the counter, partly because of lack of competition between banks and partly because of the traditionally high number of non-working women who handle the family money and who accept long queues.

In this context automation does far more than make the business of cashing cheques and of debiting and crediting an individual account cheaper. (Estimates by the American Bankers' Association suggest a cost per transaction in an ATM of 15–50 cents, a quarter of that for an across-the-counter transaction, while the cost of automatic debiting at a point-of-sale terminal could be half that of clearing a cheque.) It stands to bring a whole new section of customers to banking, to enable finance to match the needs of a world of working women and dual-income households and to gain customer loyalty for a central system to meet all financial needs.

The advantage for the banks is that such services need no longer be supplied by their branches. Precisely because customers can, through an automated system, manage the full range of financial transactions from insurance to purchases and investment, they need no longer go to a bank for their checking needs, a thrift or building society for their savings or a brokerage house for their investments. From an office or using a machine in the wall they can plug in their cards and effect their own transactions.

In one way, technology at the retail end of the business favours the large banks. Lower costs, the benefits of volume, the spread of their business have given them an advantage that new technology will tend to reinforce. But in another way technology opens up the field to new competition. ATMs can be installed at relatively low cost and, provided that the basic telecommunications within the country are there, can ensure a wide geographical coverage for any financial group, thrift, banker or broker. Within regions local banking groups can combine forces to compete with larger state or money-centre banks, pooling central computing facilities and allowing, relatively easily, mutual use of facilities. Once these have been installed, such groups can offer no-frills banking at least as efficiently as, and often at lower cost than, large banking groups with their higher over-heads.

Merrill Lynch's entry into the retail banking business with its cash-management accounts in the late 1970s would not have been possible without the cards and the automation that enabled customers to transfer and debit funds from their investment accounts with rapidity. For any organization with a strong retail branch system, be it a brokerage house in the USA like Merrill Lynch or a retail stores group such as Sears Roebuck, technology made it possible to add a full range of banking and other financial services to its basic service of stock investment or retail credit. Even in Europe, where the banks have not been restricted (as they had in the USA) by national net-works and a wide range of services including stocks and insurance, it is not necessarily the big bank groups that have taken best advantage of technology. While it has been the French bank Société Générale that has run the pioneering point-of-sale scheme in central France, it was the French co-operative bank, Crédit Agricole, that matched it with a rival scheme in Limoges. The first group to offer home bank-ing in Britain was not one of the London clearing banks but the Nottingham Building Society together with the Bank of Scotland, one of the leading Scottish banks that has decided to formulate a deliberate strategy around home banking, offering loans and services direct to the home.

Technology has thus become as much a battleground as an area of co-operation in the financial world. There are banks, such as Citicorp, that regard it as too central to share with others and are thus de-veloping their own system within America. Others are co-operating in rival groups. But, as with pipeline and rail transport of gas and oil a few generations ago, banking technology has now aroused in the bigger groups the same protective instincts and the same fears of new competition. And it may yet give rise to the same questions about government intervention to force equal access to networks at a fair price.

While in retail banking technology has been led as much from Europe as from the USA and the struggle for possession has been between banks and other financial instutitions as much as within the banking fraternity, in wholesale banking technology has been led very much more by the U S A and by the major banks. The impact of technical advance has been at least as great. Automation of interbank dealing, the settlement of cheques and the provision of regular debits and credit on accounts, the transfer of large sums and foreign-exchange transactions developed rapidly from the 1960s on. The kinds of advance talked about in terms of home banking and point-of-sale terminals is obviously of much more immediate use to the office than the home. Put a personal computer on an office desk and the finance manager or the shopkeeper can have at his disposal an immediate view of his balances, his debits, his credits, his stocks and liabilities, his foreign-exchange exposure, his forward requirement for raw material cover, his sensitivity to interest rates.

It was the American money-centre banks, eager to give their corporate customers as full a service as possible and facing severe competition for their loyalty, that first saw the possibilities. By offering companies the services of their own computer systems, coupled with the advantages of the automated interbank system within the U S A and internationally, the banks could develop cash-management systems for clients under which the corporate treasurer could, at the push of a button, review fully his financial position, and the bank's promises of advice and management with respect to his various accounts could be made most effective. For corporations in the U S A that have national sales and are impelled to keep a myriad different accounts with different banks across the country the benefits of the corporate overview are considerable.

The services provided by money-centre banks are even more useful for international companies with accounts in national banks around the world. The offer, made possible by international communication, of detailed and immediate control of a host of varying national ac-counts in different currencies, each of them earning or paying dif-fering rates of interest, has given the major international banks, and particularly the New York banks, an enormously attractive selling point. It has also made them, for the first time, real contenders for corporate business with the local banks. Previously the tendency had been for companies to set up accounts with local banks in each country of operation. Once it has become possible to centralize information and to make settlements internationally, either through a bank's own system or through a shared system such as S W I F T (the Society for Worldwide Interbank Financial Telecommunication), then the game will change. Corporations may still prefer to keep local accounts with local banks because of their knowledge of the region and their ability to handle employees' payments, pensions and insurance according to local requirements. But cash management has become a large business for banks, and it is one in which the American banks have a clear lead. Little wonder that the established banks in London and Tokyo, as well as in Stockholm and Frankfurt, fear that this will be the Trojan Horse with which the New York institutions will storm the citadel of domestic banking in the major capitals of the world.

Yet it is not on the provision of financial services, the 'intermediation' of finance, that technology is having its most revolutionary effect. It is on the marketplace itself – the commodity markets, the stock exchanges, the foreign exchanges and the money-markets dealing rooms. There its impact has been rapid and profound.

Walter Wriston is right. Finance is information – or misinformation. He who hears the news first stands to gain most. For money is made in the markets less by getting it right in an absolute sense than by being ahead of market sentiment. The first newspapers were sheets, produced in Germany, giving information about the markets. Reuters, the international news agency and now the largest provider of information internationally, started off by giving financial news. It made its biggest breakthrough in 1849, when it introduced pigeons to plug a gap in the telegraph lines between Paris and Berlin. One of the founders of the Rothschild dynasty made his first fortune by hearing the news of Waterloo a day before his competitors and investing his money accordingly. The first transatlantic cable, completed in 1866, was promoted largely by the US financial community, then still heavily dependent on European finance to fund its growth. One of the first practical uses of the telephone was its installation on the floor of the New York Stock Exchange in 1878, two years after its first test.

Three things are essential for the effectiveness of a market. One is information about the product being offered, be it apples or shares in a Korean contractor. The second is the offer to sell and the offer to buy at a price. And the third is the assurance that, once the deal is done, payment will be made. When the two dozen brokers doing deals under a buttonwood tree agreed to form the first stock market in New York on 17 May 1792, when the government and the financial powers stepped in following the scandals of the unrestricted broking and jobbing around Jonathan's Coffee House and Garraway's in London to pass the stock-jobbing Bill of 1696 and the brokers themselves set up a central stock exchange in Threadneedle Street in 1773 to regularize their activities, when the Japanese Government encouraged the establishment of a stock exchange in Tokyo in 1874 to deal in the bonds by which the *samurai* class had been paid off when feudalism was abolished in Japan, the aim was to form a club with rules and regulations to ensure that information was centralized and dealing carried out fairly and openly.

The dealing system might be an 'open-outcry' system, under which lots are offered and the brokers shout out, as at an auction, to buy them – the method favoured by commodity exchanges, where lots are of uniform items and volumes are enormous. Alternatively, they might be the bid-and-offer system used in stock exchanges, when the broker is offered two prices, a buying and a selling price, and chooses whether to take one or other or to bargain for it. But in either case it has been on the floor of the exchange that the action has been centred and that the rules of transparency, equal opportunity to all buyers and sellers and trustworthiness in payment have been imposed.

Technology has long been used to mechanize the processes of the marketplace. The telegraph allowed investors and brokers all over a country to keep in touch with the exchanges. The electric stock-ticker was installed on the New York Stock Exchange in 1867, enabling the brokers to do away with the messengers who had previously had to run from the floor of the Exchange to their offices around Wall Street with the latest price information – although messengers, with their distinctive buttons, are still in evidence on most exchanges. Computers have been installed to record price changes and to clear deals. Electronic display boards have begun to replace handwritten notices on blackboards – the 'Big Board' of the New York Stock Exchange and the sector boards of London – although many exchanges prefer to keep on chalking up price changes as they occur.

All these developments have, however, confirmed the position of the trading floor as the centre of activity. What modern technology is now doing is threatening the role of the exchange floor itself. In the 1960s the refinement, alongside computers, of screen display (videotext) of rapidly changing information gave birth to a series of companies anxious to offer their services – to install the equipment and place the information on the desks of dealers around the financial centres. At the beginning of the 1970s. Telerate and Quotron in the USA, Reuters, Extel and Datastream in Europe all began to offer their clients terminals that not only would display prices fed to them by banks, brokers and dealers but also could change the information live, or on-line, at the originator's request.

The most immediate use of this terminal trading was in the foreign-exchange and money markets. The players in the markets were banks and large corporations, which could be relied on to manage their own settlements or at least to define for their own dealers the limits of exposure on each other's business. The range of instruments could be displayed on a single screen, and the number of institutions dealing in the market was relatively clearly defined. From the early 1970s onwards Reuters and Telerate developed one of the fastest-growing businesses in the whole communications field.

This was all the more apt because Reuters, which had been founded in 1848 by Julius Reuter (later Baron Reuter) as a financial news service, had developed into a news service for newspapers after Gladstone's repeal of stamp duties. It had had to be rescued by the Commonwealth newspaper proprietors, at the prodding of the government, during the Second World War, but its financial news service – the Reuter Monitor, introduced in 1973 – was to prove to be the tail that wagged the dog, and ultimately fattened it again, when the newspaper-proprietor shareholders made a public offering of shares in June 1984, a year after Telerate, a financial information service founded in 1970, had shown just how valuable the market was, with a share offering that valued it at $900 million. The dealing rooms of the banks and institutions had become the battleground for these two companies by the end of 1984, with Telerate claiming 24,000 video screens in forty-one countries and Reuters claiming nearly 40,000 in 100 countries.

While the dealing-rooms of the money markets are being revolutionalized by the videotext services of such companies as Reuters and Telerate, the stock markets have been equally challenged by the development of NASDAQ, developed by the National Association of Securities Dealers in response to the crisis of excess demand for over-the-counter (OTC) shares in the late 1960s. OTC shares are shares usually in smaller and newer companies that are unwilling, or lack the history or substance, to go for the more formal listing requirements of the American Exchange, the New York Stock Exchange or the other exchanges in the USA. Instead they are brought directly to market, with a less regulated and detailed prospectus, by brokers and dealers who trade them with anyone willing to buy. They are a riskier but potentially much more lucrative investment than fully listed shares traded on the floor of an exchange.

In the days of paper, telex and telephone they were also a chaotic market. Between 1964 and 1968 dealings in OTC securities in the USA tripled, grossly overstraining the loose market's ability to handle the demand. By 1969 complaints were averaging fifty a day, and the much feared Securities and Exchange Commission (SEC) was forced to intervene, demanding that the Association put its house in order.

The result was the NASDAQ system, installed in 1971 and consisting of 20,000 miles of leased telephone lines connecting terminals in every dealer's office and tied into a central computing system that recorded prices, deals and other information. The dealer screens provided three levels of information. The simplest level displayed the average prices for all the stocks on the OTC – that is, the median between the bids and offer prices keyed in by members willing to make a market in a stock. The next level up allowed the dealers to see the actual bid and to offer quotes themselves. The top level allowed the market-makers to put in prices for display around the computer market. The dealer who was willing to make a market – that is, to quote a price at which he was willing to buy and a price at which he was willing to sell a particular stock – had only to key in his prices, give an indication of the volumes in which he was prepared to deal and then change the prices as demand moved the market and his own position. All the buyer or seller had to do was to look on the screen for the range of bids and offers being quoted by various dealers and then call one or more when he wanted to make a deal. The Association ensured that the prices were honoured by the market-makers and that the system operated efficiently. Transactions could take place between dealers watching screens in any part of the country.

The effect was dramatic. Within the next dozen years the share volume rose by more than sixteen times, and the number of terminals in use rose from barely a few thousand in 1972 to 40,000 in 1978 and more than 120,000 in 1985. By then the volume of share dealing, at more than 16 billion shares with a value of some $200 billion, made NASDAQ the third largest stock exchange in the world, smaller only than those of New York and Tokyo and greater than those of London, Zurich, Bonn, Toronto and Paris put together. And all of this through the medium of telephone lines.

It is hardly surprising that the stock exchanges of the world have reacted so strongly to this threat to their hold on stock trading or that regulators have become so concerned at the potential loss of control in a system where dealing can so easily move off the floor and on to the screen. Once technology has allowed a dealer to receive instant information on bid and offer prices for any cash or paper commodity, be it a currency, a financial future or an equity share, then it is but a short step to his being able to undertake the other functions of completing the deal and even settling the sum on the screen as well.

In 1980 Reuters introduced a Dealer Service, enabling dealers in the foreign-exchange and money markets to trade on the basis of the prices displayed before them through a high-speed telex-type system linking all the dealers in the market. Using a special code, the dealer can contact a bank quoting a bid or offer on the Deutschmark, for example, give it an order and then key in the deal on his screen. Following the success of this service, Reuters has since formed a link with Instinet (Institutional Networks Corporation) of the USA to offer a similar service in international stocks throughout Europe.

Instinet itself was an electronics system, started in 1969 and backed by Merrill Lynch and other groups, aimed at providing a low-cost trading network roughly along the lines of the foreign-exchange market, for institutions buying and selling shares in bulk. Among its two hundred broker/dealers are nineteen of the top twenty American firms. More than a hundred institutions belong to the system, which traded 320 million shares in 1984. The system is fully automated: the dealing in some 3,500 quoted stocks is done on the screen. There is little need – according to the participants at any rate – of regulation or guarantee of payment, as the members are all large groups in their own right, trading on their institutional reputation rather than membership of an exchange. There are no limits to the volume of any transaction (one single deal in 1983 was for $19 million worth of stock). As Instinet's chairman, Bill Lupien, a former trader on the Pacific Exchange who founded the service because he saw the opportunity of using the screen that gave out the information to bring in the order, has said, 'All markets are electronic. Nobody trades by post.'

'We have tried very hard,' he argued in one interview, 'to reproduce through the computer what you can get from an exchange floor. People claim there's no atmosphere on the screen – but we have a way of letting customers know what the level of interest is in any stock. You can only know that vaguely on a floor, but we can tell you exactly how many people are looking at it.'

Instinet quotes not only US stocks but also foreign stocks and options on stocks and currencies from the Chicago Board Options Exchange (CBOE), traditionally the markets most resistant to automation because of the large sums involved and the activity and volume brought by 'locals', the independent floor traders. But even this area of dealing activity is potentially removable from the exchange floors, at least in so far as it is a market for institutional players such as the banks and large corporations. The London International Financial Futures Exchange (LIFFE) was founded in 1982 very much with the institutional investor in mind. It has a high degree of automation in quotation and in settlement, although the open-outcry system of floor trading was left in between. In early 1985 an even more radical approach to futures and options trading was opened in Bermuda with the start-up of trading on Intex. Founded in 1981, again with Merrill Lynch's assistance and headed by a former Merrill Lynch trader, Eugene Grummer, and subject at first to a series of delays to ensure that the technology was right, Intex allows fully automated trading from afar. Market-makers tap in their bid and offer prices on contracts in gold, US Treasury securities and freight. As dealers watch the figures move on their screen, be they in London, New York or anywhere else, they key in what they want; within a matter of a few seconds the deal is done and the parties at both ends receive confirmation in the form of a printout from their desk-top computers.

NASDAQ, meanwhile, has been busily extending its own technology. In 1979 it made its price display immeasurably more sophisticated by including and ranking the up-to-the-minute best bid and offer quotes on the top 190 stocks and including the price at which the last deal was done within ninety seconds of the transaction. On his screen the dealer could now see the market moving as instantly as if he were on the floor of the exchange. In 1983 NASDAQ started up a fully automated dealing facility with its Computer-Assisted Executive System (CAES), which was designed to enable small lots to be dealt with on the keyboard. The reason for the small-lot limitation on automatic dealing in shares is simple enough. Market-makers are happy enough to deal at a quoted price for a small lot. For a larger lot both they and the other parties want to be in a position to haggle and to trade and to enjoy the security of direct conversation to confirm the deal. Small lots can be easily keyed in, and recorded on a central computer, without the need for direct negotiation. As with money-market dealing, however, there is no reason why this cannot be extended to large-lot dealing when the parties concerned are reputable institutions known to each other. Nor is there any reason why, theoretically, it could not be extended to global trading in stocks. The computer on the desk-top in Hong Kong is, after all, in contact with the computer in New York just as directly as a dealer's terminal in Boston. The only difference is the time zone.

The threat to existing floor exchanges has been made clear enough by the experience of the London Stock Exchange in the run-up period to its introduction of a new automated system of trading in autumn of 1986. As the various brokers jostled for position and the Stock Exchange mulled over which system to introduce, two of the major financial firms in London, Goldman Sachs of the USA and the UK merchant bank Robert Fleming, started to make markets in certain stocks off the floor, while Reuters turned up to offer its Instinet service as an alternative, and much faster, route to a new automated dealing system.

The stock exchanges have responded to the threat of off-floor trading by investing heavily in automation themselves and by seeking government support for their privileged position in stock-dealing on grounds of investor protection. Over the last decade, for example, the New York Stock Exchange has introduced the Designated Order Turnaround (DOT) to handle orders for fewer than 600 shares fully automatically by connecting the member firms directly with the Exchange's computer. Orders are routed via the Exchange to the appropriate trading post on the floor, bypassing the floor brokers, and are then passed back, once they have been executed, to the member firm. The price is fixed at the last traded price for the stock, ensuring for the small investor a reasonable price for his transaction and, for the broker, a low cost for small deals.

In Canada Toronto has pioneered the Computer Assisted Trading System (CATS) to enable dealers to trade directly on the screen and to promote small-lot trading. The system has already been sold to Zurich and is likely to be installed in Paris. Meanwhile London has plumped, after some years of research, for a system based on NASDAQ, called Stock Exchange Automatic Quotations (SEAC). Under this system, due to start operating in 1986, the new market-makers formed by the merging of brokers and jobbers will quote offer and bid prices and report last trades into a central system, EPIC, which will then distribute the information to members of the Stock Exchange and others. Actual dealing will be done on the floor except – as in New York, Toronto and on other exchanges – in the case of small deals, when full automation of deals will be introduced.

With automation on their own floors, the exchanges are also

combining both to increase the activity, and hence the attractiveness, of their markets and to defend themselves against the growing international spread of non-floor systems such as N A S D A Q. Since 1978 the U S A has had a Consolidated Quotation System, which gathers last-deal information from the exchanges throughout the country and then displays in each the national best bid and offer, so that the dealer in New York, for example, can deal in Chicago should the price be better there for the stock in which he is interested.

More recently there has been a growing trend towards international link-ups. The Montreal Exchange, in heavy competition with the bigger Toronto Exchange, has started an electronic link-up with Boston. Toronto, in reply, is linking up with the American Stock Exchange. London is discussing greater co-operation with the New York Stock Exchange. The Chicago Mercantile Exchange has joined with the Singapore International Monetary Exchange. Montreal, Amsterdam, Sydney and Vancouver are now linked in options trading of gold, silver and other metals.

Technology has become both the means and the object in an international struggle for territory between communications corporations, between the exchanges and between the non-floor trading systems. The struggle is likely to grow more heated as the decade progresses. The rapid development of international communications through satellites and through fibre optics will make it relatively easy for a dealer in one country – a dealer in a farmhouse in the back of beyond anywhere between Scandinavia and South Africa and Australia, indeed – to deal in shares on his home computer anywhere in the world. He does not need to belong to an exchange or to use an exchange member. He will not, in theory, even need to go through a broker or agent at all. The job of exchanges, of brokers and of regulators will be to try to make sure he does. But so long as communications allow a dealer to quote for stocks outside the exchange of the country in which he is operating, any attempt to confine trading will be an uphill task.

In early 1986 the London Stock Exchange found itself locked in intense and public competition with dealers in international stocks over the question of just who was to supervise the business. The international dealers – banks like Citicorp and securities houses such as Nomura and Merrill Lynch – argued that the twenty-four-hour trading of stocks was better kept off-floor and within a looser association on the lines of that of eurobond dealers. The Stock Exchange, desperate to get this activity under its wing, insisted that equities dealing should be supervised by one central body – itself. The international dealers argued that their size and reputation were sufficient to ensure fair play in a market largely confined to professionals. The Stock Exchange urged that rules were still required to protect the investor.

Just as the competition between various types of market is hotting up, so is the competition for the technology and for the provision of information. The major computer manufacturers (IBM, AT&T, Ericsson of Sweden, the Serge Dassault electronic group in France, British Telecom in Britain and the major Japanese electronics groups) have all seen in finance a major growth area for information technology – perhaps *the* growth area. And most have viewed the next phase as being dominated by desk-top terminals that will use and adjust both information from a central source and graphics and calculations to suit their own requirements.

On the one hand, this has induced the major financial groups, led by Citicorp and Merrill Lynch, to provide the central service on which customers, be they dealers, institutions, corporate treasurers or just plain investors, can base their own financial management programmes. Merrill Lynch has teamed up with IBM in Imnet; AT&T has joined forces with Quotron; Citicorp is offering services via Reuters. At the other end the discount brokers, especially the US brokers now owned by the big commercial banks, are beginning to offer systems that enable the small investor, with his home computer, to dabble in shares. 'RIP the trading floor,' declares one West Coast dealer in the USA.

If he is right, the development will raise some grievous questions. The floor markets of the world have developed not merely as a means of making trade more effective by centralizing the trading but also as the means by which the ordinary investor can be sure that he is going to get the best price available and not be trodden on by the professionals. And they are the institutions through which the regulatory authorities, be they the SEC in the USA or the Department of Trade in the UK, can exercise some control over malfeasance, keep a finger on the direction of investment and have some confidence that a rush at any one time out of stocks, or out of a particular stock, or the collapse of any one firm can be contained. Reuters or Telerate provide the conduit through which market-makers may quote their prices, but they do not act as the referee or guarantor in transactions. Nor can individual brokerage houses, however large they or their parents are. In one sense, technology has opened up the field for the small player and small broker by putting at his disposal the information and the computing power available to the major-league players. But in another sense the development of off-floor markets such as Instinet and Intex is geared very much to the professionals, to the institutions dealing in large lots and to the groups whose names guarantee, or should guarantee, their creditworthiness.

It is partly for these reasons that the floor will not disappear, although the paperwork might. Governments will not allow it. Nor are the major investors likely to desert it completely. The experience of the Cincinnati Exchange, which at the beginning of the 1980s had made a strong bid to become the automated centre of a national exchange in the USA, is an example of the difficulties of transposing dealing, simply on the grounds that it is technically feasible, to centre trading wherever one wants. The exchange did not have the volume, the presence of the major traders or the history to play the dominant role. When the New York Stock Exchange improved its own dealing systems to compete, the brokerage houses quickly drifted back East. It is not that the screen cannot provide the excitement of the floor: for a whole generation of traders the changing figures on a terminal are a much more natural form of dealing than the chaos and noise of a trading floor. But gossip and rumour, and the proximity of like-minded people, are essential to a market.

Technology will not alter this. What it is doing is to make the competition over where the market is concentrated that much more intense. There is no room for an infinite number of major international exchanges. The middle-sized stand to fall, and the big to lock horns, in ferocious competition for the number-one spot. What technology is also doing is to make it impossible for national regulators to turn the clock back. Communication, as Wriston foresaw, makes isolationism in finance more difficult than in any other field. These days money travels as an electronic impulse along the wires just as fast as words. If it is to be controlled, technology will have to be used by supervisors, not fought against.

THREE

THE MARKETS

'Those whose eyes are glued to the screens and ears to the telephones of the world's exchanges have missed the point,' a furious British Prime Minister, Mrs Margaret Thatcher, told an audience of oil men meeting in London in February 1985. And she went on to declare that Britain was not just an oil country and that its currency should not be tossed around at will by currency dealers reacting to every newsflash about a walk-out in OPEC or a price-cut threat by Nigeria.

Irritation with the apparent refusal of international markets to 'look at the fundamentals' is nothing new to politicians. The 'gnomes of Zurich', as Prime Minister Harold Wilson termed them, have always been an object of scorn and fear for heads of government frustrated by movements in the value of their currency. President Kennedy inveighed as much as President Johnson against speculators against the dollar in the 1960s.

But in this case there were special reasons for Mrs Thatcher's ire. Over the previous month the pound, which in 1980 had shot up to as high as $2.45 on the currency exchanges, had fallen to as low as $1.04. When a spokesman briefed newspapers, on 12 January 1985, to repeat Mrs Thatcher's long-held view that governments should not inter-vene in the markets, his words had the opposite effect to that intended. The markets took it as a signal that the British would not mind seeing the pound breach dollar parity for the first time in history. The UK Treasury was forced to react. Interest rates, which had already been raised 1 per cent the previous Friday, were slammed up a further 2 per cent, and the Bank Rate, the traditional indicator of the government's interest-rate intentions that had been abandoned in the general de-regulation of markets a few years before, was reintroduced. It was, as even members of the British Cabinet were prepared to admit, the biggest change of course in economic policy of Mrs Thatcher's premiership.

There were other reasons too for the receptiveness of the audience to Mrs Thatcher's complaints. The oil industry was going through the same traumas of market speculation as dealers marked down prices on the commodity markets of New York and London at the merest rumour of a split between the oil producers. ('What is all this about the spot market and oil futures?' asked Mrs Thatcher's husband, Denis, a former director of the Burmah Oil Company, of one of the oil barons sitting next to him at the dinner. 'We never had anything like it in my day.' 'I agree,' said the oil-company chairman. 'Why, do you know that we traced one cargo of Brent crude from the North Sea through a chain of no fewer than sixty-three purchases before it was even produced?') Oil, which for the last generation had been the most important commodity of them all, one that was traded internationally almost entirely through the hands of the main oil companies under long-term contracts, had now become a speculative commodity, being traded not even as a real cargo but as pieces of paper promising future delivery that could be bought and sold like any other piece of commercial paper. At the height of speculative fever in the weeks before Mrs Thatcher spoke a record 36.3 million barrels of oil, worth about $1 billion, were traded on the New York Mercantile Exchange in a single day, changing the price of oil that had not yet been produced, and was not due to be delivered for three months, by a $1 per barrel in a matter of minutes. No wonder that some of the more old-fashioned oil men believed that the time of madness was finally upon their industry.

The dealing-rooms of the financial centres of the world have taken off. On any one day an average of $150 billion, and as much as $250 billion, worth of foreign exchange is traded around the globe, double the volume of five years before. Less than 10 per cent (only 5 per cent, according to some calculations made by the Federal Reserve in the USA) reflects the real requirements of companies that actually need foreign currency to pay bills and to pay for goods. The rest is pure trading – by banks, by corporations and by institutions managing their foreign-currency portfolios, positioning themselves in the market, rebalancing their assets and liabilities constantly on the screens of their trading-rooms.

Bits of paper have now been introduced to speculate against other bits of paper, and one type of borrowing has been crossed with another to produce entirely different products. On the day in August 1984 when the New York Stock Exchange traded a record 236 million shares worth $7.9 billion on face value, an almost exactly equivalent sum ($7.8 billion) was made in futures on stock indices – that is, promises of delivery, on a set date in the future, of a purely notional balance of stocks making up the stock exchange index. In 1984 the volume of futures dealing in Treasury bonds on the Chicago Board of Trade, at $8 billion a day for thirty-year bonds, was double that of the dealing in the bonds themselves, and on an active day trading can top $25 billion worth of futures on thirty-year bonds.

The market, as well as the marketplace, is being changed out of recognition. And for the same reasons. Technology has made it possible to trade huge volumes on screens and on the exchange floors. What is more, it has made it possible to develop increasingly sophisticated and complicated products such as options (when the investor takes out the option to buy or sell a share, bond or commodity at a future date, at his discretion), swaps (when the borrower can swap, for example, his fixed-rate debt, raised in one country with the borrowings in floating-rate debt raised by a company elsewhere), financial futures, hybrids, revolving debt and a whole new menagerie of bonds that separate interest from principal (Treasury Investment Growth Receipts, etc.) or that allow borrowers to choose when, and in what form, to draw down their borrowing facilities (Note Issuance Facilities, Revolving Underwriting Facilities, etc.). The 'synthetic bond' has come to the markets, as plastics have come to industry.

Deregulation has made possible both the internationalization of the markets and the breakdown of traditional barriers between the long-term bond markets, the short-term money markets and the more recent medium-term debt markets and between various types of instrument. It has also made possible – the system would not have been able to cope otherwise – the spreading of risk in a world made vulnerable by the volatility of exchange rates, the explosion of prices and the fluctuations in interest rates.

The Bretton Woods Agreement of 1944, signed by all the major industrial powers of the West in New Hampshire, was intended to, and indeed did, open the post-war world to free trade and the convertibility of currencies. But it was convertibility based on fixed exchange rates, backed by the provision of short-term aid from the new International Monetary Fund (IMF) to tide any country over short-term problems. The collapse of the agreement in 1971, when it was no longer able to cope with the strains being put on the dollar (the reference currency) and the successive devaluations of various countries, opened up a quite different era of floating rates that ultimately made it exceedingly difficult to control exchange rates. First the USA at the beginning of the decade, then the major European countries (including Britain) in 1979, and finally Japan at the

beginning of the 1980s, abolished exchange controls. Banks and institutions were now free to invest freely abroad and to switch their
funds to wherever offered the greatest return or the least risk.

Alongside this freedom of capital, however, also came increasingly
volatile exchange rates and interest rates as inflation took hold of
various countries and the economic performance of the industrial
nations, which had seemed to be converging in the 1960s, diverged
again in the 1970s. Vietnam hit America and its markets particularly.
The energy crisis of 1973–4 threatened some currencies, such as the
Japanese yen, more than others. The tremendous growth in pension-
fund and institutional holdings and the expansion of interbank
dealing produced money flows that dwarfed any central-bank efforts
to resist them.

Individual governments could not – they still cannot – keep themselves immune from loss of confidence in their currency. But freedom
of currency movement has also served to intensify the differences
between national performance and to increase the volatility of currencies. Once investors had changed their approach, because of inflation, from one of looking for returns over set periods of time to one
of seeking to protect themselves from the effects of price rises or
exchange-rate falls, and once they could move their funds around the
world freely, the markets themselves were bound to respond with
new products and radically new techniques.

The traditional form of borrowing or investing in bonds at fixed-
interest rates over a set period of time gave way to floating-rate bonds
issued at rates that moved in line with the interbank market and were
to be repaid over much shorter timespans. The investor was assured
that his investment would broadly – although not at every moment –
keep pace with inflation. The borrower was assured that he would
not suddenly be caught out by a fall in interest rates or a change in
conditions. Internationalization of the markets at the same time
enabled investment houses, merchant banks and commercial banks to
offer instruments that could take advantage of the differences in terms
between countries, so that borrowers could raise money in different
markets at different rates in order to minimize their costs and investors could move their funds around to maximize their returns.
And as both investors and borrowers grew more sophisticated, so
new products were developed that enabled companies to swap their
obligations, investors to convert their bonds into equity shares or
different currencies and banks to take advantage of their spread of
customers to organize flexible instruments that could be made

short-term or long-term, moved into one currency or another and switched from floating- to fixed-rate interest at will.

Much of this change has been pioneered in the eurobond markets over the last two decades. Ironically, the market was set off not by deregulation but by its opposite. There had long existed a pool of 'eurocurrencies' – that is, deposits of a currency held outside the country of issue. Following the Second World War a number of countries, such as those in Eastern Europe, preferred to keep their dollars outside the U S A for fear of sequestration (not an idle threat in view of what was to happen later, when Iran's financial assets in the U S A were seized in the hostage crisis). To this pool were steadily added a pile of dollars held by American corporations and banks to circumvent the domestic rules (Regulation Q), which put a ceiling on interest rates in the U S A and forced banks to keep a proportion of their deposits in non-interest-bearing Federal Reserve Accounts.

It was not until President Kennedy introduced the Interest Equalization Tax (I E T) in 1963 (to be buttressed two years later by the Voluntary Foreign Credit Restraint Program, limiting the amount of foreign loans that U S banks could make from their American offices, and by President Johnson's insistence in 1968 that U S companies raising money for foreign operations should raise it abroad) that the foreign borrower grew really interested in issuing bonds in the eurodollar market. Before then government municipal authorities, major companies and international institutions had been happy enough to borrow directly in New York, where the bond markets were well established, where there were plenty of investors and where the rates were good. Almost overnight the tax, levying a penal rate on American investors buying foreign bonds, forced borrowers into the eurodollar market. Growth was spectacular. Between 1966 and 1980 the size of the eurobond market grew by an astonishing average of 28.4 per cent per year from $17.4 billion in 1966 to $575 billion in 1980, well over 80 per cent of it in dollars. By 1985 it had topped the trillion-dollar level, and new issues were running at the rate of $135 billion a year (see Table 1). After the market in U S government bonds and the U K gilts market, the eurobond market is now the third largest fixed-rate market in the world.

For the regulatory bodies, for the economists and for much of the outside world the fascination of the eurobond market lay in the fact that it was unsupervised. Because it was a market in deposits held outside the country in whose currency they were denominated – deliberately so, for that was the intention of the authorities of the U S A

Table 1   The rise of the eurobond market ($ million)

	1963	1970	1980	1983	1985
Number of issues	13	128	310	526	1,357
Value	147.5	2,762.0	26,423.0	46,376.5	135,676.2

Source: Euromoney.

in restricting their home patch – it had none of the listing requirements, the prospectuses and the regulation, that bond issues in domestic markets had. Because it was a truly international market existing
only on the telephone and in separated bank accounts, it had none of
the rules on banking prudence that domestic banking industries
had. And because the bonds were issued to the bearer without any
registration of the holders, it had the ineffable air of secret funds and
tax evasion. Who was the investor in all these bonds? The Belgian
dentist. That was the archetype.

'Twenty years ago, when this label first came out,' said a eurobond
trader quoted in the magazine *Euromoney*, 'doctors were revered,
lawyers were taken seriously, but you could kick the hell out of
dentists. The dentist was the professional you could revile. Veter-
inarians stood higher, because they were kind to animals.'

Be that as it may, the Belgian dentist was no fool. He could see
good untaxed rates made the cheaper for him by the low costs of the
market; he could sense the need to get into currencies more secure
than his own; and he could see the advantage of anonymity. If the tax
authorities and legislators of the USA became worried, as they did
towards the end of the 1970s, there was always somewhere else that
the business could go. The UK actively encouraged the business
with low reserve requirements on bank reserves, relatively loose,
informal regulation and little tax on foreign investors in London.
Luxembourg, which became the booking centre for the German
banks, offered terms that were just as attractive. Switzerland kept its
doors, although not its tax rates, open. Without expressing it quite
their way the Europeans, and especially the Germans and the British,
wanted a eurodollar market because they were anxious to prevent
their own currencies from becoming too internationalized. There
were plenty of safeguards to ensure that the Belgian dentist was kept
comfortable and anonymous.

For the finance industry, however, the importance of the euromarket was not so much its dental architecture as its technique. In the

first place, it was a bond market – that is, a market for long-term
fixed-interest paper borrowings issued by corporations, governments
and municipalities at a time when the domestic bond markets of
many of the European countries were becoming more and more dominated by government debt. The chief players in this huge and exploding market were not the commercial banks but the underwriters,
the merchant banks of London, the investment houses of the U S A
and the universal banks of West Germany and Switzerland. The
American commercial banks were proscribed, by law, from underwriting securities in the U S A and were slow to learn to do so abroad.
The U K clearing banks had grown lazy on the protected profits of
their position in the domestic U K banking scene. Although some
had bought into merchant banks in the early 1970s, the clash of
cultures proved too severe too often. Only the select ranks of the
universal banks of Europe, the banks able to underwrite securities
and to deal in retail banking, were used to this kind of market.

There persists a dispute over who did, or did not, create the first
euroissue at the beginning of the 1960s.* But much of the credit must
undoubtedly go to Sir Siegmund Warburg and his bank's origination
of the $15 million six-year issue for the Italian Autostrade road group,
guaranteed by the Italian state industrial holding company, I R I. Sir
Siegmund, who died in 1982, was one of the most formidable figures
of post-war merchant banking. A member of the long-established
Warburg banking family of Hamburg, he had set up in London in the
1930s, when anti-Jewish sentiment in Germany prompted a number
of the leading Jewish commercial families to send their young abroad.
He always preferred to call merchant banking 'private banking', set
great store by personal contacts, relied heavily on graphology for
recruitment and developed one of the most innovative investment
banks either side of the Atlantic.

During the late 1950s and early 1960s he had formed a close relationship with Kuhn Loeb and Co., and it was the experience that he
gained through this Wall Street firm (later merged with Lehman
Brothers) of raising bonds on the U S market that helped him and his
partner, Gert Whitman, to develop the idea of using external dollars
for European bond issues. The Autostrade issue was organized and
marketed by the bright young men whom Sir Siegmund liked to
gather around him – Ian Fraser, later chairman of Lazard Brothers of
London, and Ronnie Grierson, the son of a German immigrant to

* See Ian M. Kerr, *A History of the Eurobond Market: The First 21 Years* (London, Euromoney
Publications, 1984).

Britain in the 1930s, who was later to chair the Orion Bank. The style of the deal, its youthfulness and originality, was typical of a type of dealing that was dominated from the start by the investment and corporate banks – Kuhn Loeb itself, White Weld (whose European operations were to become, by a circuitous route, part of the Crédit Suisse–First Boston combine that has dominated much of the Euro-bond underwriting through the 1970s and 1980s), Deutsche Bank, Kredietbank of Luxembourg and Morgan Guaranty (which organized the first clearing operation for the market).

These were ideas banks. In the fierce competition that developed to gain a share in the action of the world's fastest-growing market there was constant pressure to produce new ideas that would persuade borrowers to issue notes or take out loans in eurocurrencies and to take advantage of the freedom of the market. During its first decade the market was geared almost exclusively to fixed-rate bonds, but at the beginning of the 1970s the eurobond market, like all the capital markets of the world, was thrown dramatically into reverse by the energy crisis, fear of inflation and the volatility of the dollar. Suddenly fixed-rate, long-term bonds were the last things that the investor wanted or the borrower could get.

The market took off largely with the aid of the FRN, pioneered in the early 1970s by White Weld, Morgans and Warburgs again as a means of guaranteeing long-term debt to the borrower at a rate that would move with inflation and was thus attractive to the investor. By the mid-1980s FRNs have grown to form 40 per cent of the overall eurobond market. Other instruments followed: floating-rate, short-term CDs, Perpetual FRNs, Revolving Underwriting Facilities (RUFs), commercial paper issues. At the same time, until 1981–2 at least, bonds themselves were supplemented as a means of long-term borrowing by syndicated loans – loans spread among a group of banks, each of whom agrees to share a part – as a means of meeting developing-country needs and recycling OPEC's surplus dollars.

The bastard child of the financial world had become the exemplary son. As deregulation has gathered pace in the mid-1980s the idea of a separate market kept aside from the main domestic financing pools has given way to a merging of those pools in a single flood of inter-national money. Many of the laws and rules that once made the eurobond market so distinct a European phenomenon have been abol-ished. The IET was effectively lifted in 1974 as the earthquake of the energy crisis forced the USA and every country to seek capital, not to refuse it. In 1981 the US Monetary Control Act began to ease the non-interest-bearing deposit rules for US banks. At the same time, in December 1981, the Federal Reserve at last allowed New York to set up an off-shore banking facility enabling banks in New York to accept non-domestic deposits and to make eurocurrency loans free of tax. The last remaining major stumbling block to euro-currency markets springing up in the USA, Japan and West Germany was the 'withholding tax' levied on bond issues. But by the end of 1984 this too was being dismantled as first the USA and then, as a direct consequence, West Germany abolished taxes on the interest or dividends to non-residents borrowing on their domestic markets. Even Japan, which had once seemed to have set its face against off-shore banking facilities in Tokyo until the 1990s at the earliest, began to discuss the possibility of allowing a New York-style facility and of abolishing its withholding taxes on euroyen bonds.

To the surprise of many who were concerned that London would lose its position as the eurocurrency market centre, the effect of this deregulation has not been to switch the action from Britain, Luxembourg, Hong Kong, the Cayman Islands or the Bahamas to New York, Frankfurt and Tokyo. In the first years following the US action there was a sharp increase in US issues of eurodollars and renewed interest on the part of governments and corporations in Europe and Asia in issuing bonds in America. But there was also a record increase in activity in the eurobond markets of London. The effect of deregulation and more sophisticated communications has been a global merging of markets, not a shift in international markets from one centre to another.

Investor preference for the anonymity of bearer bonds (the USA still insists on registering bond issues) is one reason. Residual tax problems are another. But the chief reason is that, as tax and regu-latory differences become less important to the choice of location, so convenience, the presence of other banks, the availability of facili-ties and the preferences of the participants grow greater. The capital markets are becoming a single unit. Where they are centred is a matter of history and the preferences of the institutions.

This has long been true of the interbank market, especially since the era of floating rates dawned in 1971. Communications have made interbank dealing relatively simple. You look at your screen and, when you want to deal on one of the prices quoted, you ring the bank concerned or use the Reuter dealer super-telex to make the deal and to get your confirmation slip from a printer attached to the screen. The interbank settlement systems allow efficient settlement procedures. It is the job of the dealers and their managers to ensure that risk is controlled by the amount of their exposure at any one time and by the limits set out on their dealings with any one bank.

The currency market remains the biggest and the fastest-moving in the world. On an ordinary day Hong Kong opens at 8 a.m. to do perhaps $8 billion of business, clearing up the open positions left in New York the previous night, testing out the various currencies (above all, the dollar) for what they might hold in the bigger markets. Some dozen banks will be quoting prices, all of them for dollars, most for sterling and a select group of half a dozen each for the other major currencies, such as the yen, the Deutschmark, the Swiss franc. At about the same time (a little earlier, in fact) Tokyo has opened dealing. The market is as big as Hong Kong's (see Table 2). But there are not as many foreign banks quoting as yet, and the Japanese banks are only slowly coming out of a century of tight and detailed regulation. It is the yen and the dollar that are being quoted here in general until London and the European markets open up just as the Asian markets are closing.

Table 2 The major foreign-exchange centres: estimates of average daily turnover ($ billion)

	1979	*1984*
London	25	49
New York	17	35
Zurich	10	20
Frankfurt	11	17
Tokyo	2	8
Singapore	3	8
Hong Kong	3	8
Paris	4	5
Total	75	150

Source: Group of Thirty, *The Foreign Exchange Market of the 1980s*, November 1985.

All the financial centres of Europe will be making markets in several dozen currencies – their own, the dollar, sterling, the Deutschmark, the Swiss franc and lesser currencies. But the biggest centre by far is London. On an average day it might do between $30 billion and $50 billion worth of business. On a hot day, twice this. Well over a hundred banks will be quoting rates for the currencies, and virtually all the traded currencies, from the peso to the pfennig, will find at least a couple of banks to put a quote on the screens.

Taking their initial cue from Hong Kong, the London banks will start to move their rates. On an ordinary day the margins between buying and selling will be pretty tight, a cent or two on the dollar against sterling, a pfennig on the D-mark against the dollar. The dealers scan their screens throughout the morning, turning the 'pages' to see what banks are quoting on particular currencies, buying and selling according to whether they are 'long' (in surplus) or 'short' (in deficit) in a particular currency, moving in and out usually within a few minutes of deciding which way they are going. Rarely will any one deal be exposed for more than a few minutes. Banks like to keep their books balanced, neither short nor long by very much at the end of the day or during it. Nevertheless, they deal constantly in the major currencies, watching for movement. When it comes, it's seen in the spreads being offered. Suddenly the banks will start to change their quotes as they react to each other or to a flash of news about the Middle East, about the price of oil or the death of a prime minister. From a fraction of a cent, the differences between buy and sell prices move to a cent or more. The dealers pick up the excitement. The manager comes out on to the floor from his glass-walled office within the room. On a really dramatic day, when the central banks move in to push a currency one way or another or a single piece of news drives all the markets in one direction fast, the figures on the screen change continuously as the banks widen their spreads deliberately to discourage buyers or refuse to quote at all.

When the markets were at their most volatile at the beginning of 1985, and the central banks decided that they would have to do something to stem the remorseless rise of a dollar that was threatening to make half of the U S A's traditional export industries uncompetitive and to leave the pound drowning beneath pound–dollar parity, the central banks decided to intervene in a series of telephone calls between their heads and finance ministers during the weekend 23–24 February. Central banks had tried intervention before and had failed all too often against a market whose size and momentum dwarfs even the reserves of the Germans and the Japanese. In 1981 the Japanese, at the U S A's behest, had spent more than $2 billion in a fruitless effort to stem the fall of the yen against the dollar. In September 1984 the Bundesbank, the German central bank that has always displayed an eager appetite to 'burn the speculators', had spent nearly as much in a single day (the infamous Black Friday) to drive the dollar down to less than 3.20 D-mark, only to see it return to that level within a month.

The secret, as one of the Bundesbank's top officials explained, is in the timing. In February 1985 (as again in September) the banks, led once again by the Bundesbank, were determined to get it right. On Monday, 25 February, they did nothing, but on Tuesday Paul Volcker, head of the US Federal Bank and the most authoritative figure in international banking, used a congressional hearing to warn the markets that they had pushed up the dollar quite enough. When Volcker speaks the markets begin to look at their exposure. By Tuesday night the foreign-exchange markets of New York, the second biggest in the world, began to mark down the dollar a few cents. It was just as the markets attempted to absorb this message the following morning in London that the central bankers chose to act. 'I've never seen anything like it,' said a dealer in a London bank. 'At one moment the screens were still, with practically no trading. The next moment they all came in – the French in Paris, the Bundesbank in Frankfurt, the Bank of England in London, the Bank of Italy in Rome. Hell, even the Czechs and the Russians were selling. And every time you tried to hold the dollar by buying, wham! They hit you by selling a few hundred million dollars more. For nearly twenty minutes there was pandemonium. You didn't dare deal. The screens didn't have a quote from half the banks.'

And then it was all over. Amid a heap of screwed-up paper, empty drinks cans and half-eaten sandwiches, the markets settled. In a single half-hour the dollar was down 6 per cent against the D-mark to where the central bankers had aimed their sights – just below 3.30 Deutschmarks to the dollar against over 3.50 the day before. Sterling was back to above $1.10. The central banks started to buy a little again to recoup their dollar sales after spending in the region of some $6 billion in a day. (No outsider knows the figure precisely: the only indication of its size was the figures for reserves at the end of the month.) The next time the markets were to see action like this was in September 1985.

This time intervention was not simply a matter of the central banks pitting their wits and limited reserves against a market that could soak up the entire foreign-currency reserves of the ten leading indus-trial nations in a day's trading. It had full political backing and pre-paration. The transfer of James Baker from the White House to the Treasury, to be Secretary in place of Donald Regan, had ushered in a much more politically sensitive and internationally minded economic leadership in the USA. Perhaps even more important in this instance was the move of Beryl Sprinkel, Assistant Secretary for International

Affairs and a firm opponent of currency intervention, out of the Treasury. The intensity of industrial demands for protection and the growth of congressional feeling on this score, reinforced as senators and representatives returned to their home state for the summer, demanded presidential response. If it could not be protection, a drop in the value of the dollar to more competitive levels seemed the only positive alternative. The Japanese, frightened by the strength of U S public feeling against their exports, were ready for action. The U K, which had fundamentally changed its economic policy to one of supporting sterling, also demanded action. So did West Germany.

The result was that where only a few months previously the Group of Five (the five major industrial members of the I M F – the U S A, Japan, France, Britain and Italy) had been discussing an inter-governmental study concluding that positive exchange-rate inter-vention was unnecessary except to smooth out short-term blips in the trend curves, one month later the new U S Treasury Secretary gave the go-ahead for secret preparations for just the sort of deliberate intervention on which the report had turned its back. During the late summer and autumn of 1985 officials and central bankers prepared for a secret meeting of the finance ministers of the Group of Five to tell the world that the dollar was to come down. The meeting took place, at U S intervention, at the Plaza Hotel in New York on 22 September, just before the annual meeting of the full I M F in Seoul, South Korea, two weeks later.

This time the secrecy worked despite the number of officials involved. Nothing leaked until the Friday, just before the markets closed. The ministers met and came out with their prepared state-ments. The dollar, it was agreed, was considerably overvalued. The five countries had agreed to take all necessary action to bring it down. Their statements were words only, but they were enough, on the following day, Monday, 23 September, to force down the dollar by 3.5 per cent in a single day and to get the yen up to 210.0 and the D-mark up to 2.70 against the dollar without the central banks spending a single penny. Their intervention came later as a stunned and uncer-tain market came back to test their resolve in a series of feints. The 'Plaza Agreement' (as it became known) was a milestone, the first fully international agreement on currencies since the end of the Bretton Woods agreement. By October/November the dollar was down to 2.50 D-mark and 200 yen, and the market, for the time being, seemed prepared to accept a completely new level of exchange rates.

The presence of the central banks, the size of the flows and the volatility of the prices make the currency exchanges into a market unique unto itself. The players are all major financial and industrial institutions. They are dealing in cash. The banks are not compelled to sell or buy at the prices quoted. Their rates are 'for information only', whether they wish to deal with you depends on the quantity and your own credit rating. When a bank reaches the limit of its exposure to another bank, no more deals. When all the banks mark down a fellow institution, his source of funds dries up within minutes.

Yet this type of trading has increasingly become the rule rather than the exception. The eurobond market is, in its way, just as fast and as free. Turnover in the secondary market in eurobonds (the buying and selling of bonds once they are issued) exceeded $1.5 trillion in 1984, no less than 50 per cent up on the previous year, making it twice as large as the New York Stock Exchange and four times the size of Tokyo, NASDAQ, Paris, Toronto, AMEX, West Germany, Zurich and London put together. The dealing is done on screens. The market-makers put in their bid and sell prices and the quantities in which they are prepared to deal. The dealers can ring up to make a deal anywhere in the world. Clearing is through the automated Cedel and Euro-clear clearance systems.

Now the domestic markets of the major countries are being drawn into this international dealing network. Some 20 per cent of the outstanding US Treasury bonds in the USA are owned by foreign institutions. In some recent years the Japanese have bought as much as 40 per cent of new issues. Deregulation, plus the need to attract foreign capital to fund government and corporate investment, have progressively removed the tax obstacles to foreign holdings of domestic bonds and equities. Internationally known shares in such companies as Sony, ICI and IBM are being traded in the form of American Depository Receipts (ADRs) – that is, receipts for the actual stock held by US banks or ordinary equity held by investment banks and dealers in all the main centres – across wires, on screens and out of hours.

Go to the dealing-room of any major brokerage house or bank in Hong Kong or Tokyo, Sydney or Johannesburg, New York or London, and no longer are there a few people dealing in eurobonds and US Treasury bills in one room and a couple of salesmen charged with ringing up institutions and banks to sell the bonds in another. Instead, there is now a single room, small or large, equipped with endless cables and ranked electronic screens hung from the ceiling,

giving the latest prices and news; thick carpets; a continuous stream
of talking; and still a lot of paper, if only to wrap the sandwiches. A
row of equity dealers will abut dealers in government debt and
municipals; opposite them will be the market-makers in currency
instrument and futures. If it is a big dealing-room, foreign equities
and eurobonds will be included. The salesmen, charged with off-
loading bonds and equities and making markets in them, will be side
by side with the dealers. At the beginning of the day the occupants of
the room will meet to hear the position of their group – what needs to
be sold, what needs to be bought, what has happened in the market to
the east or the west. At the end of the day they'll hand in their
positions to their colleagues in the next centre. The game is played
not with paper money but with ever-moving figures on little green
screens.

The result of this concentration of intellectual and electrical power
is not simply the 'globalization' of markets, the merging of domestic
markets into one great dealing game: it is the creation of ever more
products that can be traded and ever more novel ways of raising
money that cross the boundaries between currencies, between debt
and equity and between long-term and short-term borrowings.
'Securitization' as the current buzz word describes it, means, in the
narrower sense, the pooling of loans that bring in regular repayments
and interest – mortgages, leases and car loans, for example – in
units that can be sold off as income-bearing bonds or even as self-
liquidating assets in which shares can be sold. In the broader sense,
however, securitization describes the process that has come to dominate the market: the conversion into paper of more and more borrowing that can be bought and sold in a secondary market.

The break with the past is dramatic. In the old days – the basis,
indeed, of the financial markets for several centuries – a corporation
or institution went to different markets to meet its differing needs. If
it wanted a long-term loan at fixed interest to fund its development,
it would go to the bond market and issue fixed-interest bonds. If it
wanted to increase its general funds for expansion or for a take-over,
it issued shares on the stock exchanges, a cheap way of raising cash
but at the expense of giving away some of its equity. If it needed
short-term funds to tide it over cash-flow gaps it usually went to its
bank to get overdraft or loan facilities, which it could draw down as
needed. Now it goes to the market to issue paper that can be used
long-term or short-term, can be switched from fixed to floating rate
and may contain elements of debt or equity. Commercial paper (notes

for up to 270 days), short-term bonds (maturing at less than five years), medium-term bonds (maturing at between six and fifteen years) and long-term bonds (maturing at over fifteen years) are progressively being melded into one.

Two of the most important contributions of the eurocurrency markets to this process in their earlier years were the development of international dollar CDs in 1966 and, in 1970, the introduction of FRNs. A CD is a negotiable note issued by a bank in exchange for a large deposit. The depositor can keep the paper, taking the interest and redeeming his deposit when it is due in a matter of a few months' or years' time. But he can, in the meantime, sell the certificate in the market for cash. For the borrower it has flexibility. For the bank it is a means of creating a liability (in bank terms, perversely, a liability is a deposit with a bank, while an asset is a loan made by it) that is more attractive to depositors and a more dependable source of funding than a simple deposit. The beauty of the eurodollar CD was that it greatly enhanced the ability of non-US banks to raise dollar funds and thus join in lending dollars to others – a facility that was to have unfortunate repercussions later on.

The effect of the FRN was even more extensive. Not only did FRNs revolutionize the traditional form of fixed-rate financing; now borrowings would move in line with market rates – fixed either against US Treasury bill rates or against LIBOR for eurodollar funds, calculated from the rates offered by a number of banks and traditionally fixed each day at 11 a.m. FRNs also became an alternative to, and a substitute for, medium-term syndicated loans in international finance (see Table 3), growing to provide one-third of all new bond issues on the eurobond market by the end of the 1970s and over half by the mid-1980s, as corporations and governments replaced syndicated loans, taken out at the interest rates that banks could offer, by FRNs made at rates that their own credit rating could obtain. By 1984 the total volume of dollar FRNs had reached $60 billion in both domestic and eurodollar issues and facilities.

The 1980s have seen the traditional bank loan overtaken by ever more sophisticated packages of finance that take advantage of evolving deregulation in particular markets and fluctuating rates of interest and currency in the international markets. On the one side, a host of new types of borrowing have been evolved to enable the borrower to take out a general loan that he can then use in various ways, as and when he wants to. The Note Issuance Facility (NIF) gives a corporation the option, when it wants, to issue notes to raise short- or

Table 3 Size of major bond markets at year-end 1984 (nominal value
outstanding, US$ billion equivalent)

Bond market	Total publicly issued	As a percentage of public issues in all markets	Central government
US dollar	2,653.0	56.7	873.0
Japanese yen	779.2	16.7	477.6
Deutschmark	299.1	6.4	64.9
Italian lira	185.4	4.0	126.8
UK sterling	152.0	3.2	132.1
Canadian dollar	121.7	2.6	49.9
French franc	110.5	2.4	27.6
Belgian franc	78.1	1.7	34.0
Swedish krona	75.7	1.6	38.6
Danish krone	71.0	1.5	26.1
Swiss franc	55.9	1.2	4.6
Australian dollar	50.2	1.1	27.7
Dutch guilder	48.0	1.0	28.0
Total	4,679.8		1,910.9

Source: Salomon Brothers.

medium-term funds through a group of underwriting banks. The
Revolving Underwriting Facility (RUF) does the same thing,
allowing a company medium-term funds at short-term rates through
the issuance of commercial paper. If the paper is not taken up, then
the banks guarantee to issue a loan instead, making RUFs a hybrid
between a straight loan and commercial paper. The basic difference
between them is the underwriting guarantee. In two years, according
to Salomon Brothers' estimates, the volume of NIFs arranged increased nearly tenfold, from $2.7 billion in 1982 to $20 billion in
1984.

The flexibility between instruments within a single borrowing
facility has been extended with astonishing rapidity. NIFs and
RUFs have been made even more sophisticated by the addition of
the right to issue the notes in a choice of currencies. 'Perpetual'
FRNs have been developed as an alternative to equity and have
been quickly taken up both by banks, anxious to increase their equity–
debt ratios, and by governments, which can get good terms on the
interest rates with low currency risk, since the notes need never be
paid back. To all these facilities have been added options allowing
borrowers to review them at regular intervals, to renegotiate their

terms, to switch from fixed rate to floating rate and to change from paper to loans.

The biggest growth of all has been in 'swaps', by which a borrower in one market swaps his debt with a borrower in another market. The idea is simply that a corporation well known in the American market, for example, may need to raise Deutschmarks to build a factory in West Germany, where he is not so well known. A bank then finds a German borrower who needs dollars but is not well known in the USA and therefore cannot get as good rates as the first company. They swap, reducing the cost to each. The technique can be used not only to swap currency obligations but also to exchange fixed debt for floating debt and short-term notes for long-term notes. It's a technique of almost infinite variety and obvious attraction to corporate or institutional borrowers that find themselves with too much of their borrowing in one currency or in one form of debt. British companies, for example, were encouraged by exchange controls to borrow largely in dollars during the 1970s and now want to rebalance their borrowings with more sterling, the currency in which most of their spending is carried out. At one time US companies may have taken advantage of peculiarly favourable terms to issue a lot of debt at the long end and may want to reduce this and raise their debt at the short end.

Only introduced to the international market in the early 1980s, swaps have almost literally taken off, tripling in volume between 1983 and 1984 to a total of $65 billion of new interest-rate swaps and between $12 billion and $15 billion of new currency swaps, according to estimates by Salomon Brothers' Bond Market Research. By then they accounted for as much as 80 per cent of all new eurobond issues in some months and, at an accumulated total of $170 billion by 1985, formed a larger market than the whole UK government debt market, enough to support a thriving secondary market in the instruments.

In most of the deals the two parties were swapping interest payments. The actual loan remained in the hands of the original borrower and the lender, thus limiting the risk involved in the swap to the maintenance of interest payments should one of the parties fail. But more and more even the loan itself is now being swapped and, by 1985, one-tenth of the market was believed to have involved swaps in the underlying loan or asset.

Some idea of the size and sophistication of the international borrowings being made in the market can be gained from recent deals. The Kingdom of Sweden, voted 'Borrower of the Year' in a

Euromoney poll,* in 1984 raised nearly $6 billion. Ten or even five years before, it might well have raised this money through syndicated loans made on the US domestic market and in the eurodollar market. Instead of using syndicated bank loans, however, it raised the money directly on the bond markets.

The object, as described by Peter Engström, head of the international loans department of the National Debt Office, was to use Sweden's return to balance-of-payments equilibrium, and thus its high credit rating in the financial community, to refinance a quarter of Sweden's $16 billion foreign debt. One object was simply to obtain lower borrowing costs; another was to smooth out the repayments profile from a bunching in the 1980s to a regular path through the 1990s; a third was to replace loans with notes.

Like other sovereign borrowers in the developing countries, Sweden had begun to borrow more on the FRN market during the previous years. But its first effort of 1984 to extend the repayment period from twenty to forty years in a $500 million issue in February failed. Investors do not like long repayment periods at tight margins, however good the fees to the underwriters. So the deal had to be repackaged by Merrill Lynch, the lead manager, with special income certificates to raise the rate of return to $\frac{1}{4}$ per cent instead of the original $\frac{1}{8}$ per cent above LIBOR. The new certificate was backed by an interest-rate swap.

Much more successful and ambitious were Sweden's next moves. In April, using Chase Manhattan and Salomon Brothers as lead managers, it issued a $1.5 billion FRN issue in the US market, at that time the largest capital issue ever made in the US domestic market. It was not just a simple FRN. Under a complex deal involving both banking and underwriting practice and steering a neat course along the Glass–Steagall Act dividing the two, the issue involved seven-year FRNs that allowed investors to sell back the notes, if they wished, at a set date each year. If they exercised this option, then Chase would loan Sweden the same amount of money. The deal gave Sweden funds that were cheaper than if it had tried a straightforward seven-year note, while the investors are buying notes that are effectively annual.

On top of this deal Sweden pioneered, using Morgan Guaranty, a perpetual FRN in the euromarkets for $750 million. Under a special 'flip-flop' clause in this deal investors could 'flip' out of the perpetual and slightly higher-yielding terms and convert to a four-year bond

* *Euromoney*, October 1984.

each year; once a year they also had the option of 'flopping' back to
the perpetual if they felt more confident. Finally, to cap the year the
Kingdom raised a $4 billion ten-year borrowing facility with the
major U S commercial banks, only a quarter of which it drew down
initially. Under this facility Sweden has three options: it can borrow
any amount at a set interest rate, varying in the spread of L I B O R
depending on how much it does borrow; it can ask the banks to bid in
offering it short-term advances, and use this option in preference if
their bids are below the first option; and it can issue short-term
notes, on a tender basis, to see if the banks offer to take them up at an
even lower price.

For the Swedish government the effect of this series of deals,
according to Engstrom, was to reduce their interest rates by about
twenty basis points, equivalent to about $20 million a year. For the
banks it meant over $100 million in fees. But for the market it showed
clearly that the bond markets were now large enough and international
enough to take the kinds of billion-dollar issue that were once the
exclusive preserve of the syndicated loan market. The bond market
had grown up.

'Globalization' has not just increased the liquidity (the amount of
money) available on the international capital markets; it has also
permitted an immeasurably more rapid interplay of ideas between
the various markets. Many of the ideas, from F R Ns to R U Fs, have
come from the eurobond markets. But the 1980s have also seen an
increasing flow of innovation in and from the U S domestic markets.

For reasons of size and history, the U S bond and paper markets
have always been much more developed than the European or Asian
markets. This has been partly a banking matter. European and
Japanese banks have been able, by law as well as by custom, to offer
their clients much more flexible overdraft facilities. At the same time
the market for long-term, fixed-rate debt in Britain and other
countries has been increasingly dominated by governments and
municipalities, which have 'crowded out' the private sector. In the
U S A, on the other hand, the bond markets have long been the
readiest source of debt for corporations and have sustained a sophisticated investment interest as well as the support of recognized
rating agencies to define corporate creditworthiness – the famous
ratings, from triple-A to C, of Moody's and Standard and Poor's.

Inflation and volatility have produced a succession of novel instruments to attract the investor and spread the reach of bond finance.
The issue of straight bonds, borrowings redeemable over a set period

at the price on the bond (at par) with a coupon attached giving a set interest rate, has now been supplemented by zero-coupon bonds, or 'streakers' as they are sometimes called, in which an interest rate over the period is worked out and the bonds are issued at the par price minus this sum. Convertible bonds are bonds that give the investor the right to convert them into the company's equity on maturity and at a specified price. Bonds with warrants give the investor either the right to buy shares in the company under certain conditions or the right to subscribe to the next issue of stocks or bonds. Subordinated debt ranks the issue below that of other bond holders but above that of shareholders. Added to this are bonds that strip the coupon, or interest, element from the underlying asset in a whole menagerie of instruments introduced in the USA in the 1980s – Merrill Lynch's Treasury Investment Growth Receipts (TIGRs), Salomon Brothers' CATs and others.

The most notorious development to come from the bond markets of America has been 'junk bonds'. Pioneered by Drexel Burnham, junk bonds were developed out of the perception that a whole range of companies that could gain only poor ratings from Moody's or Standard and Poor's, either because they were heavy-industry companies in decline or they were companies too young to have a track record, could, in a liquid bond market, offer higher coupons than better-rated bonds and therefore have investment interest. Junk bonds grew out of the gap left by the conservatism of banks and institutions in the post-energy-crisis world. They proved their worth with a whole raft of companies that managed to turn themselves around – the most famous being Chrysler – or newer companies that made their founders a fortune. Indeed, Drexel Burnham claim that if all publicly held companies in the USA were to ask for ratings, no fewer than 85 per cent would fail to reach the 'investment grade' ratings. True or not, their higher-yield performance and the relatively low rate of failures during the boom years of US expansion in the early 1980s caused the volume of issues of high-yield, high-risk bonds to soar from less than $2 billion in 1979 to over $14 billion in 1984, 73 per cent of it underwritten by Drexel. The total of $36 billion bonds outstanding by the end of 1984 made up nearly one-seventh of the whole $450 billion straight public corporate bond market in America.

They have become notorious because of the contested take-overs that have swept the USA since 1983. By forming groups of under-writers who, for a fee, agree in principle to issue small or low-rated companies with bonds on the basis of the assets of a company they are seeking to take over in the event of the take-over being successful, a number of raiders, such as Carl Icahn and T. Boone Pickens, have been able to besiege some of the greatest corporate citadels in the land, from Gulf Oil to TWA, using junk bonds to finance their bids. If the raiders are successful, then they can issue bonds on the basis of their newly acquired assets. If they fail, they usually gain more than enough from the sale of their shares – 'greenmail', as it has been dubbed – to pay the fees of underwriters, who are happy to agree to provide the facility for large bond issues that they are usually never called upon to put into effect. It was, until corporations grew wise in their defences, 'Heads I win, tails you lose' for the raiders.

The relevance of junk bonds to markets outside the USA is still to be tested. The relative constriction of the bond markets elsewhere and the much tighter controls over take-overs and mergers in the stock exchanges of Europe and Japan militate against anything like the growth that the USA has witnessed – although the concept of high-risk, high-yield paper may yet prove to have more potential than Europeans are sometimes inclined to believe.

Of much greater potential application is the issue of mortgage or loan-backed bonds. 'Securitization' is a concept that has been around for some time but has only now been taken up as a technique that could apply to a wide range of financial assets. The idea is to take fixed, long-term loans and turn them into paper that can be readily bought and sold in the bond market. For three decades the US government has deliberately encouraged this with mortgages through guarantees to the Federal National Mortgage Association (FNMA, or Fannie Mae as it is usually known), the Government National Mortgage Association (GNMA, or Ginnie Mae) and the Student Loan Marketing Association (SLMA, or Sallie Mae). Mortgages, backed by the government and insured through recognized agencies, are put into a pool and shares in the pool are sold. The investor has the advantage of a security that gives him both a regular income stream from the interest payments on the mortgages, as well as an additional pay-out once the mortgages have been paid back. The security is readily negotiable in the markets. The mortgage agency has the advantage of turning what would otherwise be a series of individual, illiquid assets into an immediate source of funds. Over the last two decades the market in the USA has grown to $500 billion.

The technique is now being broadened to include mortgages held by the commercial banks and extended to other types of loan bringing

a regular income stream, such as leases and car loans. Most of the
major thrifts in the USA have now repackaged parts of their home
loans in this way. In 1985 Salomon Brothers introduced the first
issue of Certificates of Automobile Receivables (CARs, ap-
propriately). 'We concluded,' said a vice-president, 'that there is no
fundamental difference between a car loan and a mortgage. The
collateral is different – the house doesn't rust and a car does if you
leave it out in the rain. You can't steal a house; you can steal a car.
But, other than that, a car loan is a level monthly-payment debt
instrument with a shorter maturity.'

Theoretically, almost any loan could thus be turned into a security,
from government-assisted small-business loans to computer leases.
And no doubt some investment bank will give it a whirl. With $162
billion of automobile loans outstanding and several trillion dollars'
worth of what the Americans call 'receivables' in the USA alone, even
a small proportion of the potential candidates would mean a major
trading market. By 1985 it was worth well over $1 billion a year and, on
some estimates by Salomon Brothers, could eventually outrun even
the corporate bond market in size. Nor is it limited to the USA. The
technique is just as applicable and just as attractive to European and
Asian markets as to the American. Banks have become anxious – a
matter of concern for their supervising authorities – to cash in some of
their tied-up assets. Finance companies with low corporate ratings can
see a way of attracting investors by packaging some of their best loans.
Investors in Europe are becoming interested: witness the success of
the first bonds issued by Fannie Mae outside the USA in 1985. The
potential issuers of Europe cannot be far behind.

The USA's greatest export of a financial technique in the 1980s,
however, is undoubtedly financial futures and options. Developed as a
means of sustaining growth in the sagging commodity markets of
Philadelphia, New York and, above all, Chicago, financial futures
and options have exploded on to the markets in the mid-1980s. Again,
the concept is reasonably straightforward. In a futures contract the
buyer agrees to purchase the commodity or item at a specified price
on a certain day in the future. The price takes account of inflation
and the seller's view of the likely price of that commodity when the
contract matures. In an option the buyer purchases the right, at an
initial premium, to buy or sell a commodity or instrument within a
set time. If the market moves his way, he can exercise his option. If it
moves against him, he can decline to exercise the option and simply
loses his initial premium.

Futures on commodities have been used for generations by commodity brokers, by corporations buying raw materials at a future date and by investors. They are a way of ensuring that the price of vital raw material can be fixed early on. For decades the exchange markets too have used futures on currencies for the same reason. Options have contributed an element of insurance, or hedging, to this and a means of transferring risk more broadly among the participants. Where Chicago and the other commodity exchanges have added investor interest is in applying the technique to a wide range of indices, commodities, currencies and stocks and shares. You can now buy futures on individual shares and Treasury bills, and theoretical composites of the stock exchange and Treasury bills rates, on currencies or composite currencies (like the European ECU).

The theory may be to manage risk on general stock-exchange movements, on unexpected changes in currencies and on interest rates. And that is why most large corporations and all banks use futures. But in practice they have also become a means of speculation. The Chicago dentist and the 'locals', the small traders of Chicago, rule. As the range is extended, and now that even the amateur can use a personal computer to work out the computations, the sophistication has become extreme. You take out a future and then an option on that future should it go the opposite way to your expectations. Then, when the market sentiment changes a little, you take out another option to counterbalance the first option and limit your risk. You buy a put option (that is, an option to sell) and then a call option (the option to buy). Time spreads consist of options with the same price but different expiration dates; prices spreads consist of options bought at different purchase prices but the same expiration prices; a straddle consists of purchasing both a put and a call to make sure that you are covered if the underlying item moves either way. For the seller of options it means income from the premium payment and a position that can itself be covered by options. For the investor it is a means of constantly taking a position and balancing it against the future.

Stock-index futures were introduced only in 1982. Yet by 1983 the dollar value of the trading in futures on the stock index actually exceeded the dollar value of trading on the New York Stock Exchange. In 1984 the volume of bond contracts on the Chicago Board of Trade exceeded the total volume of all commodity futures contracts traded a decade earlier. The average daily volume of Chicago Board of Trade futures on US Treasury bonds is now between twice and eight times the value of trading in the bonds themselves. The variations on the theme are almost endless, as are the new products. In the OTC market customers can buy future-rate agreements (FRAs) to fix the interest for a period or an interest-rate guarantee (IRG) or an interest-rate cap (IRC), which puts a ceiling on the upward or downward movement in interest rates that they will pay, essentially by providing an option on the FRA. The investor as well as the corporation can take out options or futures on everything from the price of gold to the price of municipal bonds.

In Chicago the Chicago Board of Trade competes with the Chicago Mercantile Exchange. Vying with Chicago, Philadelphia, New York and Kansas City have raced to gain a lead on new products in order to acquire a position themselves. Most of the exchanges in the world now have options and futures on their shares. Increasingly the financial centres of the world, from Montreal to Singapore and Sydney, are introducing or thinking of introducing futures exchanges and are busily linking up with other centres across the oceans to ensure revolving activity. 'You need a mathematics doctorate and an intimate understanding of the theories of probability even to understand the first moves on the board,' said one of Chicago's biggest brokers. He did not add that most of the managers on the dealing-room floor, let alone the institutions supposedly supervising the markets, meet his criteria.

The one piece of this global kaleidoscope that is missing is the equity market. The communications are in place. The dealers in New York, on NASDAQ and the institutional networks, quote and buy and sell British, West German, Australian and Swiss shares. The dealers in London are quoting American and South African shares. But dealing in fully listed shares within a domestic market is still limited to the members of that country's exchange, and their position is still protected by law.

The potential for change is clearly there. More and more the major industrial and commercial companies, the chemical groups, the electronics manufacturers, the big computer concerns, the automobile names, are looking on the world as their marketplace and are dividing it into three regions – the USA, Europe and Asia – for planning, marketing and investment purposes. In the words of Sir Harvey Jones, chairman of ICI in 1985, 'Today's world demands response to the market. Even our research and development is now being regionally structured.'

So too with finance. Companies like I C I or Bell of Canada now see the need to have a presence and a reputation in each of the major financial centres of the world, through separate stock-exchange quotations if need be. They also see the advantage of tapping the huge funds being built up in the institutions of each of these areas. When the British government in 1984 planned to privatize its nationalized telephone company, British Telecom, in a £4.5 million flotation, it earmarked a proportion of the shares for both New York and Tokyo. And it used local underwriters to ensure international success, just as Texaco did in the same year when it proposed a $1 billion bond issue.

Companies for some time have sought a second, or even third, listing for their shares as a means of broadening their shareholding base and increasing the potential for additional equity financing. But it is only since 1982 that companies have used international syndication as a means of making equity issues, in the form either of direct share issues or of convertibles. By the end of 1985 some £2.5 billion of issues had been done this way, from British Telecom in the U K to Sallie Mae in the U S A and the Moët-Hennessey champagne and brandy group in France. Some of these were accompanied by share listings in other exchanges. But many issues, particularly by the big names, avoided foreign stock exchanges altogether, being underwritten by securities houses like Nomura, traditional bond underwriters such as Crédit Suisse–First Boston and Morgan Stanley and the Swiss banks such as Union Bank and the Swiss Bank Corporation, whose placing power among the private investors of their country remains supreme. While a full stock-exchange listing for a Swedish company might take months of documentation and review and investor 'road shows' in New York or Tokyo, a syndicated issue through the international underwriters may be effected within four days to a week for a well-known name and within two weeks for a lesser-known name. The shares will be traded and retraded on the dealing-room floors of the institutions and the investment banks of the world. Most of the initial shares of British Telecom sold in Japan, for example, found their way back to Europe within a few days. The result disappointed the British government but hardly surprised the underwriters, who merely pointed out that they could all go back to Japan a week or a year later – the idea of carefully balanced and settled placing was no longer appropriate in an age of international dealing.

That, of course, is the challenge faced by the stock exchanges as they struggle to prevent new issues by smaller and more entrepreneurial companies from veering to the OTC markets of electronic screen trading and the international issues from veering equally to the electronic screens of the big, international securities houses and investment banks, while all the while governments and legislators demand that they uphold stricter and stricter rules to protect the investor from fraud and misrepresentation. Earlier hours, new international combinations, new technology of their own are all part of their response. But the key problem remains the very factor that gives the stock exchanges of the world their character – their origins and their history as associations of individuals in Tokyo as much as New York, in London as much as Amsterdam.

Table 4   The size of the world's stock markets, 1984: market value and turnover (fixed-interest bonds and equity, £ million)

	Market value	*Turnover*	*Domestic companies quoted*	*Overseas companies quoted*
New York	2,195,222	666,458	1,490	53
Tokyo	831,473	350,289	1,444	11
London	334,283	182,338	2,171	505
Paris	146,518	44,704	550	182
Milan	130,229	5,076	143	–
Toronto	116,253	17,445	878	55
Singapore	85,652	2,684	121	187
Amsterdam	74,961	18,614	263	300
Australia (Association of Exchanges)	70,280	21,738	1,009	18
Germany (Association of Exchanges)	67,497[1]	64,119	449	180
Stockholm	66,161	7,701	159	6
Zurich	62,645	101,930	121	175
Johannesburg	60,165	13,124	470	25
Basle	58,603	22,362	322	475

Note:[1] Does not include fixed interest.
Source: UK *Stock Exchange Companion*, 1985.

The equity markets of the world guard their privileges religiously. The membership of exchanges is limited. The terms of listing, the rights of the shareholders, the rules governing take-overs all differ widely between exchanges round the world. There is constant talk of common listing and uniform prospectuses. But no exchange is prepared to accept the changes except on its own terms. And for good reason: the right to have a piece of a company and a vote in its future is the most intimate of all financial investments, and the most traditional. Globalization and securitization are tearing down most of the national barriers. At the exchanges they are still testing their defences.

FOUR

THE PLAYERS

If you had been writing a book on international finance in the late 1970s or early 1980s, the archetypal figure might well have been a banker from one of the major New York City banks, well groomed, early forties, Brooks Brothers shirt and a leather briefcase with an airline tag on it. He would stay in the Okura in Tokyo, the Mandarin in Hong Kong, the Berkeley in London, the Intercontinental in Frankfurt. He would have been educated at an Ivy League college, or act like it, and would have spent fifteen years in the planning and international divisions of the bank. His briefcase would contain summaries of the economic performance and the prospects of the country he was visiting, but he would go to its national museum, perhaps take in an opera. He would negotiate with a lawyer and expect to meet ministers as well as officials. His job would be to arrange large syndicated loans for sovereign nations.

Today he is still around but with the tinge of the past. The man of the moment is now the dealer or salesman from the bank's dealing-room floor: mid-twenties, earning as much as $100,000, a third in salary, the rest in bonuses from a good year. Shirt-sleeved, close-cropped hair, a taste for ham on rye and low-calorie soft drinks. Jogs some mornings, goes to noisy restaurants and clubs most nights. It's a man's, or rather a youth's, world. There are not many women on the dealing-room floors of the most active banks – none in many countries. It is hype in the day and drinks with the lads in the early evening.

One city is much the same as the rest. In the Connaught Centre of Hong Kong, where the window cleaners peer in through the portholes like divers on a sunken ship, in the Marunouchi district of Tokyo, in London's golden square mile of the City or in Sydney's harbour the dealing-rooms all look alike. The dealer enters through an old-fashioned heavy mahogany door, curiously out of keeping with the metal of the elevators and the hessian-covered walls of the corridor, goes through a waiting-room equipped with tastefully upholstered settees, a few prints of local interest on the walls, a glass-topped table bearing the

Wall Street Journal and some promotional brochures. The receptionist sits at a nineteenth-century-style desk. He goes through to a windowless dealing-room to find out what has happened in the markets that have already opened.

The young man has been with his bank for four or five years and learnt his trade by sitting beside an experienced dealer for six months. This is his first foreign assignment, but it is not a bad one. Two of his colleagues from New York have just gone over to a Swiss bank for 50 per cent more on their basic pay and a guaranteed bonus of $250,000 if they stay three years. Maybe he should think of moving. He doesn't expect to stay with his bank, but then he does not see himself doing any other kind of job. They say that you are burnt out as a dealer by the time you are thirty. But then there is not much point in thinking that far ahead. It looks as if something may be going on with euro-dollar futures in Tokyo.

The name of the game is now the capital markets, and the kings are undoubtedly the investment banks and securities houses of New York – Salomon Brothers, Merrill Lynch, Goldman Sachs, Morgan Stanley, First Boston, Shearson Lehman and Drexel Burnham. Not that they are all the same. Salomons has always been a trading firm, with the best reputation for managing new bond issues, thinking up new bond ideas and dealing in anything that is dealable. 'They'd try birth and death certificates if they could make a market,' says a competitor. Merrill Lynch has always been a distributor, with the largest worldwide network of salesmen and offices of any securities company, the biggest exposures and the most relentless drive to be present everywhere, to deal in everything and to sell to everybody. When the firm was dubbed the 'thundering herd' in the marketplace, the sobriquet was not entirely affectionate. Goldman Sachs is one of the last true private partnerships. Morgan Stanley is the old style: thick carpets, heavy desks and a claim to have the closest relations with the best corporate clients. (Some accuse it of showing signs of middle-age spread.)

Nor are the investment banks and securities houses unassailable. Steadily building up their positions in the markets of Europe and the USA are the Japanese. Taken as something of a joke in the early years, the Japanese houses, with their armies of salesmen, their immense resources and their determination to succeed, have not been shy of taking on the competition. Nomura is just as big as Merrill Lynch and just as ambitious to do all and be all. When they first arrived in London its salesmen had to be restrained, by orders from headquarters, from ringing up pension-fund managers late into the evening to push for business. Yamaichi and Nikko securities are not far behind, nor are the more aggressive international banks of Japan – the Bank of Tokyo, Japan's traditional international financing arm; the Industrial Bank of Japan, its most vigorous long-term credit bank; Daichi Kangyo and Sumitomo, its biggest and fastest expanding commercial banks.

It would be a foolish occupant of Wall Street who doubted the muscle and competitive power of Deutsche Bank or the universal banks of Switzerland, the Swiss Bank Corporation and the Union Bank of Switzerland. Alongside Morgan Guaranty, Deutsche must be one of the world's best-balanced financial institutions, strong in commercial banking, strong in corporate underwriting, getting stronger in trading. The Swiss, after a poor patch of complacency and stagnation during the early 1980s, are now returning to the international fray to exploit their experience, far greater than that of any other country, of private investment needs and pre-placed issues.

Coming over from the other side of the field, meanwhile, are the big money-centre banks of the USA – Citicorp, big in everything from retail banking to international dealing because power lies with possession and position; Morgan Guaranty, for many the perfect bank, strong in its corporate relations, experienced in the international field and supremely professional in its control of risk; and others, like Bankers Trust and Manufacturers Hanover, that are turning their course towards the preserves of investment banking. And coming up from an angled position to the right and behind are the new British conglomerates, formed around the merchant banks Warburgs and Kleinworts or being built up by the British 'clearers', the big retail banks of Barclays, Lloyds, the Midland and National Westminster.

The older generation say that the fun has gone out of merchant banking, that international finance is not the same any more. The individual does not lope about the market, nurturing his contacts and dreaming up new types of deal. The banks, commercial or investment, do not have the same relationship any longer with their clients, a handshake over a loan, a knowledge of the kids and their grades. True, but only partly so. Some, like the related group of Lazard banks in London, Paris and New York, are happy to maintain that old relationship, even to concentrate on it. They can make enough money doing it. There are still the individuals with their contacts – Felix Rohatyn of Lazards, the man who helped Mayor Koch bring

New York back from bankruptcy; Lord Camoys, formerly of Rothschilds and now with Barclays Merchant Bank of London. Some of the big names of the last generation are now retired – Lord Richardson of the Bank of England, Leutweiler of Switzerland, Paul Lichtenberg of the Commerzbank of Germany and Robert Baldwin of Morgan Stanley – but the strong men still exist, like John Gutfreund of Salomons, and so does the need for contacts. The steady stream of government officials and ministers who find their way into merchant banking in their later years are not employed just for the boardroom tablets.

Nor is there any shortage of originality in today's financing. It may be different. Drexel Burnham's espousal of the cause of junk bonds has shocked some, but, aggressive though it may be, it is an expression of the old-fashioned virtues of finding a market need and moving to dominate it.

Drexel Burnham Lambert was not the first investment bank to issue junk or unrated, high-yield bonds. Shearsons gained that honour in 1976. But it was the first to see their potential and to make them its speciality. A medium-sized investment bank at the time, it had been founded in 1935 by I. W. 'Tubby' Burnham, a trader who believed that actual cash was the secret of success in the post-Crash period. Through the immediate post-war years it had grown steadily, if not spectacularly, acquiring the prestigious Drexel Firestone in 1973 (a firm that had once numbered J. P. Morgan among its partners) and the William D. Witter research firm in 1976, when it ranked about nineteenth in the list of Wall Street underwriters of corporate bonds.

By 1984 Drexel had leapt to third place, behind Salomons and Goldman Sachs; its revenues had soared to over $1 billion, and its shareholders' equity had climbed tenfold to $320 million, making it second only to Goldman Sachs among private investment firms. The weapon of its success was the explosion in the use of junk bonds and subordinated debt in the early 1980s. The secret of success was the combination of talents and ambition of its three leading figures: Robert Linton, chairman from 1977, who imposed a management style of tight strategic control expressed through daily meetings of the top managers and very loose tactical control through the wide deal-making freedom he allows his managers; Frederick Joseph, the son of a Boston cab driver and a Harvard graduate who moved from Shearson Hammill to run Drexel's corporate finance department in 1974 because he wanted to shake up the financial establishment; and

Michael Milken, the legendary king of junk-bond trading, who operates out of Beverley Hills in Los Angeles, starting work at 5 a.m., eating lunch at 10 a.m. and managing an irreplaceable and intricate network of moneyed individual share dealers like T. Boone Pickens, the Bass Family of Fort Worth, Pritzker, Saul Steinberg and Ivan Boesky.

Milken, as an undergraduate at the University of California at Berkeley, had written a thesis showing that the likelihood of high-risk bonds faltering through the failure of new companies was actually surprisingly small, considering their high returns. As a trader with Drexel he developed the contacts and the knowledge of companies and their executives that was to serve as the basis of his network of trading relationships later on. Left with surprising freedom to operate, he is reputed to have been earning, at the height of the bond boom in 1984–5, $20 million to $30 million a year in bonuses.

The selling point was simple enough. There were innumerable medium-sized and even large companies bereft of top credit rating by the rating companies in the wake of the industrial shake-out that followed the second oil shock of 1979. Drexel Burnham could offer them a speedy and flexible form of finance, through high-coupon bonds, to help them to rationalize and contract. The bonds could not be sold to most pension funds and institutions because of the rules that restricted their investments to high-rated bonds and equities. But there were many individual investors, and some more speculative fund managers, who were willing to take the risks in exchange for the greater rewards.

It is this range of new investors that has given Drexel its competitive edge. Lacking the corporate and institutional contacts of a Morgan Stanley – which was to pay Drexel the ultimate compliment of setting up a junk-bond department of its own after treating the market initially with disdain – Drexel has built up, through its traditional interest in smaller companies, a unique relationship with both the companies in need of this finance and the big players – the Steinbergs, Icahns and Pritzkers – who will invest in it. Putting together borrowers in need with investors with greed is old-fashioned investment banking in modern guise.

The art is continuously to come up with new ideas. An early-evening visit to Drexel's offices in Broad Street, near Wall Street in New York, finds a small team preparing a deal not in a heavy-tabled, portrait-filled boardroom but in the small office of one of the managing directors, half filled with exercise equipment. The team of three is discussing, for a change, the defence of a company against a hostile take-over, not the other way round. They have thought of a special issue of subordinated debt and some new techniques to make the company unpalatable to the bidder. The problem is: Will the main shareholder of the assaulted company accept, and will the besieger go away? Both come on the line at various stages. The managing director shouts his responses upside-down from an abdomen machine, then jumps out to pull on a chest stretcher, changes the price fractionally, gets acceptance, knows he has won. No champagne: there is no time. It is home to pack a case to fly to Texas in order to get a judge to lift an injunction that the firm has taken out as part of the defences.

Perhaps it is more teamwork that produces more deals than before, although the prince of junk-bond trading, Michael Milken, works virtually on his own in Beverly Hills, a whole continent's span away from New York. But teamwork today, if more extensive, is just as innovative as before – very probably more so. In the traditional terms of investment banking, the bringing together of investors on one side with corporations or governments and institutions in need of money on the other side, finance has never been so imaginative or so sophisticated. The difference is that, to package the most effective loan at a time both of volatile exchange and interest rates and of increasingly knowledgeable institutional investors, you have to know what is on offer in all parts of the globe and to have experience of the different kinds of instrument, from eurobonds to receivable securities. The difference for the financial firms is that not only must you have the ideas but you must also have the international coverage to distribute the offering, the capitalization to deal in large issues and the trading ability to move them in the secondary markets.

The investment banks (or merchant banks, as the British call them) have always had the ideas and the corporate relationships. It is only recently that they, or more particularly the American firms, have developed the size and trading capacity that modern capital markets demand. In the late 1960s and early 1970s U S firms – even those like Salomon Brothers – were not very much larger than the London merchant banks such as Kleinworts, Warburgs and Schroders. The phenomenal growth came about in the second half of the 1970s, partly as a result of the abolition of fixed commissions on May Day 1975, which forced the pace of competition, led to the disappearance of a number of middle-ranked securities houses and forced a spate of mergers, confirming the dominance of the major houses such as

Merrill Lynch. Soon afterwards the bond and equity markets of America burgeoned, increasing enormously the turnover of the major dealing houses. Then, in 1982, the Securities and Exchange Commission (SEC) dramatically changed the stages of the game by allowing 'shelf registration'. Corporations could agree the terms of an issue with either a single underwriter or a group. The underwriter would then hang on to the issue until the time seemed ripe to put it out on to the market. The rule confirmed the increasing trend of the major investment banks and securities houses to hold a major proportion of an issue on their own books to sell when the price seemed right. But to do that they needed far greater capitalization than the investment banks of old, formed of partnerships between individuals using family funds or borrowed finance, could manage. Booming markets made the financial firms attractive. High-stakes trading made capital essential. In the early 1980s a spate of mergers and acquisitions put new muscle into Wall Street and brought new financial groups into the field: American Express, which bought Shearson Loeb Rhoades in 1981 and Lehman Brothers in 1984; Prudential Insurance, which brought Bache Halsey Stuart Shields in 1981 to form Pru-Bache; Equitable Life, which bought Donaldson, Lufkin and Jenrette, one of the pioneers of the eurobond market, in 1984; Sears Roebuck, which bought Dean Witter in 1981. Even Salomon Brothers sold out, in 1981, to the Phibro Corporation (see Table 5).

The imperatives for this steady stream of marriages were mixed. Some investment firms deliberately sought mergers as a means of adding to their trading and financial muscle; others found themselves too small to compete with the large traders but too big to find a niche for themselves as investment bankers; still others, private partnerships, saw a sell-out as a quick means to real capital gain.

The once untouchable Salomon Brothers decided to merge with the giant oil and commodities trading group, Phibro, after advising Phibro's parent company, Engelhard Minerals and Chemicals, to spin off its trading subsidiary. For years Salomon, when headed by Billy Salomon in the 1970s, had refused to go public as had so many of its competitors, like E. F. Hutton and Paine Weber. 'Keep small and trade more' was its philosophy, and Salomon himself insisted on retaining a tight partnership structure. Under this partners were allotted shares according to performance and given an annual dividend on the basis of those shares. When a partner left his shares were returned to the firm to be redivided among his former colleagues, and he was paid out in cash in annual sums over time.

Table 5 Major US entrants into securities brokerage through acquisition, *1981–4*

Acquiring institution	Acquired brokerage firm	Year
American Express Co.	Shearson Loeb Rhoades, Inc.	1981
Phibro Corporation	Salomon Brothers	1981
Prudential Insurance Co.	Bache Halsey Stuart Shields, Inc.	1981
Sears, Roebuck & Co.	Dean Witter Reynolds	1981
Empire of America, F S A	William M. Cadden & Co., Inc.	1982
First Union National Bank	Salem Securities, Inc.	1982
John Hancock Insurances Co.	Tucker Anthony & R. L. Day, Inc.	1982
Kemper Group	Bateman Eichler, Hill Richards, Inc.	1982
Kemper Group	Blunt, Ellis & Loewi	1982
Kemper Group	Prescott, Ball & Turben, Inc.	1982
Travelers Insurance	Securities Settlement Corporation	1982
Union Planters National Bank	Brenner Steed & Associates, Inc.	1982
BankAmerica Corporation	Charles Schwab & Co., Inc.	1983
Chase Manhattan Corporation	Rose & Company Investment Brokers, Inc.	1983
First Union National Bank	Dis-Com Securities, Inc.	1983
Security Pacific National Bank	Commission Discount Corporation	1983
Security Pacific National Bank	Kahn & Co.	1983
Security Pacific National Bank	Kenneth Kass & Co.	1983
United Jersey Banks	Richard Blackman & Co., Inc.	1983
American Express Co.	Lehman Brothers Kuhn Loeb, Inc.	1984
Chemical New York Corporation	Brown & Co. Securities Corporation	1984
Equitable Life Assurance	Donaldson, Lufkin & Jenrette	1984
Kemper Group	Burton J. Vincent & Chesley & Co.	1984
Northern Trust Corporation	Jerome Hickey & Associates	1984

Source: Richard Aspinall (of Chase Manhattan), 'Shifting Frontiers in Financial Markets in the U S', paper for a colloquium of S U E R F, March 1985.

The partnership structure, the common form of Wall Street organizations during the previous century and before, was ideal for businesses based on client relationships but was becoming less and less appropriate for a trading world where capital needs were far higher. Volatile interest rates and exchange rates forced investment banks to accept more and more risks. Rule 415, introduced in 1982 to allow underwriters to agree the issue of bonds and to hold them 'on the shelf' until an appropriate marketing moment, made capital almost imperative if underwriters were to compete.

Salomons held to its partnership structure, as Goldman Sachs still does, because its close relationship with institutions and its dealing capability allowed it to ensure speedy distribution of issues and to spread the risks. But, in 1978 the managing partnership of the firm was handed over to John Gutfreund, a tough dealer who saw that the world was changing and that, to grow, you needed to get into more and more instruments. Oil futures were one type, and when Phibro, during the preparations for its independence from Engelhard, suggested a merger in May 1981, Salomon's executive board accepted over a weekend in July. Commercial logic was one reason. So was the offer to replace all the partners' capital with $300 million in cash with a premium of $250 million for the general, or active, partners – an offer that gave the average Salomon partner, according to the *Wall Street Journal* at the time, $7.8 million each and Gutfreund over $30 million in cash and shares. It was left to Billy Salomon, who had been kept ignorant of the negotiations until the last and was excluded even from the general partners' meeting when Gutfreund announced the deal, to bemoan the passing of the old family firm. It was left to Phibro to find that it had bought a tiger that would devour it. While commodity prices fell during the early 1980s, Salomon's profits rose. Within three years of the deal Gutfreund had become chairman and chief executive of the merged group. On 28 October he announced a restructuring that reduced the number of Phibro's workers by over 20 per cent, removed its chief executive and renamed the merged group simply Salomon, Inc. in place of Phibro–Salomon. The family name had not died.

The lure of partnership reward and quarrels over the division of spoils actually brought down the distinguished firm of Lehman Brothers and cast it into the arms of American Express. Lehman Brothers, the oldest continuing partnership in Wall Street by the time of its demise in 1984, was a firm that traced its origins back to German-Jewish immigrants in the mid-nineteenth century who had built their fortunes on the cotton trade and on aiding Southern industry after the Civil War. The last active member of the family, Bobbie Lehman, had died in 1969, and his successor, the former secretary of commerce, Peter Peterson, had been ousted in 1983 by the firm's star trader and his co-chairman, Lewis Glucksman. The overthrow had been bloody enough,* but in the aftermath Glucksman had made the fatal error of the medieval rulers of Frankish Holy Land in rewarding too fully those who were his friends and punishing too incautiously those who were not.

Like many partnerships, the annual distribution of bonuses and the division of shares in the firm were fixed by the executive committee on the basis of seniority, performance and practical political sense. Nothing is quite so sensitive to a partner than the allocation of shares and bonuses. Glucksman decided to redivide the shareholding and allocate the bonuses on a 'merit' basis; the trading arm would gain an overall share more appropriate to its growing contribution to the profits. It was logical, but it was not forgivable. After nine months of internal debate, wrangling and internecine quarrelling, Lehmans finally sold itself out to American Express to join Shearsons in the giant financial conglomerate in April 1984.

Probably the end of its independence was inevitable. Even with Glucksman's undoubted trading flare, its capital, at $250 million (like that of Salomons) was too small to enable it to extend its trading and take the knocks of a new trading world. Most of its rivals, after all, went the same way. Shearson Loeb Rhoades was induced into marriage with American Express by the merger-maker Sandy Lewis in 1981.† Dean Witter Reynolds, the product of seventeen mergers itself, went to Sears Roebuck in 1981. The Bache Group was forced into a sale to the Prudential insurance giant, partly in self-defence against the unwanted attentions of a less welcome suitor, the Belzberg family of Canada. Harry Jacobs, the man who had ousted his predecessor as chairman of Bache in the 'night of the long knives' in 1972, was himself ousted from Bache within two years by the new owners. Other mergers also had difficulties. Dillon Read, a medium-sized firm that had failed to develop a trading capability, was taken over by Bechtel in 1981, only to be set free again in a management buy-out in early 1983. In June 1984 the French banking group, Paribas, paid $100 million to take full control of brokers Becker

* See Ken Auletta, 'Power, Greed and Glory on Wall Street', *New York Times*, 17 and 24 February 1983.
† See Tim Carrington, *The Year They Sold Wall Street* (Boston, Houghton Mifflin, 1985).

Paribas, only to sell it a month and a half later to Merrill Lynch for $100 million in Merrill stock, less than half the amount that it had pumped into the group over the previous couple of years.

The mergers, the boardroom rows, the match-making and the smell of personal gain on Wall Street in the early 1980s have, in many ways, served as the warnings of, and the models for, the reshuffle now going on among the merchant (or investment) banks on the other side of the Atlantic. Like the American investment banks, the great names of British merchant banking, of the acceptance houses, as they are termed – Morgan Grenfell, Hambros, Schroder Wagg, S. G. Warburg, Kleinwort Benson, N. M. Rothschild, Baring Brothers – tend to be family affairs. All have their origin in entrepreneurial individuals and families, many of them Jewish immigrants. Most, like Barings, Rothschilds, Kleinworts, Schroder Wagg and Hambros, go back to the eighteenth and the early nineteenth century. Most grew through a combination of trade finance and the arrangement of loans for foreign governments, and most built up strong transatlantic connections and, in some cases, cross-shareholding. By the standards of the nineteenth century, they were large and well capitalized. In 1875 N. M. Rothschild and Sons had a capital of £6.5 million. J. S. Morgan, the largest of the American international houses at the time, had a capital of less than £2 million.

It was not that the British merchant banks refused to understand new markets. Three at least – Warburgs, Morgan Grenfell and Hambros – became major underwriters in the eurobond market, appearing regularly in the top ten lead managers, or book-runners, for non-dollar issues. Warburgs, the newcomer brought to London by the giant of post-war British merchant banking, Siegmund Warburg, appeared regularly in the top table for dollar issues as well. But all tended to regard small and personal as beautiful. The fat in the business was in the fees earned for advising clients on take-overs and mergers, not in dealing on your own account. Siegmund Warburg, indeed, used to warn constantly of the dangers of growing big and repeating the mistakes of the slothful heavyweights with which he had set himself to compete in Britain.

For those who kept an eye on the American markets Rule 415, allowing 'shelf registration' of issues, sounded the warning bell for a completely new round in the financing game. At first it was thought that the main beneficiaries – and the main proponents of the change, for that matter – would be the securities houses (such as E. F. Hutton) with national distribution systems. Instead it was firms (above all,

Salomons) with contacts among institutions and the ability to trade issues in the secondary market that were able to take the risks and offer corporations the means to a quick and effective form of finance, and these dominated the business from the start.

The British merchant banks and most of their European equivalents among the *banques d'affaires* were not geared up for this kind of activity. Although their increasing reliance on syndicate lending during the 1960s had forced most firms to abandon their partnership status and seek outside capital by 1970, the average U K merchant bank was still capitalized at only around $200 million by the early 1980s. Merrill Lynch, by contrast, had shareholders' equity of ten times this, at over $2 billion, while Shearson Lehman and Salomons were both capitalized at over $1 billion. On any one night Salomons or Merrill Lynch might 'go to bed' with an overnight exposure on their books of bonds and stocks of between $3 billion and $5 billion. Nomura, with a capitalization greater even than Merrill Lynch's, or Yamaichi or Nikko in Japan could do the same, as could Deutsche Bank or the Union Bank of Switzerland, using their full corporate muscle.

The merchant banks of Britain suddenly found themselves left in an inferior league; their ratings in the underwriting leagues suffered as a result. The big eurobond issues, even in some of the European currencies, were going to the Americans. The decision of the London Stock Exchange and the British government to alter the basis of trading in shares on the London Stock Exchange and to allow merchant banks and others to buy into Stock Exchange firms in 1984–5 was the spur to the merchant banks to rethink their positions and seek new partnerships: it was not the *raison d'être*.

The benefits of scale have led to an increasing concentration in the underwriting business. By the early 1980s the top five firms (the 'special category' group of Salomon Brothers, Morgan Stanley, First Boston, Merrill Lynch and Goldman Sachs) managed two-thirds of the total debt and equity issues in the U S A. One of them, Salomons, accounted for nearly a quarter. The top ten accounted for nearly 90 per cent. In the eurobond markets, where wider international competition has produced less of a concentration, the top two firms, Crédit Suisse–First Boston and the Deutsche Bank, still managed over one-third of all new issues in 1983. Even in 1984, when the lead positions came under challenge from the inroads of the Japanese and the efforts of the U S investment banks, the top ten firms managed well over 50 per cent of nearly $70 billion in new issues (see Table 6).

Table 6   The top ten suppliers of international funds in 1984

(a) The top underwriters of international bonds (eurobonds plus domestic currency bonds issued by foreigners)

Rank		Volume ($ million)	No. of issues
1	Salomon Brothers	4,794	281
2	Swiss Bank Corp.	3,977	513
3	Union Bank of Switzerland	3,342	420
4	Deutsche Bank	3,307	365
5	Crédit Suisse–First Boston	3,223	413
6	Nomura Securities	3,020	350
7	Morgan Guaranty	2,390	288
8	Daiwa Securities	2,318	293
9	Merrill Lynch	2,315	296
10	S. G. Warburg	2,269	356

(b) The top underwriters of international bank loans[1]

Rank		Volume ($ million)	No. of issues
1	Bank of America	5,862	63
2	Morgan Guaranty	5,791	46
3	Chase Manhattan	4,817	90
4	Citicorp	4,635	70
5	Lloyds Bank	3,370	93
6	National Westminster Group	3,330	98
7	Manufacturers Hanover	3,306	75
8	Bankers Trust	3,271	76
9	Bank of Tokyo	2,796	115
10	Chemical Bank	2,784	57

Note: [1] Ranked according to a system that gives special credit to bond issues or euroloans where the firm acted as lead manager.
Source: *Institutional Investor.*

Crédit Suisse–First Boston is a classic example of what makes success in modern bond markets. Erected out of the dismembered European arm of the troubled White Weld securities house in New York, it combines Crédit Suisse, one of the oldest banks in Switzerland, which became a partner with White Weld in eurobond dealing in 1974, and First Boston of the USA, which merged White Weld's European operations in 1978. Merrill Lynch took the US operations of the firm after some pressure from the authorities to mount a rescue. It has one of the best reputations in the euromarket for innovation, being the pioneer of floating-rate paper and London dollar CDs.

But, even more, it owes its success to its ability, through its Swiss connections, both to place issues with the private clients who, until recently, dominated eurobond buying, and to trade the bonds in even quite small lots through the secondary market. During the early 1980s it managed over a quarter of all new eurobond issues. Even in 1984 it was responsible for one-sixth, with a dominant position in floating-rate issues and dollar bonds.

Investment banking on the international scale is not only big business; it can also be extremely profitable – far more profitable in recent years than the straightforward business of banking or insurance or home loans, all of which have been badly hit in the 1980s by inflation, market volatility and excessive competition.

Competition has squeezed drastically the commission income that used to be the staple diet of securities firms and brokers. Increasing international competition is also squeezing the margins in the underwriting business, forcing firms to emphasize their fee-earning business of advising customers and arranging borrowings. But for the lead managers, the book-runners on an issue, the commission rate can still be as high as 2.5 per cent of the initial price, which is no mean return if you have the size and muscle to take on most of that issue yourself and not share it out among a consortium of participant underwriters who take up to two-thirds of the commission rate for their part. As the bond issues get larger, so do the book-runner's fees, or initial commission. On a fairly straightforward $200 million FRN issue the lead manager can earn up to $1 million. On a complex billion-dollar loan the total commissions can add up to between $15 million and $20 million, and the lead manager's share can be between $6 million and $8 million. Sweden and the World Bank, two of the most active borrowers in the market, paid out $45 million and $70 million respectively on borrowings of $4.5 billion (Sweden) and $11.5 billion (World Bank).

On top of that comes the trading itself. If an issue priced at $100 for each bond or share ends up trading at below this, then the difference comes out of the underwriter's commission. But if he is good enough at placing his part of the issue privately with clients such as pension funds, if he can hang on until the time is ripe to sell or if he can buy and sell cleverly enough, then he stands to increase his earnings still further.

Crédit Suisse–First Boston regularly makes a return on equity of over 30 per cent. Trading and investment banking provided First Boston, one of the group's parents, with two-thirds of its revenue in

1984, one-third from trading. Salomon Brothers' $200 million of pre-tax profits in 1984 supplied all of the group's total profits, while Citicorp's recently established capital markets division provided 18 per cent of the giant group's total profits and, with a net return of over 30 per cent, was by far the most profitable division in the bank.

A detailed study carried out in 1984 by J. P. Morgan and Co., the holding company for Morgan Guaranty, showed that, in the five years 1979–83 the profits earned by securities firms from under-writing and trading debt and equity had more than tripled, from $3 billion to over $10 billion. In 1983 underwritings had earned them $3.5 billion, three-quarters of it from underwriting bonds and debt issues, some $750 million from underwriting stock issues. Trading had earned the firms $6.8 billion, two-thirds of it from trading in debt securities. Over 80 per cent of the revenues earned from trading were made by the top twenty-one firms in 1983, fairly evenly divided between the top ten investment banks (Morgan Stanley, etc.) and the eleven wire-line securities houses (those enjoying full national coverage through their own communications network) led by Merrill Lynch. What was most galling to Morgans in the survey was that the profits of the investment banks were also much greater than those of the big commercial banks. While return on equity for the largest investment banks had averaged 30 per cent between 1980 and 1982, the return on equity of the top ten bank holding companies (Citicorp, Chase Manhattan, etc.) had been less than half that, at around 14 per cent. It was hardly surprising that the study had been commissioned by J. P. Morgan as part of a fierce lobbying campaign to get Congress to repeal the Glass–Steagall Act of 1933, which deliberately and precisely forbade deposit banks from becoming involved with the underwriting of securities on the grounds that it was this extension of their activities that had so undermined their creditworthiness in the Wall Street Crash.

The commercial banks, indeed, are the chief victims of the rev-olution that is now taking place in the international markets. Not before time, some would say. For in the 1970s they had seemed to be lords of all they surveyed, as they stepped from the first-class com-partments of jumbo jets to be whisked by limousine straight to re-ceptions given by the prime ministers and finance ministers of the world. Having seeemed for a moment, in the immediate aftermath of the 1973 oil shock, to be in serious danger (even Chase Manhattan was at one time thought to be a candidate for rescue), they had re-emerged as the chief avenues, and the main beneficiaries, of the recycling of oil wealth. Syndicated loans were the most profitable business of the decade, and they were – they still are – a business dominated by the top twenty commercial banks of the world.

The unstoppable rise of syndicated, international lending, which grew by 23 per cent a year from a total market of $260 billion in 1975 to top $1,000 billion in 1982, collapsed just as suddenly in the mid-1980s. The debt crisis, falling oil and commodity prices, the trans-formation of OPEC from net lender to net borrower on the world's markets, the devaluation of bank assets and share values – these brought to a halt virtually all but involuntary lending by the banks to the developing countries by 1983–4. Net international bank lending, according to BIS figures, plummeted from $160 billion new loans in both 1980 and 1981 to $95 billion in 1982 and $85 billion in the two following years. The experience of syndicated loans by the banks was even more severe. The volume of syndicated loans roughly halved between 1982 and 1984 (see Table 7). The loans that had once gone to the Third World, using money from the oil producers and savings from the industrial nations, were now being kept within the developed world. New lending to the developing world in 1984, at little more than $15.5 billion, was a quarter of what it had been in 1980. The industrial world, for the first time since the oil shock of 1979, became a net importer of funds from the developing world, through re-payments of loans, new deposits and exports, to the tune of $18.5 billion in 1984, compared with a net outflow of nearly $50 billion in 1981. Not only did this imply an appalling retreat from Third World debt by the banks; it also forced the banks back to lending in the industrial world at the very moment when the developed countries, government-guaranteed agencies and municipalities as well as cor-porations were turning increasingly to the capital markets as a source of funds. The derating of banks on the US bond markets had made it

Table 7   The fall of bank lending 1981–5 ($ billion)

	1981	1984	1985 (first half)
Bank lending	165	95	30
International bonds of which:	49	107.7	80.6
Fixed-rate issues	37.2	62.4	45.1
Floating-rate notes	7.4	34.4	31.3
Convertible bonds	4.4	10.9	4.2

Source: Bank of England and Bank of International Settlements.

cheaper for the borrower of credit to go directly to the market to borrow on his own name rather than from a bank that had, in turn, to depend on funds raised at a higher rate. As the volume of loans fell, the volume of bond issues grew. In 1984, for the first time, the eurobond market overtook the euroloan market. In 1985 it moved well ahead. Loans are a bank's business. Securities are, or have been, a business for the investment banks and securities houses.

The process of 'disintermediation' has been made all the more agonizing for the commercial banks by the growing tendency of companies not only to arrange their borrowings through other financial intermediaries but also to place their deposits directly in the market and to use finance as a profit centre in its own right. The rise and rise of the corporate treasurer has been one of the most persistent features of the last decade and one of the most relentless for the banks. In the USA it was a trend that set in during the early 1970s, partly because of the legal obstacles to the large commercial banks' development of a full national network. In Europe, and especially in Britain, it has started to develop as a trend only in the last few years.

Relations between bankers and their corporate clients in Europe tend to be much closer. The overdraft system, under which customers can arrange overall borrowing ceilings below which they can draw or repay money at will, make the short-term commercial-paper market less attractive for companies than is the case in the USA. From small beginnings the commercial paper market in the USA had grown to a total of $250 billion by the mid-1980s. In Europe the paper market has been almost exclusively an interbank one, tentatively gaining a foothold in the euromarkets as a corporate borrowing instrument only in 1983 and 1984. Perversely too the effect of accelerating inflation in the 1970s tended initially to have the opposite effect on companies in Europe to those in the USA. Seeing prices rise and interest rates follow more slowly, companies were tempted to raise their gearing, with the result that corporate bank loans actually increased sharply at the expense of equity issues during the late 1970s and early 1980s. The nationwide banks of Europe and of Japan benefited from a growing corporate market, which helps to explain why many of them were rather slower than the American banks to build up a position on international loans.

This position is now changing fast, even in Britain. Falling inflation and rising real interest rates have made companies think twice and three times about relying on bank loans for their borrowings. Years of contraction and 'rationalization', as extensive labour-shedding and plant closures are politely termed, have made the international companies of Europe and Japan flush with funds. GEC of Britain, BP, Unilever, Siemens, Volvo and others are all reporting 'cash mountains' that may, in the case of these companies at least, amount to more than $1 billion each. In Japan the car company Toyota, one of the most rightly run and most cash-conscious companies in the world, is known by the business community as the 'Toyota bank'. The electronic companies, such as Matsushita and Hitachi, are not far behind it, or their European equivalents, in their new-found cash reserves and their recently developed instinct to use these to their best advantage. *Zaiteku* (the high technology of financing) is bringing to Japan once again a Western whiff of commercial dealing that is new to a land dominated by traditional interrelationships.

'A generation ago,' says one of BP's top financial officers, 'the company finance director used to count up the cash balance each evening and go round to a discount house to put it on deposit overnight. And that was it. Now we've got our own traders looking at the markets and computers working out our best opportunities for making the most of our money.'

BP is now one of a growing number of European companies that, following the American example, have set up special Treasury departments to manage their exposure, cover their forward needs and use their corporate standing in the markets to best advantage. BP established BP Finance International as an in-house bank and separate profit centre within the group at the beginning of 1985. Volvo set up a corporate bank, Fortos, to bring together its various fund-raising, investment and leasing and credit operations in April of that year. In the USA General Electric Co., IBM and Xerox have long since developed subsidiary banking arms, while automobile companies like Ford and General Motors have ambitiously expanded their credit corporations. BP's Finance International is large enough to put it on a par with most of the country's merchant banks. Volvo's Fortos unit is capitalized at a level ($55 million) that makes it the fifth largest bank in Sweden.

The object of these in-house banks is partly to centralize the planning of currency, cash and borrowing needs at a time when currency and interest changes can make or break the profits of a whole group. Size is clout in the financial markets, the more so at a time when a corporation's overall credit ratings can make a difference of 2 or 3 per cent in the rate of interest that it might be paying. The banks are also there to rebalance assets and liabilities at a time when deregulation has made regrouping important in order to take full advantage of market opportunities. The growing sophistication of financing by customers in government and corporations was seen in the surge in 1985 to replace medium- and long-term loans with bonds, N I Fs and other instruments as soon as it became apparent how much cheaper these were. The extent of in-house knowledge could also be seen by the stampede of corporate purchases of financial futures and options as hedging instruments in the last few years. The management style of most corporations may be becoming more de-centralized during a period of recession, but the financial style is veering in the opposite direction.

Last, but perhaps most worrying both for corporate management and for their traditional bankers, these in-house facilities are also being used as profit centres in their own right to earn the greatest investment return from a corporation's cash reserves and short-term assets. Corporations are now becoming some of the largest purchasers of bonds, commercial paper and CDs, breaking into the areas tradi-tionally reserved for the banks and for purely financial institutions and showing every sign of wanting to act as financial institutions themselves. Given the fact that BP, for example, had a cash reserve of $3 billion in 1985, it could well regard itself as the equal of most pension funds, insurance companies and many banks. Logically there would be nothing to stop corporations from taking the final step and arranging swaps, currency exchanges and the sale and purchase of bonds without the intermediation of a bank, investment or com-mercial.

In practice there may be good reasons why they should not. Companies do not like giving away their financial plans to each other. They are too commercially valuable. Nor is it going to be that simple to break the bonds between banks and their long-term customers, least of all where the company–bank relationship is that of the German *Hausbank* or the French *chef de file*, let alone the *keiretsu* relationships of cross-interests in Japan. It is sometimes easy for the British and the Americans to forget that the banking relationships of continental Europe and Japan and the role of the universal banks of West Ger-many, Switzerland and France and the long-term credit banks of Japan are based directly on the ownership of shares in their clients, not just on common membership of the local rotary or golf club.

The old days, when customers expected from their bank managers a wide range of apparently free financial services in return for de-positing their money at the banks and allowing the banks the benefit

of the surplus on their current accounts are none the less clearly passing. The terrible word 'unbundling' is now being used to describe the
growing policy of banks and other financial institutions to divide up
the services that they offer and to charge separately for each. It is
happening in corporate finance, where investment banks are charging
higher arrangement fees and reducing the starting commission for
originating loans. It is happening to ordinary consumers as banks
charge fees as well as interest on loans and other facilities. Given the
fact that the non-interest-bearing current account is becoming a thing
of the past, the banks have little choice. Yet this, in turn, only forces
the customer to look on each service as a separate expense and therefore to seek the most competitive rate for it. Companies or individuals
may prefer to keep separate accounts at their bank branches. For
borrowings, investments, insurance and mortgages, the more sophisticated – that is, the wealthier – will shop around.

   This can only intensify the disintermediation of the better class of
corporate or individual customer, the High Net Worth Individual, as
the richer private customer has become known in financial marketing
language. As corporations with good credit ratings go directly to
market, so the commercial banks have been forced further and further
downmarket to seek higher-risk customers to sustain their loan, or
asset, business. Declining or overstretched companies have been the
one potential area of loans growth. Consumer finance, with its high
interest rates, has seemed the most lucrative.

   Yet it is in these areas that the banks are now facing their most
formidable challenge. Most banks are anxious to avoid high-risk loans
after the energy and farm loans of the post-1983 period, never mind
the problem loans to sovereign nations. But if they have been slow to
develop this business, others have not. Junk bonds have exploded on
the scene precisely because companies that are in decline or are too
young to warrant formal ratings have failed to get finance from traditional banking sources. The use of junk bonds in take-overs has
aroused concern, but their main application still derives from Drexel
Burnham's simple perception that although this market may be
riskier, it may also provide much higher returns. And – so far – the
failure rate has been relatively low. Junk bonds have filled a market
gap left vacant by the banks, just as thrifts and building societies did
a century ago, when groups of individuals founded community
savings and loans schemes (often intended to be temporary until the
loans were paid off) to supply the long-term lending on houses that
the banks were reluctant to provide.

The same, it could be argued, is true of consumer finance: credit cards and in-house instalment facilities backed by finance companies developed rapidly during the 1960s and 1970s because of the banks' failure to seize the market early on. US restrictions on national branching of commercial banks played a part, but so did the sloth of regional banks in the USA, the clearing banks of London and the main commercial banks of Japan, content as they have been to live off regulated interest rates and non-interest-bearing accounts.

As the banks now try to tackle this area, driven by the decline of non-interest-bearing checking accounts and the desertion of credit-worthy corporate clients, they face formidable competition from established competitors that are, if anything, even better capitalized than they are. Sears Roebuck and J. S. Penny, both of which have developed national instalment and banking facilities in their stores, are as well capitalized in their finance divisions as most money-centre banks, and far bigger if the whole group is taken into account. Ford and General Motors have expanded their automobile instalment subsidiaries to become sizeable financial companies in their own right. The development of ATMs and the potential of ETPOS networks have greatly reduced the competitive advantage of bank-branch networks, the more so in the USA because of the branching restrictions. As long as you have a network of shops, you can offer a full range of services just as effectively as, and quite possibly more cheaply than, the banks. To the consumer the name of Sears is just as good as that of the Bank of America. In instalment finance of purchases the stores and car companies actually have an advantage, in that they are the point of contact. And it has been, because of the high interest rates charged, a profitable business. In the bidding struggle between the House of Fraser and Burtons for the Debenham chain of stores in Britain, it was Debenham's finance subsidiary, Welbeck, that was regarded as the plum, and certainly the most lucrative part, of the Debenhams empire. Even Marks and Spencer, the best-known clothes store group in Britain and traditionally the most reluctant to develop parallel businesses, by 1985 had bowed to logic and announced a credit card of its own.

If the banks have problems in competing for loans business, they are encountering equally severe competition for funds. For centuries the strength of the banks has been based on their ability to raise funds more cheaply than other financial institutions. Once depositors started to desert them for other, higher-interest forms of investment, and once they themselves were forced by fluctuating interest rates to seek more varied forms of funding, they found themselves turning to the wholesale markets for a larger and larger proportion of their funds. Yet here they were competing directly with corporations and other financial institutions whose credit rating was just as good as theirs and, indeed, often better after the problems of sovereign debt and the difficulties of Continental Illinois Bank led to a general derating of the banks. If they could no longer get their funds more cheaply than their competitors, how could they offer a more attractive service to their customers? 'The bank is dead,' goes the cry. 'Long live the financial supermarket.' And even financiers of long experience and innate conservatism now lean back in their chairs round the main financial centres of the world and ask, with all seriousness, how the traditional commercial bank, as the customer has known it so long, can survive the competitive pressures on every side of its business.

It is a question that will dominate the rest of the 1980s. It may not be fully answered even then. Yet it is in many ways an unreal question. The banks lie too much at the centre of the financial system simply to waste away, like the Byzantine Empire, falling finally to the new competitors. They remain collectors of deposits and lenders of loans on a scale that dwarfs that of most other institutions (see Table 8). The advantages of a branch system for collecting deposits and making loans, and of a bank manager to assess the risk and opportunities, are too important to be dismissed just like that. Nor would the financial authorities allow the collapse of such a central part of the structure.

What will happen (what is happening) is that the commercial banks will reach into the territory of their competitors in self-defence. Not all of them will survive. Few will thrive in their present state. And not all, by any means, will choose to do the same thing. For some, only one perhaps, it may be possible to be the full-service bank – that is, strong in retail banking, with diversification into insurance, consumer finance and real estate, strong in corporate finance, both as a lender and as an originator of borrowing and a powerful presence in all the bond and dealing markets. Citicorp is trying that. What Exxon is to oil, Citicorp is to finance. It is there in every free market in the world, offering everything from bonds to currencies and insurance. It has invested in its own communications network in New York, its own transponder on a satellite. It owns Diners Club, Carte Blanche travel and expense cards and offers its own MasterCard and VISA cards in the USA. Its capital market group earns over $100 million a year. It has bought into the UK brokers Vickers da Costa to give it

Table 8 The top thirty banks in the world ($ million)

Rank		Assets[1]	Deposits	Capital and Reserves	1984 pre-tax profits
1	Citicorp	142,732	90,349	6,426	1,544
2	Daichi-Kangyo Bank	119,082	95,527	2,988	540
3	Fuji Bank	115,117	90,712	3,254	590
4	BankAmerica Corp.	113,710	94,048	5,119	453
5	Mitsubishi Bank	110,701	87,719	3,154	540
6	Sumitomo Bank	107,629	85,798	2,427	613
7	Banque Nationale de Paris	98,996	83,840	1,496	324
8	Sanwa Bank	96,482	76,619	2,575	469
9	Crédit Agricole	92,434	59,979	3,832	n.a.
10	Crédit Lyonnais	90,497	78,469	1,028	309
11	Société Générale	87,137	76,745	1,181	202
12	Barclays Bank	85,153	73,753	3,008	758
13	Norinchukin Bank	83,094	73,643	420	136
14	National Westminster Bank	82,717	75,775	3,048	776
15	Industrial Bank of Japan	81,723	71,544	1,944	436
16	Chase Manhattan	81,632	59,680	4,023	629
17	Tokai Bank	76,088	65,332	1,910	314
18	Deutsche Bank	73,393	67,664	2,446	608
19	Manufacturers Hanover Corp.	73,062	44,206	3,287	565
20	Midland Bank	71,111	65,461	1,949	156
21	Mitsui Bank	71,062	60,309	1,725	267
22	Bank of Tokyo	66,150	52,811	1,600	361
23	Long-Term Credit Bank of Japan	65,443	57,864	1,361	230
24	Royal Bank of Canada	64,403	59,016	2,846	643
25	Mitsubishi Trust	61,671	56,664	1,345	152
26	J. P. Morgan	61,214	38,760	3,734	703
27	Taiyo Kobe Bank	59,786	38,760	1,083	224
28	Hongkong and Shanghai	59,757	54,085	2,671	n.a.
29	Mitsui Trust	58,448	49,946	1,195	n.a.
30	Sumitomo Trust	58,036	52,291	1,358	166

Note: [1] Less contra accounts.
Source: *The Banker*.

an equity dealing arm in Tokyo and Hong Kong as well as London, has put itself forward as a market-maker for gilts in London, offers discount brokerage services for New York, has consumer finance and mortgage lending offices in fifty-five US cities, became the first foreign bank to gain full clearing-bank status in Britain in 1985 and has bought failing thrifts in Florida, Illinois and California. It is seeking constantly to test the limits of government regulations confining its actions: through the purchase of a bank in South Dakota to carry out insurance, through the establishment of industrial banks in Tennessee and Kentucky, through the founding of a bank in Maine. Wriston once said that the bank's ambition was to offer anybody anywhere virtually any financial transaction – an aim that is almost staggering in its conceit. Citicorp is not a bank that believes in hiding its light under a bushel or its offices behind discreet brass plaques. But if any bank has the scale as well as the gall to fulfil this mission, it is Citicorp.

Other banks may also try to offer a broad range but with a more limited focus. Of the American banks Chase Manhattan is probably the most ambitious to achieve both national representation through the regulatory constraints and an international banking presence, although it has moved into the underwriting field less forcefully than Citicorp. Sumitomo, Daichi-Kangyo and Mitsubishi are perhaps the banks most advanced in balancing a strong national banking network in Japan (the Japanese do not have the US geographical restrictions on branching, but they do have the Glass–Steagall restraints on underwriting) with an aggressive capital-markets expansion abroad. From South-East Asia the Hongkong and Shanghai Bank has emerged as one of the most interesting international banks, building up its wholesale position through acquisition.

The universal banks of West Germany, Switzerland and France have always had coverage of both retail and wholesale finance. What they have tended to lack is the international reach, other than in former colonies. The clearing banks of London, on the other hand – Barclays, National Westminster, Lloyds and Midland – have had the international reach but have lacked the capital-markets experience. All these banks will try to even up the balance by aggressive expansion – the West Germans (or at least Deutsche Bank) abroad and the British clearers into merchant banking. But, big though they are, it is very difficult to see them offering either the range of products that Citicorp does – it tends to go into its markets, then flood them with every conceivable product – or the total geographical spread. None is likely to have its own satellite transponder, for example.

Even within these various groups there are differences of emphasis. Of the French banks Paribas remains perhaps the most international. Of the British banks Barclays and perhaps National Westminster are closest to achieving the aggression and planning required to play a major role in investment banking. Among the German banks Deutsche appears to have pulled ahead of its rivals, the Dresdner and Commerzbank, in their challenge to the big U S money-centre banks. Among the Swiss, who have tended throughout their history to be strongest on investment, the Swiss Bank Corporation and the Union Bank of Switzerland would seem to have the strongest international ambitions.

For other banks it will be a question of choosing on which field to concentrate their ambitions, and the trick will be to choose a field in which they can predominate. Morgan Guaranty is perhaps the best example of a bank developing a fully rounded international position from its strength as a wholesale commercial bank with particularly good relations with governments and with large corporations. Like Citicorp, it is pushing hard against the regulatory boundaries of U S banking but keeping itself to wholesale banking, with strong and expanding merchant bank operations in Japan, Hong Kong, London, Brussels and Germany.

Bankers Trust is now going down the same road, to the point of telling its ordinary deposit customers that it no longer wishes to maintain that end of its business. Instead it has gone far further than any other bank to 'securitize' its loan portfolios, selling off the loans to investors as interest-bearing securities to give it liquidity and using this liquidity to build up its corporate business in all forms, from eurobond underwriting to loan and fund management.

Bankers Trust's decision to give up retail banking in favour of what it termed the 'merchant bank route', a hybrid of corporate and investment banking, was an unusually farsighted and, for the time, courageous one. It was made in 1978, when the bank, under the chairmanship of Alfred Brittain, decided that it needed to take a completely new look at itself. 'The bank had suffered badly in the 1970s,' recalls David Beim, head of the bank's corporate banking and himself a recruit from First Boston, 'from over-lending on real estate and poor results. It really had to decide whether to go down the retail route or to withdraw to the wholesale side. Although it had a strong chain of two hundred branches in New York, it was a fiercely competitive area, and any expansion would have required large investment. On the other hand, we had a long tradition of wholesale banking going back to the First World War. The bank decided that it had to be this way.'

The consequences of this decision was not simply the sale of the bank's whole branch network but also the realization that, if it was to take the wholesale route, this would mean going all the way – hiring traders, establishing a real presence in the major bond markets of the world and developing a much closer relationship with the corporate customer and all his needs, from mergers and acquisitions to commercial paper issues. Undaunted by its initial failure to sell the retail chain to the Bank of Montreal, Bankers Trust has stuck to its logic, and pushed it even further, under the almost evangelical energy of its young president, Charles Sanford. By the early 1980s it had decided to repackage all its corporate loans as tradeable paper in order to give it greater liquidity, to spread its risks and to force it to improve its asset quality. By 1987–8 it hopes to have 'securitized' in this way over 90 per cent of its loans, the traditional assets of the banking industry.

At the same time it has pushed hard against the limits of money-centre banking in the USA, becoming particularly active in the commercial paper and private placement markets, to the considerable consternation of the more conservative in the investment banking industry. Indeed, in an effort to create a corporate merchant-banking feeling it calls its senior managers 'partners', eschews memo writing and tries to gather its senior management, like partners in a firm, into regular, informal morning meetings.

'Diversification of risk is the only free lunch,' Charles Sanford is fond of saying. He might also add that the diversification of product, turning high-grade, low-earning assets into complex, 'unbundled' products, is the way to rapidly improving returns. As a self-defined intermediary in the flow of funds from investor to borrower, taking a fee from each, Bankers Trust by 1984 was earning the highest return on equity of any of the largest fourteen bank-holding companies in America and had shot to number three position in terms of returns on assets.

Despite the doubts of critics, who worry about is vulnerability to wholesale finance and its dependence on trading profit. Bankers Trust's path is likely to be followed by an increasing number of banks, not just in the USA but elsewhere too. Among the Japanese banks the long-term credit banks, and particularly the Industrial Bank of Japan, are most likely to emphasize the strategy of wholesale banking. Because of their past as lenders of long-term funds to industry, they have strong links with corporate clients and little experience of retail banking. Among the European banks, Commerzbank of Germany and perhaps Paribas of France will assume a similar corporate concentration.

Manufacturers Hanover ('Manny Hanny'), on the other hand, is now moving from the large customer to the smaller customer with its rapid expansion of offices throughout the USA and abroad and its purchase of the CIT Corporation from RCA for $1.5 billion. The purchase took it into the area of small and medium-sized company loans and finance, which fits neatly with its strength in leasing and banking for the real-estate industry. Bank of America, once one of the world's largest financial institutions and the most profitable in the 1970s, has been forced to cut back dramatically since it found itself overwhelmed by bad loans. In the summer of 1985 it stunned the investment community with a $338 million loss for the second quarter, the largest quarterly loss in banking history. The strategy of its new president, Samuel Armacost, is to invest in order to become the largest consumer banking group in the USA on the one hand and to contract in order to concentrate nationally and internationally on corporate finance on the other.

A quite different but even more ambitious approach is meanwhile being pursued by another West Coast bank, Security Pacific. From a relatively small regional base, Security Pacific has followed an extensive path of diversification through acquisition, mostly of small and medium-sized companies but including a London broker (Hoare Govett), a Swiss private gank (Ralli Brothers), eight discount, municipal and wholesale securities brokers in the USA as well as a series of retail finance, mortgage and insurance operations, two German consumer banks (Bankhaus Bohl and WIFAG Bank) and a Japanese finance company (Honda Chiyo). The logic is that of opportunity and diversification rather than of any grand strategy. But it has been enough to make Security Pacific into America's seventh largest bank-holding corporation, with over one-third of its revenues coming from non-traditional services such as broking. Where Citicorp sees the world as a series of markets into which to sell its services, Security Pacific's voluble boss, Dick Flamson, sees the world as a place of endless, barely related opportunities in which he can build a 'loose confederation of separately managed businesses'.

That, of course, is what worries many observers about the banking industry's Gadarene stampede towards diversification. In the first place, it brings the banks straight up against some formidable competition from non-bank institutions, many of them just as large as, and in many cases better positioned than, they are. The one group with the power and the reach to take on Citicorp is American Express. It has, through its credit-card and travel network, an international presence that is as big as any bank's and a technological investment in communications, ATMs and electronic fund-transfer systems that is well advanced. On to this it has built, through a dramatic run of acquisitions totalling $1.5 billion since 1981, a rock-solid base in the international capital markets, starting with the purchase of Shearson in 1981 (to which a trouble-ridden Lehman Brothers was added in 1984). Investors Diversified Services (a Midwest marketer of investments) in 1983 and the Trade Development Bank of Switzerland in the same year.

The problem of integrating these units into the Express conglomerate have proved a great deal more intractable than American Express officers seem to have expected. The Trade Development Bank of Switzerland had been built up by the Lebanese billionaire Edmond Safra. It was bought in the hope that Safra could help the American Express International Bank on its way to new heights. Within two years Safra departed after a taut and fractious round of negotiations intended to prevent him from competing with his old masters. Not long after, in the summer of 1985, David Weill, the former head of Shearsons who had been catapulted into the position of president of the whole corporation, left after a long dispute over the future of the loss-making Fireman's Fund insurance subsidiary. Integration is more than an accounting procedure, and it may, according to observers, be the end of the decade before American Express and Shearson Lehman become one. Yet if size and determination have anything to do with it, the group, the largest manager of money in America, will be very much in the top rank of heavyweights.

Wherever the banks go, they will come across such competition. At the retail end of the business Sears stands as the largest retailer of finance to the domestic consumer in the USA. Its instalment credit service goes as far back as 1911. To that it has added life and property insurance through its Allstate subsidiary, broking through its purchase of Dean Witter, real estate through Coldwell Banker, savings through the Sears Savings Bank and advanced ATM and POS systems as well as home banking through a joint operation with IBM. With revenues of over $10 billion a year from finance and insurance, Sears can already claim to be a nationwide, major financial institution. With total revenues of nearly $40 billion, it is certainly big enough to take on bank competition. In partnership with the First Bank of Chicago, it also aims to become a major trading, and trading finance, force in the world. By the end of the decade shoppers not from just the USA but from Europe and Asia too may be able to walk into stores and find there, among the handbags and the perfume, financial counters offering them credit, loans, investment, insurance and house finance. J. C. Penney is attempting the same thing in association with First Nationwide Savings and its own insurance companies, as well as combining with oil companies on fund transfers. European retail store chains are considering similar initiatives.

The threat of more aggressive action by the commercial banks in the field of consumer finance has in turn prompted a growing conjunction of forces among the regional banks and thrifts, often in combination with retail stores and insurance companies. In Britain the building societies – promised new freedom by a recent government report recommending that they be allowed into a wide range of banking activities previously forbidden them – have been among the pioneers of electronic banking. In continental Europe and Japan the regional banks and co-operatives have not been slow to see that mergers and co-operation may be the only way to survive, given the costs of automation and the competition for deposits and loans.

Part of the prize being sought in this struggle for the consumer customer is the individual with capital and the individual with a mobile pension and accumulated savings. Somewhat belatedly, banks and retailers have woken up to the fact that, while recent economic restructuring in the industrial economies has widened the gap between the haves and the have-nots and between those in work and those out of work, with potentially tragic results for the future, it has also created a far broader class of comparatively wealthy individuals who borrow and invest sizeable sums at the same time – perfect bank customers, in other words. Their numbers have been enormously increased by the growing number of executive women and the size of new electronic industries in which entrepreneurs are able to capitalize their wealth quickly through the OTC markets. It has been calculated that in the USA alone there are now more than 1 million millionaires – that is, people with assets worth more than $1 million. There are possibly five to ten times as many with liquid assets of $500,000. Total personal assets in the USA have been variously estimated at between $6 trillion and $10 trillion. Three-quarters of the wealth is concentrated in the top 10–15 per cent of the population. In Europe the total sum may be nearly the same, but the wealth is probably concentrated in fewer hands. The market in High Net Worth Individuals has become a supremely appealing target for consumer finance groups.

It is a market that can be approached from a number of different directions. Insurance companies, such as the Prudential and American Can (through its purchase of Ticor, Associated Madison, Transport Life Insurances and Penncorp Financial) have considerable knowledge of customers through their traditional insurance business and are now starting to sell to the same customers the investment expertise that they have accumulated as major investment institutions. Credit-card companies and retail stores are equally well versed in the wealth of customers and have direct and regular access to them by mail. Banks, and particularly local banks, have similar knowledge, as do the brokerage houses such as Merrill Lynch. The automobile companies have as wide a network of outlets, through dealers, and as much knowledge as any. The key question for all of them is whether this sought-after group of potential customers will go for personal service – (for example, the banks and brokers and in-store finance shops) or for the cheapest and speediest form of finance (for example, the automated and home-banking services now being offered).

For the banks the corporate market is likely to be no less competitive, and for similar reasons. There is strong competition from non-bank institutions (defining a bank here as a company that takes deposits and makes loans to clients), and they are all tending to head for the same group of highly creditworthy customers. Besides the investment banks and securities houses, there are the insurance companies specializing in corporate finance, of which the Aetna Life and Casualty Company is perhaps the most ambitious internationally and Connecticut General–INA Union the most aggressive in the USA. There are the in-house banks of the major corporations, now beginning to seek advisory business outside their own family or companies: the GEC group of Britain; Xerox, which has now centralized its leasing and loans business in one division; the General Electric Corporation, through its General Electric Credit Corporation (GECC). There are also the major international accountancy firms, anxious to use their entrée into companies and their knowledge of corporate finance to sell more than bread-and-butter auditing services. Arthur Andersen, Peat Marwick, Coopers and Lybrand, Price Waterhouse, Arthur Young, Ernst and Whinney are all firms with more than $1 billion in revenues. Two such firms, Price Waterhouse and Deloittes, planned to become even bigger through a merger that was finally aborted in 1984. Six of the top eight firms now have corporate-finance divisions to which they are busily recruiting merchant bankers to help advise clients on fund-raising as well as on tax and costs in their business.

The area of keenest competition, eventually to be the greatest bloodbath, is the raising of money for corporations and governments. It is here that all the competitors are moving to lock horns – the securities houses, the investment banks (which are becoming virtually indistinguishable from each other), the new financial groupings of American–Shearson and Prudential–Bache, the new competitors from Japan and Europe, the consortium capital market groups such as Orion and, of course, the major commercial banks themselves. These have some advantage of size and the capital they can bring to bear on dealing. It is easy to forget how big the top banks are compared with the investment banks. Citicorp is capitalized at $6 billion, three times as much Merrill Lynch and six times as much as Salomons. The top twenty-five commercial banks are capitalized at over $50 billion; the top twenty-five insurance companies at nearer $60 billion. The top twenty-five securities companies are capitalized at less than $10 billion (see Table 9). And the difference is even greater in Britain, where the total capitalization of the top five merchant banks, even after the spate of mergers of 1983, was only $1 billion, compared with Barclays' capitalization of over $4 billion.

Their greatest disadvantage is a cultural one. The bank manager is brought up to assess creditworthiness in a borrower. An investment banker or securities underwriter, particularly in today's world, has to understand exposure – the exposure of large overnight positions in securities, the exposure of an agreement to take an issue on his own books at a price that he may not be able to recover from the market. The history of the efforts by British clearing banks to buy into mer-chant banks or to develop their own during the 1970s is not an encouraging one, nor are American Express's efforts in the same field. When the Midland Bank of the UK attempted to inject some entrepreneurial spirit into its merchant bank, Samuel Montagu (owned jointly with Aetna), by recruiting the Swede Staffan Gadd in 1980, the relationship came apart within three years. He wanted expansion; Midland wanted caution after the débâcle of its take-over of Crocker National Bank in California. He wanted freedom; they wanted committee control. He was replaced by the former head of the country's Foreign Office officials, Michael Palliser.

Nor is it only commercial banks that have found it difficult to

Table 9   The top twenty U S securities firms, ranked by capital ($ million)

	1984 capital	*Offices*	*Employees*
Merrill Lynch and Co.	2,214.6	1,085	42,232
Shearson Lehman Brothers	1,896.0	354	15,293
Salomon Brothers Holding	1,731.8	10	3,293
E. F. Hutton Financial Services	1,019.9	413	16,842
Dean Witter Financial Services	1,237.0	645	18,840
Goldman Sachs and Co.	859.0	16	3,903
First Boston	659.0	17	2,709
Prudential Bache Securities	617.9	331	12,870
Paine Webber Group	572.4	283	10,978
Drexel Burnham Lambert Group	561.2	60	6,543
Bear, Sterns and Co.	500.0	12	3,920
Morgan Stanley and Co.	355.3	7	3,084
Stephens, Inc.	320.1	1	195
Donaldson, Lufkin and Jenrette	310.9	25	3,600
Thompson McKinnon, Inc.	243.5	154	4,284
Kidder, Peabody and Co.	242.6	74	5,765
Smith Barney, Inc.	207.0	104	5,400
Spear, Leeds and Kellogg	205.0	10	1,124
A. G. Edwards and Sons	176.1	258	4,385
Van Kampen Merritt, Inc.	170.6	8	221

Source: *Financial Times.*

combine the qualities of a good trader with the discretion of a banker. Lehman Brothers, one of the weakest of the investment banks at the beginning of the 1970s, had been rescued from the brink of disaster by the apparently perfectly matched joint leadership of Peter Peterson, the man with the style, the contacts and the management ability, and Lew Glucksman, the man who lived for the trading floor. It was Petersen, indeed, who, recognizing the need for trading strength, raised Glucksman up to be co-chief executive in 1980. Yet in 1983 Glucksman suddenly turned on his colleague, forced a 'me-or-you' showdown and pushed Petersen out. Morgan Stanley, the most blue-blooded of the Wall Street merchant banks, did not even start a full trading department until 1973 and has suffered for it. Sandy Weill, another of Wall Street's natural traders, failed to survive the translation to the more bureaucratic style of the American Express financial conglomerate and the big-company management approach of its chief executive, James Robinson.

The answer of the day to this problem of culture appears to be to buy dealing talent and merchant-bank experience virtually at whatever cost. Teams of specialist dealers are now being induced to cross the streets of London and New York (the Japanese still take a rather dim view of this kind of behaviour) by salaries that are beyond the wildest imaginings of the most senior executives in manufacturing industry. Even highly paid lawyers are known to be envious. As they change employers, occasionally pursued by legal actions to prevent them from taking with them their old firms' clients as well as information, the specialists erode to some degree the old spirit of banking; formerly it was about personal relationships, which were stable because the bank officers were stable in their jobs. 'Unbundling' has come to mean more than simply breaking down services into separate fee-paying profit centres. It is people too who are being separated out as profit-earning items.

As the Morgans and the Citicorps jostle with the Salomons and the Merrills and then again with the Barclays and the Kleinworts, the Warburgs and the Deutsche Banks, and these again with the Nomuras and the Sumitomos, the commissions in the world's capital markets are being squeezed to a pittance. There are now over a hundred financial groups dealing regularly in the international bond markets. Some – probably several dozen – are going to fail, collapse on the battlefield in a heap of debts or retreat to their home patch, licking their costly wounds.

PART TWO

£ $ ¥ £ $ ¥ £ $ ¥ £ $ ¥ £

THE THREE-LEGGED STOOL

FIVE

THE FIRST LEG: NEW YORK

'As the world economy becomes increasingly interdependent, the financial services revolution has become more important in providing the fuel. New York has been the principal beneficiary,' David Rockefeller, the city's best-known name, declared as New York's financial services industry burgeoned in the mid-1980s.

It was no idle boast. After the dark days of threatened bankruptcy at the end of the 1970s the business of money brought a wave of new funds to the city. Wall Street, which had seemed a poor second cousin to the rising skyscrapers of the big commercial banks in mid-town Manhattan, was now a place of steel skeletons and rising glass again. The two huge towers of the World Trade Building were fully let at last, even if the upper storey did have to be evacuated when a cyclone threatened. The hotels were filled with financiers and investors visiting the 'capital of capital,' as the New Yorkers proudly proclaimed. In the globalization of finance New York was very clearly the first and biggest centre of all.

And with good reason. The USA is the source of half the world's capital. New York, for all the challenge of rival centres in Chicago and Philadelphia and San Francisco, and for all its self-inflicted wounds of metropolitan chaos and urban decay, is the point through which the ever-growing movements of money come and go. It contains by far the largest stock market in the world, is the centre of by far the greatest concentration of financial institutions and the source of many of the capital-market groups that are dominating the markets of the world. If the banks and investment houses of Europe and Japan now send their brightest young talent for a stint in New York, just as the commercial families of Europe sent their scions to Florence, Milan and Pisa in medieval times and the bankers sent their sons to Germany and to Paris at the end of the last century, it is because New York is where the techniques of trading, the experience of markets and the excitement of dealing are meant to be.

The reasons for this are not all the most salutary. The biggest draw of the American markets in recent years, and the biggest base on which many of the securities and investment houses have thrived, has been the enormous and growing size of the US deficits. The accompanying ballooning of the market for US Treasury bonds and the regular new supplies of bonds put up for auction have ensured that American government debt has become the key reference point of interest rates all around the world and, perversely, the greatest supporter of the dollar. Continual efforts by the finance ministers and central bankers of the world to play down the central role of the dollar in world finance and to pull up the use of other currencies like the yen and the Deutschmark have been thwarted by the suction of the world's investment dollars into Treasury bills. Japan has at various times in the last few years bought as much as a third of new Treasury bill issues and the proportion of total US debt that Japanese institutions held at the end of 1985 had reached well over 20 per cent. Another 10 per cent was held by the Swiss, the West Germans and other global investors. Just who is dependent on whom in this one-way flow of funds is a moot point. America now relies on foreign purchases to sustain its debt funding. But the world's institutions are now too heavily overbalanced towards dollar holdings to seek actively a collapse of the American currency. Either way, events have made New York, always the world's capital of equity finance, the capital of its bond markets as well.

What all those eager young teams of Japanese bankers and the high-flyers of Europe's financial institutions are coming to New York for, of course, is not simply money and a portfolio full of Treasury bonds. That was the story of New York in the days of syndicate banking, when the waiting-rooms of the banks were filled not with Europeans but with Latin American finance ministers. Nor are they coming to learn the structure of the USA's domestic financial market – important though the US experience of interest-rate deregulation and legislative change has been.

From that point of view, the USA, the world's largest economy and its biggest financial unit, remains something of a curiosity: it has been legislative restriction rather than free-market liberalism that has determined development. The experience of the Wall Street Crash and the succession of bank failures in the early 1930s was a more searing one for the USA than for perhaps any other country. Its response was to reduce the freedom of banks both in the variety of financial activities they could carry out and even in the geographical extent to which they could develop retail banking. The reaction of European governments, by contrast, was to tighten controls on smaller competitors rather than to restrict the larger financial units, and this process was pushed further in Japan and West Germany, where the authorities and the bankers attempted to rebuild the big groups in order to help finance the industrial groups.

The result, in the U S case, has been that New York houses the most aggressive international banks in the world because these banks have not had room to expand within the American market. For them it has been 'export or die'. The reverse side of the coin is that the troubles of the money-centre banks – Continental Illinois most dramatically but many of the New York banks as well – have threatened the over-stretched banks of the U S A far more dangerously than those of most other countries because they have lacked the firm national retail base enjoyed by Deutsche Bank in West Germany, Barclays in Britain or Crédit Agricole in France. Equally, the deregulation of interest rates in the early 1980s has had a far more drastic impact on the thrifts and smaller banks of the U S A than it has had (as yet, at any rate) on the building societies of Britain or the co-operatives of Japan.

In that context the U S A has had much to learn from Europe and Japan. The experience of the universal banks of continental Europe is in many ways the model of which the money-centre banks of New York would like to base their own future. The system of 'overdraft' finance in Britain and Europe, at bottom a revolving borrowing facility, is in several ways more flexible and more effective for the customer than the U S system of commercial-note issues by corporations.

Many of the techniques of syndicate lending and the development of F R Ns and R U Fs originated not in the U S A but in the euromarkets of London, the brainchildren as much of European investment banks as of their U S counterparts. In the arts of traditional investment banking, and in advising corporations how to issue new finance and how to plan and conduct take-overs and mergers, the English merchant banks were for long regarded as the best in the world. The U S government borrowed the services of Schroders to teach it about the short-term money markets in the 1920s. Some of the most successful take-overs in the 1970s were engineered in the U S A by British merchant banks acting for European corporations. In the business of portfolio management it has been the Swiss to whom the industry has traditionally looked up. In the techniques of government funding, the issue of 'tap' stocks, the use of the discount houses as a means of determining price and supply and the refinement of perpetual bonds, the London gilt-edged market has been far and away more sophisticated than the U S Treasury bill auction markets.

Hong Kong and Sweden were well ahead of the U S A in developing A T Ms, computerized clearing systems and home banking. High wage costs and, in the case of Scandinavia, wide dispersal of the population forced the pace. Point-of-sale systems, allowing transactions to be cleared automatically from the sales desk of local stores, were promoted in France ahead of most of the United States. Merrill Lynch has little to teach Nomura or its colleague investment and securities houses about the marketing of securities to the public and their distribution through a nationwide network of high-street offices and salesmen.

Many of the financial techniques and products that have been introduced in the U S A and widely copied elsewhere have in fact been the result of the rigidities and peculiarities of U S regulation rather than the freedom of its markets. The cash-management funds pioneered by Merrill Lynch thrived because banks were not allowed to offer commercial rates of interest on investment accounts. Junk bonds grew so successfully because the rating system of bonds pushed out into the cold a whole category of corporate borrowing at a time of economic recession and structural upheaval. The restrictions, unique to the U S A, on branching by the big commercial banks have also led to the pursuit of a number of innovative techniques to get round them. Cash-management services for corporations are a case in point. U S companies have needed them because they have been required to use a wide variety of different banks throughout the various states in which they operate. Cash-management services are a way of centralizing information and, potentially, of providing companies with a national banking service. Branching restrictions have also encouraged the major banks in North America to invest heavily in developing on-line electronic funds transfer networks.

The peculiar vulnerability of U S banks to the debt problems of Latin America, their lack of a strong domestic retail base and their lopsided expansion through loans to particular industries or regions have also forced on the U S A a particularly strong corporate paper market. Corporations have been able to borrow at cheaper, or 'finer', rates in issuing their own paper rather than in borrowing from the banks because they have been able to grow bigger than many banks and because their own credit rating has ended up higher than that of the crisis-affected banking community. Those conditions have not existed in Europe and Japan to anything like the same extent.

Yet the financial world has not been beating a path to New York simply to gaze at the peculiarities of the American system. Financiers arrive to learn the techniques of capital-market financing, to find out about the latest products from the futures and the bond markets and to see, in the USA today, a vision of what other markets may be in the future.

The techniques and the ideas stem from the USA's unquestioned pre-eminence in corporate finance. Be it in the corporate bond markets or in the New York and American exchanges, New York is the biggest, most active and the fastest-moving centre in the world. No other country has developed a commercial-paper market for companies on anything like the same scale or with equal sophistication. The New York Stock Exchange is three times as large as Tokyo's and eight times as large as London's. A roll call of the new instruments of today's world capital markets – variable-rate and convertible bonds, bonds with warrants and deep-discount bonds, financial options and futures, securitized mortgage and automobile-leasing pools – is a catalogue of innovations by American banks in American markets. Any major international company considering launching itself on the global stock market thinks of issuing simultaneous share offerings in New York as well as its home market. When Reuters went public, shares were on sale in New York at the same time as London. When the British government wished to offer public shares in the state utility British Telecom, it did so in New York, through American investment houses, as well as London. In being able to handle huge issues without a hiccup, the New York Stock Exchange has shown what 'liquidity' means. NASDAQ has demonstrated to the world what electronic trading is all about.

What the rest of world also wants to learn about from the American experience as it embarks on the same road is deregulation, decontrol, and its effect on the structure of financial institutions. The dismantling of 'Regulation Q' controls on interest rates in the USA, and the consequent impact on thrifts and regional banks, has been the pointer to what the Japanese may now face as they do the same in their market. The British decision to end fixed commissions in the London Stock Exchange, with all that this implies for the mergers of some large firms and the disappearance of others, comes a full ten years after Wall Street ended fixed commissions on what was to become known as 'May Day', 1 May 1975.

That decision, it has to be said, was not the product of pure free enterprise and commitment to the ideas of open competition. Just as in the case of London's Stock Exchange ten years later, May Day was the result of a determined and belated effort by the SEC and the members of the New York Stock Exchange to prevent the institution from becoming redundant.

The threat came most directly from the development of off-floor trading (particularly from NASDAQ, by the computer-backed, screen-trading system developed for unlisted securities in 1971) and more broadly for the sheer growth of volume on the Stock Exchange and its increasing dominance by institutions buying and selling in bulk or in 'block trades.'

The failure of the traditional paper-based and floor-concentrated system to cope with the rise in business was a great embarrassment. In the expansionary years of the 1960s volume growth on the New York Stock Exchange tripled, to the extent that in the 'back-office crisis' of 1967–70 the Exchange had to shut on Wednesday afternoons and restrict its opening hours to catch up with orders and settlements. Over 150 Exchange members went out of business altogether, unable to cope, while others, including Goodbody and Company, the fifth largest brokerage house in the USA with over a quarter of a million customers, had to be rescued by Merrill Lynch. Desperate to keep up with the growth, firms like Goodbody had rushed to expand staff and invest in new technology, thus landing themselves with huge over-heads that proved too burdensome when the market swung and volumes went down by over a quarter.

At the same time, the nature of stock-exchange business was fundamentally altered by the growing dominance of the institutions as buyers and sellers. Despite the justified reputation of the USA as a share-owning democracy – about 20 per cent of the American population owns shares, compared with 12 per cent in Britain and less in most European countries – the ownership of shares and, even more, trading in them was becoming progressively more concentrated in the hands of the institutions.

By the beginning of the 1970s the institutions – the pension funds, mutuals and insurance companies – were responsible for something like two-thirds of the non-member trading volume on the Exchange, while block trading, deals in blocks of shares of 1,000 or more, accounted for over half the total volume. The institutions, resisted strongly by the member firms, started to press not only for reduced commissions but also for direct membership of the Exchange so that they could handle their own purchases.

If they were not going to get it on the floor of the Exchange, there was every chance that they would get it off the floor. The introduction of an automatic quotation system by the National Association of Securities Dealers in 1971 was originally seen simply as an expedient. Until then the dealers had been held back by the mechanical difficulties of developing effective trading in unlisted securities in the over-the-counter market. There was no system of 'specialists' with the task of providing quotes in the stocks. The physical constraints of trading off the floor made it difficult for both buyers and sellers to see clearly whether they were getting the best price. Once NASDAQ was introduced, however, the picture radically altered. It was possible to process bids and display them on screens quickly. The market became more transparent. And, once the institutions overcame their initial worries, they began to provide increasing liquidity to the market and increasingly large volume deals, thus making it more attractive, in turn, to the company raising money. To over-the-counter shares the dealers added trading in listed shares, dubbed 'third market trading'. Further, institutional buying power enabled securities houses to make private placements of company paper or shares, bypassing the market altogether.

Faced with a market that was threatening to overwhelm the brokers and their staff and with the possibility that the Exchange might lose its position as the central market altogether, the SEC and the members of the Exchange were forced to act. The first move was negative – to stop the introduction of institution membership. The problems that this raised in terms of conflicts of interest and dealers acting on their own account were forcibly brought home in a report by William McChesney Martin, a respected former president of the Exchange, in August 1971. The report was backed by Congress, which four years later ordered the SEC to forbid brokers to transact business on behalf of affiliated institutional accounts. Nor would the Stock Exchange budge from the rule (Rule 390) forbidding members to deal off the floor of the Exchange.

On the other side, to make the floor more attractive the Exchange did agree to the abolition of fixed commission rates from 1 May 1975, with some complaints and not a few dire warnings of the blood that would be spilt in the aftermath. Together with the SEC, the Exchange also acted to improve the administration of the Exchange, to speed up its settlement process and to make it more attractive to institutional clients. After a series of experiments with alternative systems, including going over almost entirely to terminal-to-terminal dealing through a national, central system, the Exchange finally introduced the Intermarket Trading System in 1978, which allowed immediate communication but not the execution of orders on a national clearing system.

The experience of the May Day 'big bang' was both more far-reaching and less drastic than many on the floor had feared. Despite an early effort by the major securities houses to hold the fall in rates to single figures, commissions tumbled rapidly, particularly for institutions. By the end of the 1970s these were paying nearly 60 per cent less on deals than before May Day. The fall in commissions for smaller investors, however, was much less dramatic, at around 20 per cent. Indeed, rates on deals of fewer than 200 shares actually increased. In this sense May Day, as many had feared, had the effect of accelerating the trend away from the small investor in the USA.

It also had the effect of shaking out the Exchange itself, although not necessarily in the ways that market opinion had suggested. Some of the most respected names in the market – Shearsons, Dean Witter, Bache and Paine Webber – were taken over or merged. A number of the middle-rank names disappeared altogether, while some smaller firms, which had been expected to go under, in the event managed to survive in a specialist function. Where the largest twenty-five firms had less than half the industry's revenues and capital at the time of May Day, by the beginning of the 1980s this proportion was reaching up to two-thirds.

Competition over commissions was not the only reason for change, of course. The huge sums required to invest in new electronic equipment and computerized dealing-rooms tended towards concentration. So did the steady rise of block trading. Only the larger firms could handle effectively such large gobbets of shares. Commission competition, however, did force the big securities houses to seek to expand their income in other ways. One was to increase their range of market activities, especially into the commercial-paper market. Others were to seek more products to sell to their clients and to use their distribution networks to greater effect.

Merrill Lynch's Cash Management Account and Money Market Fund, introduced in 1976, were part of this process. They proved to be much more. They challenged directly the banking and interest-rate structure of the USA. Where the USA's corporate debt markets were relatively advanced by international standards, its domestic banking markets were not. The Crash of 1929 in Wall Street and the banking collapses thereafter had resulted in a series of Acts laying down new rules on securities issues and strictly segregating the roles of securities and investment houses on the one hand and the commercial banks on the other. The Glass–Steagall Act of 1933 was based on congressional feeling that some of the banking problems of the time arose from the banks' activities in the securities markets. It effectively prevented commercial banks from entering the underwriting field for nearly fifty years and became the model for similar legislation in occupied Japan after the war.

At the same time, the actions of both the Federal government and the state legislatures, impelled by pre-war anti-trust fervour, also prevented banks from developing interstate banking facilities and imposed tight controls on banking mergers. Hence where European banks, especially in Germany and Switzerland, were able to grow on an expanding retail network, those in the USA were not. The money-centre banks, licensed by Federal authorities, were forced to seek growth abroad, and they have done so with a vengeance in expanding their international lending during the last two decades.

The situation was made supportable, both for regional banks struggling to grow within local confines and for money-centre banks struggling to grow without a regional base, by the regulation of interest rates. 'Regulation Q', covering short-term interest rates, was, as in Japan, partly aimed at consolidating the position of local financial institutions – banks and savings and loans institutions. It was also aimed at ensuring monetary stability and reasonable management of the repayment of public loans accumulated during the war. So long as the pace of inflation was moderate, which it was during most the 1960s and into the early 1970s, it was defensible. But the inflation of the mid- to late 1970s, fuelled by the Vietnam war and accelerated by the energy crises of 1973 and 1979, made such a policy more and more difficult to sustain.

Merrill Lynch's Cash Management Account was both the signal and directly a cause of the end of the regulated banking era in the USA. The idea came to Merrill Lynch in an almost classically hesitant way. Its then chairman, Donald Regan (later President Reagan's Treasury Secretary and White House Chief-of-Staff), had begun to develop a future for the securities firm as a financial 'department store'. He had asked Thomas Chrystie to head up the planning effort and to use some of the research he had commissioned from the Stanford Research Institute into what the financial customer of the 1970s might want.

The use of credit cards or chequing accounts did not figure largely in the report. But the topic did come up in discussion. Both Chrystie

and the Stanford Research Institute advisers claim to have convinced
the other of the idea. But, either way, by the end of the discussions
Chrystie had flown back to New York with the idea of linking a credit
card with an investment account at Merrill's. Regan was quick to see
the possibilities. A team was put on to the project, and by the autumn
of 1977 Merrill launched its Cash Management Account, on a trial
basis, in selected towns in Colorado and Georgia. Linked with a Visa
credit card issued by a bank, the Cash Management Account enabled
customers to establish an investment account that would allow them
to invest in stocks up to the credit allowed under law (50 per cent
in most states) and to withdraw cash or borrow up to the same
limit. When the account was in cash credit, the surplus was
invested in the money markets. When the account holder drew
down his cash, he could borrow up to the limit of his share holdings
at a few percentage points above money rates.

The account was not an immediate success. Local banks in Colorado, and in other states as the scheme was extended, furiously
objected to it as a form of banking in disguise – 'It looked like a duck,
walked like a duck and quacked like a duck,' said one state supervisor.
The minimum funds limit to establish an account seemed high at
$20,000. The workings seemed cumbersome: 'a complicated form of
overdraft', Paul Volcker called it. Within Merrill Lynch many
regarded it as a wasted and potentially politically harmful effort. But
gradually it caught on. Regan, abandoning the traditions of the firm,
offered bonuses to the salesmen selling the account. The 1979 oil-
price hike caused widespread concern over inflation and a burgeoning
desire by the wealthier investors to combat it. Gradually word got
around that, using a Merrill Lynch credit card or cheque book, you
could keep an account that earned interest when in balance and cost
less than a bank loan if you went into debit. Quite simply, the account,
copied widely since in Japan and Europe, offered ordinary investors
short-term returns that were far higher than those offered by the
banks by putting their money into funds that were then placed directly
and securely into the money markets. Suddenly the Cash Management Account took off. Within a matter of months savers were moving
their funds from thrifts and from banks into these new money accounts, and Merrill Lynch's competitors were producing similar products of their own. The response of the banks was to plead for release
from the interest-rate controls that had made life so comfortable for
them for so long. The response of other savings institutions such as
the thrifts – caught particularly badly by their practice of lending

long-term at fixed interest and funding this from short-term deposits that could not be protected from the competition at a time of rising inflation and volatile short-term interest rates – was to demand greater freedom of investment to balance their books. In the end the authorities had no option. Over the period 1979 to 1984 interest-rate controls were phased out, and the banks and savings institutions were given latitude to spread their wings into new markets.

The story of the development of financial institutions in the U S A since then is very much one of a constant straining at the regulation of markets and institutions as the various players have vied for a place in each other's territory and as new products have been developed to blur the boundaries between past market compartments. Indeed, it could be argued that the U S A has been innovative less because of its freedom than because of the peculiarities of its constraints.

Commercial banks have found their own room for action limited by rules preventing them from spreading into securities underwriting or developing nationwide retail networks. Thrifts have found themselves pinioned, as in other countries, by a structure that has traditionally confined them to borrowing short and selling long. The commercial-paper markets, the new hybrid products, futures and options, have been promoted, at least partly because of the tightness of S E C control on equities following the Wall Street Crash. Just as other countries, the U S A has found itself caught between the pressure to tighten regulations (in the wake of the Continental Illinois collapse, the troubles of the thrifts in Ohio, California and Maryland and the cases of fraud that have erupted among financial firms selling new products) and the irresistible tide of competitive change that demands ever greater deregulation.

The greatest pressure for deregulation has come from the commercial banks. Shaken by their over-exposure to Latin America and weakened by the desertion of their corporate customers, they have sought the capital markets as their new hunting grounds, however over-culled the prey. Governments have readily allowed them to participate in the Treasury bill market, in the interest of the Federal Reserve as much as of the banks. But the money-centre banks have also been pushing hard at the boundaries of securities dealing. Discount brokers were quickly seized on as a natural route to diversification. They could be regarded as a logical extension of the banks' chequing business. Discount brokers have captured 15–20 per cent of the retail market in small lots of shares. Led by Bank of America, which acquired Charles Schwab and Co. in 1982, and Security Pacific

National Bank, which acquired two discount brokers the following year, the banks leapt at the opportunity to move into this part of the business.

At the same time, the commercial banks have also tried to expand the territory defined for them by the banking Acts of the 1930s by extending A T M systems and promoting telephone and mail services across state boundaries and by using the opportunity provided by the problems of thrifts to press home their case for buying non-banking institutions such as real-estate firms.

It is the two areas of securities dealing and across-state purchases that will be the main battlegrounds of the future development of U S financial institutions. In the field of securities underwriting the commercial banks can, and do, try to edge their way forward by moving into the blurred territory of securitization of loans and mortgages, by dealing in futures and options and, most dramatically, by providing guarantees for commercial-paper offerings. Between 1978 and 1983 stand-by letters of credit rose four times, from $26 billion to $120 billion. In the end, however, the future of the commercial banks' encroachment into the securities area will depend on a full-frontal breach of the Glass–Steagall Act, a cause for which they are lobbying hard. And that in turn will depend on the popular image of the banks, which has been severely dented by the Continental Illinois collapse and by political irritation with the banks over their sovereign lending. The banks may see the Glass–Steagall question as one of fair competition between them and the investment and securities banks; Congress will tend to see it more in terms of reward or favour to a group of institutions that it instinctively distrusts because of their size and now dislike because of the debt problems that they have brought on the nation.

Yet those very international debt problems will continue to pressure banks to push at the limits of domestic interstate banking as well. Here the case of the big commercial banks for equity is undoubtedly strong. U S law has, for the last fifty years, been based on a rigid definition of banking, involving both lending the deposits on the one side and other forms of financial activity, whether securities trading or insurance, on the other.

The weakness of this division lies in the grey area of 'non-bank banks', that is, institutions such as thrifts that are regarded as not fully commercial banks in the sense that they specialize in one form of banking or another. It is a grey area that non-banking financial institutions, like the investment houses and insurance companies, have been able to exploit much more effectively than the commercial banks. Insurance companies in the first half of the 1980s galloped down a broad avenue of financial purchases from securities houses (Prudential–Bache, Equitable Life–Donaldson, Lufkin), as have other financial groups such as American Express, Sears Roebuck and the Phibro Corporation. They have also been able, as in the case of J. C. Penney, First National Bank, American Express and the Boston Safe Deposit and Trust Company, to move heavily into the field of non-bank banks.

The commercial banks in their turn have attempted to cross the same boundaries in the other direction, particularly through the purchase of thrifts but also through the development, as in the case of non-banks, of service that can be provided across the country without constraint and without going through branches, thus avoiding the restrictions on branching that cover banks and not other financial institutions.

The move has not occurred without opposition both from the Federal authorities and, more particularly, from state legislatures anxious to protect regional interests against what they see as the overweening power of the money-centre banks. And so far it is the regional interests that seem to be winning. After a series of moves by state legislatures, led by Massachusetts in 1982, to allow interstate mergers between banks of neighbouring states, the Supreme Court in June 1985 delivered a landmark decision to support the 'regional compact approach'. The decision – bitterly attacked by Citicorp, which had sought a Federal overruling of the state decisions, and strongly criticized by Paul Volcker of the US Fed., who feared the 'balkanization of American banking' – freezes the geographical growth of banking in the USA at a regional level.

At the time of the decision legislatures of seventeen states had passed reciprocal regional banking laws, leaving New York, California and Texas as the biggest stand-outs. A wave of interstate mergers and take-overs was poised to follow, creating a peculiarly American picture of a national map divided into six major banking regions, each developing strong banking groups in its respective area but excluding eighteen of the country's largest twenty-five banks, based in New York or in other non-participating states.

It is not a stand-off that can last. For its proponents the Supreme Court's decision will provide a breathing space in which the regions can throw up banking groups with sufficient capitalization to compete with the money-centre banks, to invest in automated facilities and, quite possibly, to spread their wings into bond trading and non-banking activities. But eventually these groups, if they do become strong, will want to expand beyond their own regions first into the rest of the country and then, no doubt, into the rest of the world.

Nor is it likely that the money-centre banks will rest where they have, for the moment, been halted. Citicorp has already used the thrift crisis to take over ailing savings and loans institutions in California, Illinois and Florida, while it also won the right to open a bank in Maryland in return for investing in a central credit-card computer facility that would create several hundred jobs. Chase Manhattan has also been active in thrift take-overs. New York and California will not for ever stand aside from the regional development. New York already has laws allowing the reciprocal entry of others states' banks. If the lure of the New York state market has not been sufficient to get other states to make those arrangements so far, the threat of competition from new regional groupings is likely to spur them to action.

The development of regional banking in the USA is bound to influence its position, and the role of New York, in international finance. The US authorities sought to back the interstate restrictions and to protect the domestic banks from foreign competition by insisting, in the 1978 International Banking Act, that foreign banks coming into the USA establish their headquarters in, and restrict their activities to, one state only.

The International Banking Act has encouraged states, with some success, to bid for the entry of foreign banks, especially Florida, California and Georgia. Put together with the regionalization of the USA, recent law has done its best to shore up the position of a number of regional centres in competition with New York.

So too have the efforts of various regional and commodity exchanges – the Chicago Board of Trade, the Chicago Mercantile Exchange, the Philadelphia Exchange, the Pacific Exchange as well as the American Exchange in New York. All have used the development of futures and options contracts, both on commodities and on financial indices and stocks, to keep volume growing at a time when trade in commodities is declining rapidly and when NASDAQ has done much to curb the prospects of securities exchanges.

Chicago particularly has proved a veritable hotbed of new ideas. Financial futures now represent about 90 per cent of total volume on the Chicago Mercantile Exchange and nearly 70 per cent of the large Chicago Board of Trade, most of it in Treasury bonds. When the SEC opened up the market for options on OTC trade, no fewer

than five stock exchanges, as well as the Chicago Board Option Exchange (once an off-shoot of the Chicago Board of Trade, it set up to
rival its old parent on its own account), and the National Association
of Securities Dealers moved in.

The race is on to provide new specialist products on the principle
that, with ultimately limited investor appeal, it is he who gets there
first who tends to gain the liquidity and to hold his position. Even the
tiny Coffee Sugar and Cocoa Exchange in New York came up with
its own 'first' in 1985 – a futures contract guaranteeing cash payment
on a specified date based on the official Consumer Price Index for
wage-earners. But product innovation is not an infinitely extendable
road to growth. A consumer market even of the size of the USA's
will have limited sums available for each new vehicle and will therefore be constrained with respect to the volume of its secondary dealing
in futures or options.

The great advantage of the American markets of Chicago, New
York and elsewhere is the powerful presence of 'locals', the brokers
and small firms that make their living by dealing, buying and selling,
every day, all day – taking positions, selling short or selling long to
make a profit for themselves and their clients. The floor of the
Chicago commodity markets or the New York Stock Exchange is
quite different from anywhere else in the world with the possible
exception of the old and now merged exchanges of Hong Kong. In
Chicago and New York new technology is seen not in cleanliness and
order but in great tubes, ungathered wires and suspended screens.
The floors themselves, above all the commodity markets, remain a
pandemonium – of noise, of paper, of continual swirls around groups.
Daytime is one long auction of shouted offers and screamed bids.
You declare your quantity. You shout your price. The garish coloured
jackets and the pitch of the voice are critical. Your bid does not get
noted if you are not immediately recognizable.

Other futures markets are trying to achieve the same floor excitement: the London International Futures Exchange, the new
exchange in Singapore. But they do not achieve it because they remain
essentially institutional markets. The big buyers and sellers are the
banks, the investment funds, the big block traders. That, argue some
of the leading members of the London futures market, is the inevitable
trend of the future. The day of the small man is passing. But that is
not so in the USA. The locals there still provide between 40 and 60
per cent of the trading. It is they who give the market its sense of
constant movement and uncertainty. And it is their presence, probably

more than anything else, that has given the Chicago markets their
liquidity – their tremendous depth. You can deal in almost any quantity
with speed, and the market will take it. The excitement cannot be
recreated. It is very difficult, for example, to imagine a market so
dominated by a few main brokerage houses as that of Japan managing
anything other than the most stultified start to its proposed futures
market. There may simply not be room for locals' markets other than
in the USA. But as long as the locals are there, US markets will be that
much bigger and that much more exciting than anywhere else.

In the meantime the exchanges of the USA have to worry about
the faltering growth in the number of companies coming to the floor
markets for full quotation and the apparently irresistible rise of the
NASDAQ market – now the third largest securities market in the
world after New York and Tokyo – as a national off-floor market.
The American Exchange, which has traditionally specialized in listed
medium- and small-sized company quotations between the OTC
market and full listing on the 'Big Board', has found its total number
of listings halved within a decade. The New York Stock Exchange
has shown virtually no growth in listings over the same period.

One answer has been to go abroad to find new companies and to
extend the pool of investors. A study carried out by the New York
Stock Exchange into prospects for 'Big Board' listing could find only
275 candidates in AMEX and NASDAQ quotations. It readily
counted some four hundred foreign companies with the size, history
and reputation to do so. Hence there has been an increasing marketing
effort to build on the examples of ICI, British Telecom and Reuters
and to get major companies abroad to seek direct listing; hence also an
effort to extend trading hours and to seek link-ups with foreign exchanges in order to increase trading. Toronto has recently sought a
link with AMEX and several other American exchanges. The Chicago
Mercantile Exchange pioneered a direct link with the Singapore Monetary Exchange under which a settlement agreed in one market could
take place in another. The Philadelphia Exchange, which has made a
niche for itself in currency options, has opened discussions with
London's futures market. Volume growth has been seen as the necessity of market life and internationalization as the way to achieve it.

Whether the high hopes of the various markets will be fulfilled is a
more dubious question. The cost and administration of gaining full
New York Stock Exchange listing has been enough to restrict to a
handful the foreign companies seeking such a step. By the end of 1985
there were still only twenty companies outside North America (in-

cluding Canada) listed on the 'Big Board' and no queue behind them.

Nor was the start to direct link-ups between markets that impressive. Again the costs were high and investors in Singapore, for example, reluctant to extend their trading to Chicago. It was a question of getting accustomed to new patterns, argued enthusiasts for globalization. Given time, it would develop just as financial futures had developed. No, answered the rival Chicago Board of Trade, what was wanted was direct access to the American market through extended trading hours, not an expensive, continuous trading system between centres. Yet extended hours were welcome neither to the traders nor to the supervisors of the SEC, for whom keeping track of dealing became much more difficult. Almost everyone accepted the globalization of markets. What many doubt now is that it will lead to a massive move of trading between regions rather than the concentration of trading on certain centres within regions.

If the doubters should prove wrong, it is likely that the USA will attract large sums of foreign capital to all its centres and not just to New York. The scale of American savings, the relative underweighting of pension funds and insurance in foreign stocks and the experience of trading are there. If, however, the doubters prove correct, the opportunities for regional centres to achieve real growth through internationalization must be considered questionable. Certainly, banks will set up regional offices and purchase regional distribution networks, as the Japanese have already done in California and the Europeans have done in Texas. But the attractions of state banking have been considerably reduced by the problems of oil loans in Texas and the agricultural contraction of California and the Midwest, as well as the effect on Florida of the difficulties of Latin America. Without the ability to go nationwide from a regional headquarters, most of the major banks of Europe and Japan will feel reluctant to invest a great deal purely locally. And the same is probably true of regional exchanges. Investors still prefer proximity to a market, and the ability to deal in new financial products locally will blunt their need or desire to go abroad, other than to the main money centres.

New York's position is assured because the players are there, the communications are in place and the markets are already huge. Other centres of the USA and of Canada – which is having to debate the role of its three main markets in Toronto, Montreal and Vancouver – are going to have to survive on a speciality that they can internationalize or, at least, become internationally famous for.

SIX

THE SECOND LEG: LONDON

Four years after the newly elected Conservative government, under Mrs Thatcher, abolished exchange controls in 1979 as a symbol of the new freedom that they were bringing to the markets, officials of the Bank of England did a study of how the top twenty institutions were arranging their foreign investments. The total outflow was not too dramatic. There had been, in the first year, a rush by institutions to take advantage of the new situation to increase their holdings of foreign assets, the more so when sterling soared to record heights on the foreign-exchange markets. But it had been, in most cases, a once-and-for-all adjustment of portfolios, the pace of which slackened after a few years. What did shock the officials was the channel through which this outward flow of money passed.

The fund managers of the major funds were asked two questions: one was how much of their investments in Japanese, Canadian, Australian shares or government bonds were made through a member of the London Stock Exchange or its affiliates abroad; the second was how much of their real-estate investment abroad was done through a British firm. The answer to the first question was only 5 per cent. The answer to the second question was about 50 per cent.

The conclusion was an extremely disturbing one. For the last twenty years of progressive manufacturing decline in Britain, the one optimistic assumption had been that while industry's contraction might be irreversible, at least the City of London remained the financial centre of Europe and second only perhaps to New York in the world. London's insurance and commodity markets, the inheritance of a century of British imperial and trade dominance before the First World War, remained the most truly international of their kind. British invisible foreign earnings from financial services were the largest in the world and for long had made up for any deficit on visible trade. Britain's major banks were among the top ten in Europe and were as large as all but their very largest American counterparts. British merchant banks, or investment houses, were renowned for both their style and their skills as corporate advisers. The London

Stock Exchange, one of the oldest anywhere, had taught most other nations their trade.

If, as now seemed possible, the City of London was failing to get even the business of British institutions when they had the freedom to choose, what hope was there for the country as a whole, which now lacked the economic base and the domestic resources of France or West Germany, never mind the USA and Japan. London would have to be a Hong Kong, relying on its wits, if it was to survive as a major financial centre. But could it?

The emerging debt crisis was showing up severe weaknesses among some of the major London clearers, Lloyds Bank in particular. Midland Bank's financial results had been damaged by a problem-ridden take-over of the Californian Crocker National Bank. The insurance market was coming under strong competition from New York, and Lloyd's, the most venerable insurance market of them all, was sullied by a series of losses and scandals that had aroused some of its most important investors ('the names', as they are known) to threaten legal action against the governing council. The traditional commodity and freight markets – the Baltic Exchange, the metal exchange – seemed old-fashioned and in danger of being bypassed by the new electronic markets of the USA and Asia. The British merchant banks, fine though their reputation was, were beginning to look small and underfinanced by comparison with the American and Japanese houses that were setting up in London. At one time in the period 1983–4 even the future of the eurobond market looked threatened by the establishment of the International Banking Centre in New York and proposals to end withholding taxes on foreign holders of American bonds.

Government concern over the City's loss of international competitiveness, and particularly the worries of the Bank of England, were to influence profoundly the course of deregulation in the 1980s. Formally the Bank of England, a bank originally established by private concerns to raise money for the government in 1694 and only nationalized in 1946, is charged with supervising the banks and the financial structures of the country. Informally it acts as the City's sponsor within the government and its unofficial club manager.

While the Japanese authorities faced with the same questions across the other side of the globe could afford to take a hard look at the balance of risk involved in decontrol of Japan's internal markets, the Bank of England was dominated by the fear that, unless the British moved ahead with reform, the country's position could be lost. The

Bank's job became increasingly one of persuading and cajoling conservative elements in the City to accept the necessity for change in the interests of world competitiveness.

The immediate impetus for change came, as in the U S A, through the law, and the law applied to a very specific part of the City – its Stock Exchange rules. Like most other areas of the City of London, the Stock Exchange is essentially a club. It had been built up out of the needs of trade and the wealth of investors during the eighteenth and nineteenth centuries and given order by a set of largely self-imposed rules, developed to avoid the kind of scandal that first impelled the brokers of London to form an exchange in the early eighteenth century after the South Sea Bubble shock of 1720. If the Exchange boasted proudly the motto 'Our word is our bond', it was no more than a reflection of the fact that the Stock Exchange, like the Lloyd's insurance market or, for that matter, the fur, metals or gold markets, was made up of a group of individuals who held personal rather than corporate membership of the club, who pledged their own wealth to honour any debts and who exercised voluntary control over membership and codes of conduct.

In 1979 the Office of Fair Trading, Britain's more limited version of the Anti-Trust Department of the U S A, launched an assault, through the courts, on the Stock Exchange's system (common to most countries) of charging fixed commissions on all share purchases or sales. The assault was very much in the mood of the time. Professionals – doctors, lawyers, opticians and others – were coming under increasing attack from consumer groups for their membership restrictions and their fees. House buyers were starting to breach the legal profession's former monopoly of conveyancing, or transferring legal ownership of property. The government had set in motion the ending of fixed charges for spectacles and was looking at the cost of pharmaceuticals.

The Office of Fair Trading's attack was further supported by the Treasury and the Prime Minister, who were voicing increasing concern and anger over the commissions theŷ were paying out for the issue of government paper, or 'gilts'. The gilt-edged market, because of the Bank of England's control, was a tight-knit one, limiting the number of firms that could be involved and paying relatively high commissions on most issues. As the volume of gilts being sold and traded on the market soared throughout the 1970s, so the Treasury found it more and more unreasonable that it was having to pay standard commission on what was, by its nature, large-volume business in which the lots were sizeable and the main purchasers big institutions. Determined to cut the cost of government debt, instinctively critical of any sort of cartel (the more so in an upper-crust establishment such as the City) and anxious to prove that the government would spare no one in its championing of free competition, the Prime Minister, Mrs Thatcher, barely concealed her own belief that the gilts market was little better than a rip-off.

In this atmosphere Sir Gordon Borrie, Director General of the Office of Fair Trading, deliberately picked the Stock Exchange as a test case of professional restrictions on free competition. It seemed a good target. The City was unpopular in the country and had long been regarded as a haven of privilege and wealth operating against the interests of industry and employment. Its rule book, a huge tome several inches thick, gave precise ground for legal attack. Not least, there was the precedent of May Day in the USA, showing that deregulation could be effected and that the system could survive the shock to the benefit at least of the large clients, the institutions.

The wheels of the law, however, grind slowly. After the initial burst of enthusiastic public acclaim for the move and political approval, the case was buried beneath the steady research of the lawyers preparing for court. It was in this overcast situation that Cecil Parkinson, the new Secretary of State for the Department of Trade and Industry, in whose ambit the Office of Fair Trading was, called for a meeting with the Stock Exchange Council chairman, Sir Nicholas Goodison, in June 1983. Fresh from the most resounding electoral victory this century, with good contacts himself in the City and determined to start his first ministerial post by clearing the decks of all outstanding issues, Parkinson thrashed out a deal with Goodison. The government would let the Stock Exchange off the hook of legal action on grounds of competition if it voluntarily agreed to abolish, within a set time, minimum commissions and if it opened its doors to wider Stock Exchange membership.

The outside world, the media and Parliament greeted this move as a shocking betrayal by a Conservative government, acting, as so often in the past, to protect its City pals and its moneyed interests. Sir Gordon Borrie muttered in his tent of the government's shameful behaviour. Most of the City at the time thought it was a compromise very much in their favour. A few wiser heads, in the Bank of England and the Treasury, argued not so much that it was a good thing but that it was necessary. The legal action, said Sir Kenneth Berrill, a former head of the Cabinet Think Tank who had retired from government service to become chairman of the international equity brokers Vickers da Costa, had had the effect of 'freezing rather than releasing change'. It had become urgent that the City should be released from the past and allowed to get on with preparing for the new world of changing international finance. Nonsense, retorted the Office of Fair Trading: the Stock Exchange would have done nothing without the threat of legal action.

Those most involved with the decision were aware of its importance. Parkinson, a shrewd man who had visited the USA (and whose political career was to be interrupted soon after by the public scandal surrounding the pregnancy of his mistress), claimed that it was a piece of firm decision-making, which had forced on the City change that would otherwise have had to wait years for a court judgment and almost certain appeals to higher courts. Goodison, a man of considerable subtlety of mind, equally claimed the victory for the Stock Exchange – a victory that substituted a modest embrace for what would otherwise have been legal rape. The City had been freed to get on with its affairs in an orderly and voluntary manner.

The worry of the government was that, unless the City did get on with it own business, it would simply be overtaken by events. The worry of Goodison and the Stock Exchange Council was that, unless the City was allowed to move with the times, trading would move from the floor on to green screens and to off-floor trading that would leave the Stock Exchange redundant. What neither Cecil Parkinson nor Nicholas Goodison appears to have appreciated fully at the time was just how far beyond the walls of the Stock Exchange the combination of commission abolition and freedom of Stock Exchange entry would take the change.

The problem lies in the unique structure of the London Stock Exchange. Unlike its counterparts in the USA or Japan, the British system has traditionally been based on a division not only between banks, which are restricted from underwriting shares on the market, and investment and securities houses, which are able to deal in stocks on the market, but also between brokers (the agents who buy and sell stocks solely on the orders of a client) and jobbers (who deal in stocks held on their own books). A client wanting to buy or sell stocks would go first to a broker who, acting on his commission, would then go down to the floor and tour the jobbers holding that stock. He would ask each the selling and buying price, or bid and offer price, without revealing which interested him particularly. Having found the best price, he would agree the transaction. Equally, a corporation wanting to raise money on the Stock Exchange or to buy shares in a potential take-over candidate would normally go first to a merchant bank, which would use a broker to do the buying or launch the issue.

The separation of functions ('single-capacity' as it is called) so dear to the heart of traditionalists on the Exchange has been based not simply on tradition but also on a profound belief, arising from the Stock Exchange's own origins in the South Sea Bubble scandals, that such a separation was the only safe way of protecting the interests of the client. With a broker acting solely in the interests of the client and working on a straight fee or commission, and the jobber gaining his percentage on the actual dealing, there was, so the purists argued, no temptation for the broker to persuade his clients to buy shares that he was holding on his own account or to sell shares that he was short of. The problem of erecting artificial 'Chinese walls' around divisions within a group in order to prevent conflicts of interests did not arise because there was no need for it to arise. Each unit in the market concentrated on its own function.

To survive, however, such a system needs minimum guaranteed commissions if most of the brokers are not be forced out of business in a scramble for business though commission-cutting. The jobber makes his profit from dealing in shares on his own account, buying them at one price and selling them at another. The merchant bank, or investment house, receives fees for its advice from its clients. The independent broker has neither guaranteed source of income. His only alternative to set commissions is either to become a low-cost, high-volume discount broker – a course that, to judge by the American experience, would leave few in the market – or he can hope that the client is prepared to pay him voluntarily a high commission for his research and advice, which (again on American experience) is unlikely. If he cannot do either he has to seek to diversify, joining a bigger bank grouping in which he becomes part of the client service and/or seeks to gain profits through direct dealing, or jobbing. The trouble with the merger route is that you lose your independence and probably a good deal of attraction to your client as well. The trouble with dealing is that, in order to make money and to cover risk, you have to have size. That most of the City of London institutions, formed into partnerships, patently did not have. Except for the jobbers they had never needed it.

Whether the Stock Exchange understood that in removing the brick of set commissions it would bring the whole house down around it is not clear. Certainly some of the most internationally minded figures did. Jacob Rothschild, a member of the great banking dynasty and a nephew of the baron, was an early proponent of the theory of 'supermarket' financial conglomerates. Gaining a reputation as something of an *enfant terrible* in the City for his view, he split from the Rothschild merchant bank to set up his own investment house and to establish, through merger and acquisitions, the organization about which he preached.

With a speed that left some of his competitors (not least in his own family) breathless, he built up an international financial conglomerate, making one of the first purchases of a broker (Kitcat and Aitken), taking over the Charterhouse Group with its merchant bank subsidiary, Charterhouse Japhet, buying a half-share of L. F. Rothschild, Unterberg, Towbin and, finally, seeking a merger with the Hambro Life insurance and fund group headed by Mark Weinberg. The moves – particularly marriage with Hambro Life, with its retail strength – which promised a financial group of considerable strength and reach, were hailed by much of the press and thoroughly disliked by the City, which doubted whether such a rapid agglomeration of purchases and mergers could be run effectively. It was never tested. First in, Jacob Rothschild was also first out. Charterhouse Japhet was sold to the Royal Bank of Scotland, Rothschild's stake in Kitcat and Aitken to another bank with 'Royal' in its name, to the Orion Royal Bank of Canada. Jacob Rothschild was several hundred million pounds the richer for his sales, leaving the City to wonder whether this was shrewd deal-making or prescience of troubles ahead.

Others, like John Berkshire of Mercantile House, a financial grouping built around the money-broking business, had sufficient knowledge of large-scale international markets outside the Stock Exchange to understand what the business of dealing entailed and moved carefully within the wholesale markets. Merchant banks such as Kleinwort Benson and Warburgs, which had established offices in New York partly to gain more from the transatlantic mergers and acquisitions that ebbed and flowed with the relaxation of exchange controls and the volatility of the currency markets, had enough experience of what was happening in New York to see the way of the future and to seek American-style investment-bank groupings.

But the majority of brokers and jobbers in the London Stock Exchange, and in the provincial stock exchanges even more, did not. Most saw the Parkinson–Goodison agreement for what it seemed on the surface, a reasonable enough compromise that got them out of a potentially bottomless hole of legal action. The agreement had allowed the Stock Exchange time – three years until the end of 1986 – before the rule book had to be changed and commissions abolished. This was partly to give the Stock Exchange Council an opportunity to take its members along with it. But it was also to give it time to introduce the technology that was essential if it was to end single-capacity and recording deals automatically in a way that would prevent market manipulation. As for the question of dual capacity, this was mentioned, but there was no firm statement that it would necessarily come. That was left to the market to decide, as was the question of just how the market should be opened up to new entrants – whether corporate membership would be accepted, whether outside firms could take over all or only part of member firms. Gradualism and compromise, those two key English themes, were assumed to be the order of the day.

When the major players woke up to the full implications of the new situation, however, time was the very last commodity that seemed to be available. There followed one of the most extraordinary periods of mergers, sell-outs, auctions and arguments among member firms that the City has ever seen (see Table 10), as each broker and jobber desperately looked around for partners and new capital, fearful of being left behind when the starting bell went and uncertain of the new rules, and as partners in the firms suddenly became aware of the once-and-for-all opportunity of making a capital gain that lay before them. Sir Martin Jacomb, then deputy chairman of the merchant bankers Kleinwort Benson, called it 'taking partners before the dance begins'. Others described it as just a mad scramble that would come to no good end.

Those with plans already laid were quick off the mark in arranging to sell themselves to the most appropriate, or the highest, bidder. Vickers da Costa, a medium-sized broker with strong international ties and a valuable asset in an established securities licence in Tokyo, sought refuge in a major American bank, Citicorp, which was eagerly seeking entry into the inner circle of the UK clearing houses. The merchant bank S. G. Warburg was equally quick to move in to take a minority stake (the maximum allowed initially was 29.9 per cent) in the leading jobbers, Akroyd and Smithers, before going on to expand this with a deal for a holding in the government brokers, Mullens, as well as Rowe and Pitman. Most of the big American financial groups, including Chase Manhattan, Shearson Lehman–American Express and Security Pacific, moved in, as did the Union Bank of Switzerland, Skandia of Sweden and the Hongkong and Shanghai Bank. Within barely a year of Cecil Parkinson's announcement

Table 10   The City marriages, with dates of announcement

Banks and financial groups	Brokers	Jobbers
British		
S. G. Warburg (Mercury Securities)	Rowe & Pitman (international) (Aug. 1984) + Mullens (the Gov. Broker) (Aug. 1984)	Akroyd & Smithers (Nov. 1983)
Kleinwort Benson	Grieveson Grant (June 1984)	Charlesworth & Co. (Oct. 1984)
Hill Samuel	Wood Mackenzie (June 1984)	
Barclays	De Zoete & Bevan (Mar. 1984)	Wedd Durlacher (Mar. 1984)
National Westminster	Fielding Newson-Smith (July 1984)	Bisgood, Bishop & Co. (Feb. 1984)
Hambros	Strauss Turnbull (Mar. 1984)	
Mercantile House	Laing & Cruickshank (May 1984)	
Charterhouse J. Rothschild	Kitcat & Aitken (Nov. 1982)[1]	
Samuel Montagu (Midland Bank)	W. Greenwell (Mar. 1984)	
N. M. Rothschild		Smith Bros. (Dec. 1983)
Grindlays Bank[2]		
Exco	Capel-Cure Myers (July 1984) Galloway & Pearson (May 1984) Laurie Milbank (money broking) (Dec. 1984)	
Morgan Grenfell	Pember & Boyle (Oct. 1984)	Pinchin Denny (Apr. 1984)
Guinness Mahon		White & Cheesman (Apr. 1984)
Britannia Arrow Holdings	Heseltine Moss (Nov. 1984)	
Baring Brothers	Rowe & Pitman (Jan. 1984)	Wilson & Watford (Dec. 1984)
Charter Consolidated		
Foreign		
Citicorp (US)	Vickers da Costa (Nov. 1983) Scrimgeour Kemp Gee (Aug. 1984) J. & E. Davy (July 1985)	

Parent	Firm	
Chase Manhattan (US)	{ Laurie Milbank (Nov. 1984) { Simon & Coates (Nov. 1984)	
Shearson Lehman–American Express (US)	L. Messel (July 1984)	
Security Pacific (US)	Hoare Govett (June 1982)	
Merrill Lynch (US)		C. T. Pulley (July 1984) A. B. Giles & Cresswell (June 1985)
Dow Scandia (US)	Savory Miln (Sep. 1984)	
North Carolina National Bank	Panmure Gordon (Dec. 1984)	
Canadian Imperial Bank of Commerce (Can.)	Grenfell & Colegrave (Apr. 1985)	
Orion Royal Bank (Can.)	Kitcat & Aitken (Feb. 1985)	
Hongkong and Shanghai Bank (Hong Kong)	James Capel (Aug. 1984)	
Union Bank of Switzerland (Switz.)	Phillips & Drew (Nov. 1984)	
Crédit Suisse (Switz.)	Buckmaster & Moore (Jan. 1985)	
Bank Centrade (Switz.)	R. Nivison (Jun. 1985)	
Banque Bruxelles Lambert (Belgium)	Williams de Broe Hill Chaplin (Dec. 1984)	
BAII (Luxembourg)	Sheppards & Chase (Apr. 1985)	
National and City (Ireland)	Dillon & Waldron (Sep. 1984)	
FBD Insurance (Ireland)	Maguire McCann Morrison (May 1985)	
Smurfit Paribas (Ireland)	Doak & Co. (July 1985)	
Crédit Commercial de France (France)	Laurence Prust (June 1985)	
Paribas (France)	Quilter Goodison (Sep. 1985) (from Skandia of Sweden)	
Gironzentrale (Austria)	Gilbert Eliott & Co. (May 1985)	

Notes: [1] Later sold to the Orion Royal Bank. [2] Now owned by the Australia and New Zealand Banking Group.

eighteen of the top twenty brokers and all the major jobbers had entered into some sort of marriage. By the end of 1985 some fifty deals had been done at a total cost of between £600 million and £800 million. Only the Queen's broker, the stately Cazenove, stood apart.

The key to the 'musical chairs', as it was quickly dubbed, was the need for each to find the partner who most nearly made up for his own deficiencies when the floodgates of change were finally thrown open in 1986. The brokers were the men with the clients, particularly among private individuals, the expertise in particular markets and, in the case of half a dozen, an edge in the all-important gilts market. The jobbers did not have the client base, but they did have the all-important experience in dealing and carrying the risk of large quantities of stock on their books overnight.

The obvious and logical step would have been to put brokers together with jobbers. But that ill suited the nature of the people involved. 'You know the real difference between brokers and jobbers?' asked one of the country's largest pension-fund managers. 'It's that the brokers up there went to private schools, to Marlborough and Eton, while the jobbers down there went to state schools. And the brokers have always despised the jobbers and thought that their job was easy. Do they have something to learn,' he added.

That is not strictly true. The senior partners of most of the jobbers were very much upper-crust. But it is undoubtedly the case that there is a difference of culture in Britain between those who deal with clients and those who trade. The whole history of division of responsibility in the City, as well as education, has ensured that this difference persists. Brokers instinctively felt that they would somehow be muddying relations with clients if they became jobbers, while jobbers instinctively worried about getting too close to people who had previously been in a bidding relationship with them.

Even without these cultural differences, there was the overwhelming problem of capitalization. The structured nature of the market had allowed jobbers to remain relatively undercapitalized by American standards. Even when protected by the Stock Exchange rules, the need for increasing reserves to cover the risk of dealing losses had forced a steady merger of jobbers during the 1960s and 1970s. Hence the multi-name plates on their doors. But it was still possible for jobbers to hold comparatively small amounts of stocks on their books overnight and to keep risks within tight margins so long as the competition between them was limited and the lots being bought and sold remained relatively small. Once the market was turned over to open competition, and to global competition at that, a jobber would have to increase his resources by a factor not simply of one or two but of ten or twenty. Merrill Lynch might go to bed with an overnight exposure of between $2 billion and $3 billion dollars. Few jobbers had an overnight book of more than a few hundred million dollars.

The problem of capitalization has been crucial to the City of London. By the very nature of partnerships, Stock Exchange firms have extremely limited resources of their own (see Table 11), while, because of their history in private hands, the merchant banks have equally tended to need relatively small capital assets to fund a business that has been largely a fee-earning client-relationship service. Dealing on their own account would put them into a different ball game altogether.

Table 11   The capitalization of UK merchant banks, 1984

	Equity capital (£ million)
Kleinwort Benson	215
S. G. Warburg	140
Schroder Wagg	125
Hill Samuel	123
Morgan Grenfell	116

Source: Financial Times.

The hunt for partners in the City thus became a search not just for logical alliances but also for adequate resources. For some the extent of change was not worth it. Better, they argued, to remain small, personal professional advisers acting in the interests of a limited number of clients and maintaining a niche in the marketplace. But for most, even if they did not wish to become global players, a reformation around larger groups, and particularly around money, was inevitable. Hence the first move, by Vickers da Costa, was quite deliberately to fall into the hands of the institution with the greatest resources of all, Citicorp. Hence too a number of brokers particularly sought arrangements with foreign institutions, such as Shearson Lehman and Chase Manhattan, that had dealing experience and resources and the ambition to spread out. Only the Japanese, cautious of entering a field so filled with particular traditions and personal connections, failed to nibble at the bait.

For a number of traditionalists in the City, however, selling out to foreigners was unseemly. The preferred route was to try a British grouping around a merchant bank. The merchant banks, with their connections, their international experience and their natural advantages in a period of client withdrawal from commercial banks, were the obvious leaders. Their first step tended to be an alliance with a jobber, who could bring them experience and skills in equity trading and for whom they offered a marriage more comfortable than direct alliance with the brokers. S. G. Warburg, the creation, like so many other British and American financial investment houses, of a Middle European immigrant between the wars and one of the most aggressive of the merchant banks in London as well as a leading underwriter in the eurobond market, was one of the most ambitious, forming a large new group around first a jobber and then two brokers. Kleinwort Benson, which took an interest in Grieveson Grant in June 1984, and Rothschilds, which quickly moved together with the jobbers Smith Brothers, were two others.

A major question, on the other hand, for long hung over the intentions of the London clearing banks, the members of the British national cheque-clearing system. This privileged group of five – National Westminster, Barclays, Lloyds, Midland and Williams and Glyn (a subsidiary of the Royal Bank of Scotland) – was in many ways similar to the top five banks in New York, certainly in capitalization and in the extent of their internationalization. Their base, however, was in retail banking across the country, and their strength lay in their protected position as clearers that had lasted for most of the century. Several of them had experimented with the purchase of merchant banks a decade before, when the first signs of disintermediation had begun to appear and corporate finance seemed the wave of the future. But the experience of the Midland Bank with Samuel Montagu and National Westminster Bank with County Bank had not been an entirely happy one.

Run by bank managers who had worked their way up the branch retail network, the clearing bankers found it difficult to understand the investment-house business and socially awkward to relate easily to the aristocrats and private-school men of merchant banking. There were arguments between managements, and the two parts were never really unified. At the same time the clearers, like their fellow commercial banks in Europe, Japan and the USA, turned more of their attention to international lending. When the City revolution broke out, therefore, it found most of the clearers far more worried by, and interested in, the problems of international debt, competition from the building societies and the credit divisions of retailers than capital markets. It took as much prodding from the Bank of England as from the brighter executives within the banks to get the clearers to take part. They were led eventually by Barclays, eager to set up a merchant-banking operation of its own through the merger of jobbers Wedd Durlacher Mordaunt with brokers De Zoete and Bevan, closely followed by National Westminster, which took shares in jobbers Bisgood, Bishop and Company and brokers Fielding Newson-Smith.

The chief beneficiaries of this change were the partners and the most experienced dealers of the Stock Exchange firms. 'New York's May Day ended with brokers driving cabs,' commented Richard Lambert, deputy editor of the *Financial Times* of London. 'The City's "Big Bang" is making everyone millionaires.' That was no exaggeration. The assets that everyone was buying were more than the name of a firm and its client list; they were the contacts and experience of the operators themselves. As the larger banks moved in to buy a share of the action, and as the existing teams sought to supplement their skills by direct purchase of individuals or even entire teams from their rivals, so the price shot up in the manner of the market in star football players just before a season starts.

The first deals, for a 29.9 per cent initial share, were at prices that valued a whole firm at between £50 million and £100 million and gave its senior partners between £1 million and £2 million. Paid over time, the deals were organized in a way that was supposed to preserve the partners' loyalty for at least three years – 'golden handcuffs', as they were called. As competition intensified, however, gold proved too pliable a metal to withstand the heat. 'Golden hellos' were paid to compensate dealers for forsaking their new owners. Barclays bought into the jobber Wedd Durlacher Mordaunt, only to see eight of its main dealers seduced by Kleinwort Benson for a rumoured total £1 million in acceptance fees and a guaranteed £2 million for their first year's salary.

While the headhunters sought new recruits, the advantages of movement began to seep down to the 'marzipan set', the bright middle-rankers 'just below the icing and just above the cake'. Packages guaranteeing £250,000–£400,000 over two years were offered to analyst stars in certain sectors, heads of research and specialist dealers, while even quite junior salesmen and dealers were being offered £50,000–£100,000 a year compared with with an average wage of £10,000 a year for professionals in Britain. For those on the gravy train the professions had never seen a chance to earn capital like this. The price of country houses along the main roads of London, particularly the M4 motorway into the West Country, went up 30 per cent in a year. Flats in the centre of London shot up at the same pace. In the City a new class of privileged was created, limited in number but large in individual gain. The public looked on in amazement. The many in the City who were not part of the deals were filled with resentment.

Those among the Stock Exchange's 4,400 individual members who were excluded from the musical chairs took their revenge in the summer of 1985, when Sir Nicholas Goodison presented his two main proposals for constitutional reform, designed to take the Exchange into the new world. One was to allow outsiders to assume full ownership of Exchange firms, where they had at first been only allowed 29.9 per cent. The second, more contentious, was to change the rules to move the basis of membership of the Exchange from the individual to the firm and to establish shares in the Exchange that members could sell and new members buy.

To the Council, and to Sir Nicholas in particular, the change was essentially to shift the structure of the Exchange from the old world of individual responsibility to the realities of a new world of capitalized companies. 'It was about,' he argued, 'whether or not the members want to keep the bulk of the securities in this country and in the Stock Exchange.' Unless the changes were made, the big international securities houses would be tempted to make markets off the floor of the Exchange, dealing directly in major shares between themselves and with the institutions. Out of hours, some of the US houses were already doing that. Now both Goldman Sachs and Flemings were starting to make markets in individual sectors. The Stock Exchange needed time to bring its members with it and to prepare the technology to have a 'Big Board' of its own. But it did not, as these moves to off-floor trading suggested, have that much time.

A sizeable minority of the Exchange, on the other hand, felt that they were being bounced into change far too rapidly. It was partly a question of resentment at the sums being paid for the top brokers; those who had spent their working lives at the Exchange felt it improper that individual firms should sell out in this way. But it was partly also deep-rooted doubt about the direction of change.

At the heart of the system of individual membership was the concept of individual responsibility; at the heart of the system of single-capacity was the clear avoidance of conflicts of interest. The reformists might scoff at the qualms of traditionalists, pointing out

THE SECOND LEG: LONDON 145

that conflicts of interest did indeed occur among brokers who managed funds and could easily direct clients into shares for their own benefit. They might also argue that to cling to tradition was to cling to parochialism at the expense of any hope of London continuing as an international centre. But some formidable figures in the City, such as David Hopkinson, chairman of the M & G unit trust group and one of the biggest investors in the City, expressed profound concern that their interests as clients would not be served. David Hopkinson likened the rapid change to the stampede of the Gadarene swine and, explaining that while anybody who opposed the moves was 'immediately branded as being fuddy-duddy and not wanting change' and while there were quite 'a lot of points of detail that needed changing on the Stock Exchange', this change was 'much too fundamental in a very short space of time. We are not comparable with what happened in America.'

Fear of being taken over by the Americans worried even senior partners in firms that were part of the changes. The rash of take-overs, suggested Peter Wilmot-Sitwell of Rowe and Pitman, which had sought marriage with Warburgs, would 'swamp not simply the City, not just firms like ours but the whole City machinery', making it impossible for the historic system of self-regulation through membership of a club and 'nods and winks from the Bank of England' to remain workable.

The Stock Exchange Council's and the government's response was to insist that a system of self-regulation was not merely workable but the only way of managing change with sufficient flexibility. Despite a report commissioned from Jim Gower, a respected professor of law, which had suggested the imposition of something approaching the US SEC, the mere mention of such a statutory body sent ministers, the Stock Exchange and officials firmly back to self-regulation.

Instead of a statutory body able to control and investigate City affairs on the lines of the SEC, the Department of Trade and Industry proposed two bodies to co-ordinate regulation by voluntary professional organizations such as the Exchange, the Association of Licensed Bond Dealers and others. One was a Securities and Investment Board (SIB) under the chairmanship of Sir Kenneth Berrill, then chairman of Vickers da Costa; the other was a commission to oversee the selling of investment under the direction of Mark Weinberg, former chairman of Hambro Life, a major insurance and investment group. The problems of conflicts of interest in share dealing, suggested the Stock Exchange, could be handled, as in the

U S A, though disclosure on an electronic board that would instantly reveal the size of the price of deals as they were struck.

The Stock Exchange membership, worried enough about supervision by a government body with draconian powers, accepted the point. It also accepted as inevitable internationalization, and therefore outside ownership of firms, and passed that change to its rules in June 1985. It would have been the death knell for change if the members had not done so. But they remained sufficiently concerned about the principles of changing from individual to corporate membership, as well as the financial rewards, to refuse the necessary 75 per cent majority for that resolution. It was a blow, and one that particularly hurt American securities houses seeking a corporate seat. But it was intended less to stop the change than to fire a warning shot across the bows of the Council and to demonstrate a real concern that internationalization should not mean the end of long-established local custom.

The problems of opening up to free competition in Britain are being seen clearly in reforms in the market for government securities. It was, as in Japan and the U S A, the explosion of government debt and the consequent large-volume style of dealing that had done much to force the pressure of change in the City. Indeed, it was Britain's large debts, accrued during the succession of wars in the eighteenth century, that had helped to make London an international money-market centre in the first place. In the early 1980s the government's disquiet at the cost, and at times the difficulty, of funding its deficit through the traditional market had been a major factor in its attitude to reform of the Stock Exchange.

At the time of the Goodison–Parkinson agreement competitive pressures had reduced the number of jobbers handling gilts to six, of which two, Wedd Dulacher Mordaunt and Akroyd and Smithers, held about 80 per cent of the volume. There were, in addition, about a dozen brokers retailing government stocks in any quantity. What happened to these firms was of paramount interest to the Bank of England. It had to gain control of the market if it was to carry out its funding operations smoothly and hope to influence the money supply and interest rates. Yet it was equally attracted to the idea of being able to increase the competition and decrease the commissions on gilts. Not only was it champing at what it regarded as excessive profits among some firms retailing gilts but it – or more particularly the Treasury, which tended to regard the Bank of England as a lackey of the City on these occasions – was also irritated by a series of 'gilt strikes', when the market, expecting an interest-rate increase, refused to buy new issues of government security until the rates on them were raised. The idea of being able to sell more easily large volumes to international firms who could hold gilts on their books if necessary, and could sell them all around the globe, was extremely appealing to the Treasury and the Bank of England. Nor were they unaware of the point that in other centres, such as Tokyo, that were opening up reciprocity was the key for UK groups wishing to enter.

The Bank of England's approach was, therefore, to open up the market to as many groups as were, in its eyes, competent to take on the job. At the same time it used its influence to ensure that the existing British firms fell into good hands. Akroyd and Smithers went to Warburgs, a merchant bank that the Bank of England seemed to think particularly able to take on international competition. Warburgs also got the brokers Mullens, a private firm that, for reasons of long tradition, acts as the government's agent in the gilt market. Wedd Durlacher Mordaunt, meanwhile, was merged with the new grouping being developed by Barclays Bank, along with brokers de Zoete and Bevan. Two of the leading gilts brokers also went to British firms: W. Greenwell, whose gilts team was headed by Gordon Pepper, one of the City's most formidable gurus, went to Samuel Montagu; and Grieveson Grant joined with Kleinwort Benson.

Working largely on US lines, the Bank, in consultation with the Stock Exchange and the financial institutions, produced a new market structure for government debt. There were to be, in the first rank, a body of market-makers – those able to deal wholesale in government securities and, if necessary, to take them on their book when the Bank wanted to issue a large new issue. As the market was expected to be dominated by institutions buying in large lots, and in order to facilitate wholesale dealing, the Bank also suggested interspersing a small group of inter-dealer brokers charged specifically with dealing between the wholesalers to redistribute their risk. Retailing gilts from the market-makers to the institutions would also be money brokers, able to lend to market-makers when they were short and to finance them when they were long. Each was supposed to put up about £20 million in capital.

The most significant difference between this system and that of the USA, however, was that the gilts market was to be kept as part of, and not separate from, the equities market the Stock Exchange itself, though separately capitalized. This was not only a concession to the Stock Exchange's desire for territory; it was also deliberately designed to increase the volume and liquidity of the Exchange as a whole, and to provide some means, through the Stock Exchange, of monitoring and supervising trade. It might also encourage those international securities and investment houses that were attracted to the gilts market to deal in equities.

And attracted the investment and securities houses have been – from Europe, from Asia and from the USA. When the Bank opened up the field to applications, over sixty applied. When it closed the list and announced those approved, a total of twenty-nine had been approved, little fewer than the thirty-seven market-makers that the huge US market was able to support. Yet the London market, at £250 billion (£261 billion in 1984), is only a quarter the size of the USA's. Clearly, not all were going to survive. The more cautious and some of the wiser spirits withdrew completely. Exco, the money-broking financial conglomerate, said no. So did merchant bankers Schroder Wagg and the US investment firm Drexel Burnham.

None the less, the final list contained fourteen British groups – including, of course, all the existing players in the market – no fewer than eleven groups from the USA, including Citicorp, Chase Manhattan, Goldman Sachs, Merrill Lynch, Morgan Guaranty and Salomon Brothers, as well as Crédit Suisse–First Boston, Orion Royal of Canada, British brokers now merged with the Hongkong and Shanghai and a Swiss-backed group. It was virtually a list of the international players in the global capital markets business. They could not possibly all hope to best the competition. Give it three years, say the gloomier prophets, and the number will be down to fifteen. Not so, say the more optimistic. Competition breeds greater volume, and as the world's capital markets become integrated, so this will be just one part of the twenty-four-hour switch-around of stocks that goes on.

The reformation of the gilts market gives some idea of the difficulties facing the UK, and particularly British capital-market groups, in maintaining a competitive position in the new world of international finance. London no longer has the domestic base that would make it a natural equivalent of New York and Tokyo. The industrial and agricultural profits that helped it to become the world's banker and investor in the last two centuries, and the imperial possessions that supported its trading position, have long since contracted. Britain's Gross National Product (GNP) is now less than half that of its colleagues in the EEC. As an equities market the UK is only marginally above that of Frankfurt. As a bond market it is slightly smaller than Switzerland. Although sterling remains the third largest reserve currency in the world, its role in trade is declining. Sterling-denominated bonds account only for some 7½ per cent of the international bond market (partly because of deliberate discouragement by the Bank of England, which, like the Bundesbank, has worried about too great an internationalization of its currency).

So too with its financial institutions. The structure of its markets around small, specialized partnership firms has left it well behind the USA in experience and size as a player in the capital markets. The clearing banks do not equal the investment banks of New York in their development of dealing skills and are only just on a par with the Japanese equivalents. Even under the new groupings British institutions are still relatively undercapitalized by American standards. And, perhaps more than those of most countries, they face deep-rooted cultural problems in marrying the quite separate skills of client relationships, retail banking and dealing under the same roof. The structure of the banking market and the exclusivity of the Stock Exchange club has left them poorly prepared for the full blast of international competition.

The strains of old ways meeting new needs and practices were thrown up all too vividly in London in the insurance and metals markets, where London had long been considered supreme. Over the years 1982–5, however, a long series of scandals occurred in the Lloyd's insurance market, forcing parliamentary intervention to regularize it through new, self-imposed rules, the resignation of several of the market's most senior members and the appointment of a full-time chief executive charged with rooting out corruption and malpractice.

The scandals, and some very considerable losses, concerned the use of the money invested in the market by the 'names', by their managing agents and by the professional underwriting groups. Lloyd's had always been a market structured around the matching of private-risk money with market need through the agency of a small group of professional managers. That was its origin in the seventeenth century. Yet what the scandals and the losses of the 1980s threw up was the question not just of whether ethical standards were declining but also of whether such an informal system could cope with the kind of trading that high inflation, volatile interest rates, fluctuating exchange rates and the high intrinsic costs of expensive damage actions and individual pieces of equipment demanded. London had grown up in an era of sea trade, when the insurance of a cargo could safely be spread between a group of individuals. But how to spread the risk of a satellite or $1 billion lawsuit for malpractice or negligence? And how to cope with a financial environment in which surplus funds could no longer be set aside in simple investments to earn interest until the claims came in? The scandals of Lloyd's arose partly because of the way in which individuals were moving funds to their own foreign-registered companies to avoid tax and partly because of increasing pressure in the 1970s to re-insure and set off risks in other markets.

Lloyd's had tried to meet the demands of modern trading by reducing the conditions imposed on new 'names', by greatly increasing their number from about 6,000 at the beginning of the 1970s to nearer 20,000 by the beginning of the 1980s and by allowing the professional brokers to strengthen their hold on the market and to control more of the managing agents who put the funds of the 'names' into various underwriting syndicates. These moves raised the capital of the market and improved its efficiency. But it increasingly separated the investors on the one side from their professional managers on the other. In a series of scandals – the Savonita affair in 1978, the losses of the Sasse syndicate in 1979, the discoveries of the off-shore funds of the Alexander Howden Group, the re-insurance activities of the P C W Underwriting Agencies – the strains inherent in this form of self-regulated market came bursting out into the open. New legislation, a Lloyd's Act to replace the orginal 1871 Act that had sanctioned its special self-governing status in the first place, was part of the answer. The requirement that brokers divest themselves of managing agencies was another, as was internal reform. But by the end of 1985, when the specially appointed chief executive, Ian Hay Davidson, had resigned because he was unable to achieve the right working relationship with the non-executive chairman of the market, it was still far from clear that a solution had been found.

Even more dramatic, although less scandalous, were the events in the tin market in October and November 1985. The London Metal Exchange (L M E) had for generations been the pre-eminent non-precious metals trading market in the world, dealing in the forward-delivery of copper, tin, aluminium and other metals. It was founded, in 1877, in a room above a hatter's shop by a group of merchants who drew a circle on the floor in chalk and started trading. Like Lloyd's, it prides itself on its traditions of trust and unregulated dealing. Prices are established not by continuous trading or managed through a separate settlements company that keeps the accounts and dictates the margin. Instead a group of dealers – there are twenty-four members altogether – meet around a circle, or 'ring', facing each other, and decide the prices of the LME's seven metals in four sessions each day, each lasting five minutes. The dealers, backed by telephone booths that will pass on instructions, wait in silence for each session to begin. Dealing starts. The telephones ring. Conversation builds up and then, in a crescendo of shouting, of bid and offer, the deals are done. Settlement between the dealing groups is direct. There are no limits (as on the American markets) to the amount of movement in prices each session. There has rarely been any problem of delivery or payment. It has always been a market that worked, balancing supply and demand of key materials – until Thursday, 24 October, that is, when one of the biggest players in the whole market, Pieter de Koning, telephoned the chief executive of the LME to say that he could no longer deal in tin. De Koning, one of the market's most respected figures, was buffer-stock manager for the International Tin Council, an association of twenty-two consumer and producer countries that had, since soon after the war, been operating the longest-running commodity agreement in the world. Founded to try to prevent prices from rising too fast or falling too rapidly, the Tin Council (which the USA left in the 1970s, declaring its opposition to such cartels) operated through its buffer-stock manager, who bought tin when it was in surplus and sold it when it was short and thus kept it within certain agreed price limits.

For months the limits of between £8,500 and £9,500 per tonne had been challenged by a growing surplus of tin. New suppliers in Latin America, Bolivia and Brazil were not members and were pushing more and more exports on to the market. Demand was weak. Tin, like most commodities, was under strain. Traders, sensing a price collapse, began to sell short on future deliveries. The warning signs grew. In the summer the buffer-stock manager was able to give the speculators a bloody nose by suddenly tightening supplies when forward sales deals became due. But in October it was clear that the market was slipping away. Promised a new injection of funds by the producer members of the Tin Council – mainly Malaya, Thailand and Indonesia – de Koning attempted to maximize his position by increasing the number of forward purchase agreements and embarking on a series of 'special agreements', under which he agreed to buy tin at the prevailing price from brokers and to sell it back to them again at unspecified prices in the future or sold them tin on the promise of later repurchase at an initial outlay of fee plus computed interest. The deals enabled him to gear up his position dramatically.

But even they were not enough to cope with the market when de Koning, despairing of the promised new funds, telephoned the Exchange with the news that he could not go on. He had committed himself by the time to about £1 billion of forward sales and purchase deals and owed the banks about £350 million. The dealers in turn owed another £160 million of borrowings against his assurances. Dealing in tin was suspended until the mess could be sorted out.

The difficulty was that it could not be sorted out easily. Far from accepting responsibility for the debts of their buffer-stock manager, the members of the International Tin Council showed every sign of walking away from them on the legal ground that the Council was a limited-liability entity and that any funds put in at this stage would only be wasted, as the price of tin was bound to fall. In vain did the dealers and creditor banks plead, with the support of the British government, that such action was immoral. The harsh fact was that to reopen the market and allow a managed wind-down of the International Tin Council's position required new working capital. That the member states of the Council were not prepared to supply. The hardest line, indeed, came from Britain's own allies in the EEC, who argued that it was essentially a British problem and should be solved by the British. And while these discussions were going on, dealing in other metals on the LME contracted to a trickle as each of the dealers looked at his opposite number and wondered whether he was about to go bankrupt over the crisis.

Just as in the case of Lloyd's, the question was posed whether London could any longer persist with a style of trading that had been born a century before. And yet, just as in the case of Lloyd's, the tin crisis also showed the continuing resilience of London as a trading centre. Despite the problems, the number of investors applying to join Lloyd's actually increased sharply, while no other centre came forward to provide the particular brand of high-risk insurance that could cover a jumbo jet or a satellite. Nor was there any immediate sign that trading in metals or other commodities was yet ready to desert London as an international centre for physical forward contracts. As a financial centre its role appears to be strengthening rather than weakening.

If London no longer has the size of domestic market that it once had, it still boasts eight of the largest fifty industrial companies in the world. Its clearing banks are among the top twenty largest banks in the world. Its insurance companies and pension funds are the equivalents of, if not slightly larger than, their American counterparts.

Its commercial and merchants banks have more international experience than either the American or the Japanese banks. They, and Britain, have been at it longer. Most of the world's traders in money, in commodities and in international paper are there.

If the pessimists worry about whether British financial institutions can manage the competition, no one is any longer in much doubt about London's place in the tripartite world of markets. It has not always been so. It is easy to forget that in the nineteenth century it was Paris that was the pre-eminent banking centre of Europe and that in the first half of the twentieth century, before Nazism drove out or destroyed the best financial brains, it was Germany that had developed the most adventurous merchant-banking firms. Even today the universal banks of Switzerland and West Germany have a well developed financial conglomerate form that gives them natural advantages in the new world.

Yet the size and strength of the UK's financial institutions – its pension funds and insurance companies, as well as its major banks – the variety and liquidity of its markets and the experience of its traders have made it a natural financial centre of the European area. It has the good fortune to stand right in the middle of the world's time zones (not entirely through luck – it was Isaac Newton and British astronomers that made Greenwich Mean Time the base line of time and longitude). It has enjoyed the advantage of familiarity with language of finance, English. It has also had the attraction of following a policy of opening doors to foreign firms. Most of the big international names are represented in London and have been for a generation or more. There are 600 subsidiaries of foreign banks in the UK.

What the City lost as it strong domestic economic base contracted it has more than made up for in the size of the interbank market and its dominance of eurobond trading. Through accident as much as policy it allowed both to develop freely. As much as half of the interbank market in London may now be accounted for by the transactions of Japanese banks. But they are none the less Japanese banks set up in London, and London remains by far the largest banking centre in the world (see Table 12). Its hold on the eurobond market, threatened at times by the competitive liberalization of West Germany and New York, remains (so far) as strong as ever. The very fact that many foreign firms have proved eager to take over UK brokers and jobbers – Citicorp, the Union Bank of Switzerland, Chase Manhattan, Paribas, Shearson Lehman, Security Pacific, the

Table 12   The main centres of international bank lending, 1980–84
($billion)

	1980	1984	1984 (%)
UK	459	669	24.9
USA	165	403	15.0
Japan	107	245	9.1
France	160	178	6.1
Luxembourg[1]	108	99	3.7
Swiss trustee accounts	68	98	3.7
Belgium[1]	70	89	3.3
The Netherlands	66	65	2.9
Switzerland	67	61	2.3
West Germany	74	61	2.3
Canada	45	69	2.6
Italy	37	45	1.7
Offshore banking services	309	506	18.9
Gross lending	1,778	2,682	100.0

Notes: International bank lending is defined as consisting of foreign-currency lending to residents and non-residents and domestic-currency lending to non-residents.

[1] Excludes some lending between Belgium and Luxembourg.

Source: *Bank of England Quarterly Bulletin.*

Hongkong and Shanghai Bank, Crédit-Suisse – is a sign of international success. When, in early 1985, Deutsche Bank made the decision to move its eurobond dealing-room to London, the seal seemed set on London's status as a global centre. The question was not so much whether it could hold its position in the world but whether the British players could hold their place in it.

——

SEVEN

THE THIRD LEG: TOKYO

In the spring of 1984, during the negotiations between Japan and the USA over what was to become known as the Yen–Dollar Agreement, the US Under-Secretary at the Treasury, Beryl Sprinkel, shocked the Japanese team by physically banging the table. He was fed up, he declared, with Japanese procrastination. The Japanese were ducking their international responsibilities and protecting their financial market. It was time they changed. And the USA would insist that those changes went far further than the limited gradualistic measures now being tabled.

The Japanese side was severely taken back. It described itself, at least in later conversations, appalled at Sprinkel's manner, resentful of his accusations and puzzled by the ferocity of American demands. Why should the USA be so interested in the details of Japan's domestic financial structure? Its international markets, the greater use of the yen through the expansion of the euroyen market, yes, that they could understand. By why the insistence on liberalizing the internal market and on opening up, for example, membership of the Tokyo Stock Exchange to foreign firms? Could it be, they asked darkly, that the US approach owed something to US Treasury Secretary Donald Regan's former role as chairman of Merrill Lynch, the very firm that was most insistent on gaining a seat on the Exchange?

The misunderstanding was typical of the increasingly acerbic relations between Japan and its major Western trading partners during the 1980s. As the size of the Japanese surplus grew from 1981 onwards, as the march of the Japanese car and its video tape-recorders cut a seemingly irresistible swathe through the home industries of Europe and North America, so the low value of the yen and Japan's tight control of its financial industries appeared as yet one more example of its one-sided approach to economic relations.

Pressure, argued many in the USA and in Europe, was the only way to force the Japanese to give way on anything. They were past masters of the tactics of obfuscation and delay, so the greater the pressure, the better. And in finance at least the West had one obvious area of superiority over its rival. Finance, said some of the US negotiating officials, would be the spearhead of a services-trade counter-attack, and as soon as the obstacles placed in its path by domestic protection in Japan were pushed aside, Japan would become an international financial centre, whether it liked it or not.

Such an approach was met not only with resentment by the Japanese, always sensitive to questions of cultural superiority on the part of the West, but also with some genuine uncertainty. To them their financial structure (see Table 13) was an intrinsic and private part of the Japanese domestic scene, something that owed its present form to history and, to a degree, to American reforms imposed after the Second World War, when General McArthur reorganized the Japanese economy, broke up the major economic groupings and introduced US concepts of banking and investment houses. There might, to the Japanese eye, be a tough negotiating battle to be fought over the entry of foreign competition into the system, to the detriment of previously protected local banks or institutions. But Japan found it difficult to understand, and certainly difficult to comply with, Sprinkel's demands for all sorts of changes to local money markets and other domestic matters.

The argument between those who believe that the Japanese finally moved because of outside force and those who believe that force in this case was largely irrelevant to what emerged from the negotiations has never been settled. It re-emerges constantly in the discussions of trade and industrial questions and the liberalization of agricultural and consumer-goods markets within Japan. What is indisputable, however, is that the Yen–Dollar Agreement, finally concluded in the summer of 1984, fired the starting gun for Japan's financial revolution – and for a pace of change that few, if any, of the participants could appreciate fully at the time.

The agreement, in the form of a report to US Treasury Secretary Donald Regan and his counterpart, Finance Minister Noboru Takeshita, on 29 May, essentially covered three areas. One was the direct promotion of the use of the yen internationally through the expansion of the existing highly restricted euroyen market, the creation of a yen-based bankers' acceptance market and the abolition of restrictions on currency swapping. The second was the deregulation, over time, of deposit interest rates in order to close the gap between Japanese and American rates and hence to encourage more financial flows into the yen. The third area was the removal of restrictions on foreign entry into key sectors of the market, particularly

Table 13 Principal Japanese financial institutions at the end of 1983

Central bank	The Bank of Japan
Private financial institutions	
Ordinary (commercial) banks	City banks (12)[1]
	Regional banks (63)
	Foreign banks (65)
	All banks[2] (86)
Specialized financial institutions	
Financial institution for international finance	Specialized foreign-exchange bank (1)
Financial institutions for long-term credit	Long-term credit banks (3)
	Trust banks (7)
	(Banking a/c)
	(Trust a/c)
Financial institutions for small businesses	Sogo (mutual) banks (71)
	Credit associations (456)
	Credit co-operatives (468)
	Shoko Chukin Bank (Central Bank for Commercial and Industrial Co-operatives) (1)
Financial institutions for agriculture, forestry and fishery	Norinchukin Bank (Central Co-operative Bank for Agriculture and Forestry) (1)
	(Credit Federations of Agricultural Co-operatives) (47)
	Agricultural Co-operatives (4,356)
Other financial institutions	
Insurance companies	Life insurance companies (23)
	Non-life insurance companies (22)
Securities companies (218)	
Housing finance companies (8)	
Banks (2)	
Corporations (10) (including Shoko Chukin Bank)	
Others	
Government financial institutions	Post offices (23,490)
	Trust Fund Bureau (1)

Notes: [1] The number of institutions in each category appears in parentheses. [2] This figure excludes foreign banks.
Source: Federation of Bankers' Associations of Japan.

the previously well protected trust business, and foreign securities companies' newly won licence to become members of the Tokyo Stock Exchange.

From the American point of view – and from the point of view of interested observers such as the British, who were pursuing parallel talks of their own – the central thrust of the talks was the internationalization of the yen and the secondary issue that of access for their own institutions to the Japanese market.

In the gathering storm of mutual recrimination that developed in the early 1980s the US government soon accepted that the Japanese were not formally managing their currency. If the dollar was strong, it conceded, part of the reason was the high US interest rates compared with those of Japan and, for that matter, West Germany and Switzerland. But it could not accept that the tight control exercised by the Japanese authorities over the domestic market did not have a part to play. American industry was up in arms about Japanese price competition, and the low value of the yen was the key.

As Jeffrey Frankel, an economist on the President's Council of Advisers, recalled: 'In Late September of 1983 Lee Morgan, chairman of Caterpillar Tractor, came to Washington. He visited top officials at the White House, Treasury, Council of Economic Advisers and other agencies. As he went he left two gifts. The first was a copy of a new study entitled *The Misalignment of the US Dollar and the Japanese Yen: The Problem and its Solution* by David Murchison and Ezra Solomon. The second was a toy Caterpillar tractor made in West Germany.'

The report by Ezra, an economics professor at Stanford, and Murchison, one of Caterpillar's legal advisers, caught precisely the argument that was to lead President Reagan to ask Prime Minister Nakasone for the opening of financial discussions to parallel trade discussions when the two met that November. Its authors accepted that interest-rate differentials played a major role in currency valuation, but they argued that the unique problem for the yen was its restricted use as an international currency. Here was Japan, the second largest industrial economy in the Western world, with financial bond and equity markets far larger than any European centre, accounting for 12 per cent of the free world's GNP, 94 per cent of its exports and 7.5 per cent of its imports. Yet the yen accounted for only 4 per cent of the reserves held by the major international monetary authorities, compared with nearly 70 per cent held in US dollars and 12 per cent in the Deutschmark. In the eurocurrency market of some $2,000 billion dollars per annum the yen's proportion was even lower at around $25 billion of issues, the same as sterling issues but far less than the $100 billion of Swiss issues and the $189 billion of Deutschmark issues, never mind the $ 1,600 billion of dollar issues.

The cause was identified as the Japanese controls on the various markets that might have promoted the use of the yen: the lack of a yen-dominated bankers' acceptance market, the restrictions on the ability of Japanese banks and institutions to swap currencies and the imposition of limits on the type of borrower and the number of issues either of foreigners raising money in yen in Tokyo (the so-called *samurai* market) or of Japanese groups attempting to raise euroyen outside.

Dr David C. Mulford, Assistant Secretary for International Affairs at the US Treasury and a key figure in the negotiations, put it bluntly enough. 'Our general objective was to begin to change the environment in which the exchange rate is determined,' he told a conference in London later, 'from one based on government regulation and administrative "guidance" to one governed by market forces ... Change,' he went on, 'does not come quickly in Japan, since there is always the threat of renewed regulation by a government bureaucracy whose penchant is for regulation instead of free markets. Therefore, although I believe the effects of domestic and international liberalization in Japan are inexorable, they are also, if you will pardon the expression, inscrutable.'

It is precisely this tone of schoolmasterly censure that the Japanese find unpardonable. Their view was that they were being made victims of President Reagan's conversion to the pure Chicago doctrine of free-market forces.

They argued, with considerable statistical evidence, that Japan was, by any ordinary historical yardstick, positively leaping towards internationalization. The 4 per cent of reserves was nearly ten times what it had been ten years before. It had been in the last three years that Japan had emerged as a capital exporter rather than importer; its foreign exchanges had already been largely freed in 1980; its domestic markets were in the process of deregulation; and its concerns about the use of the yen in the eurocurrency markets were no more than the worries of West Germany or even the USA five years before. The USA might have been converted to the Chicago school of monetarist economists. Japan had not.

'On our part,' recalled Isao Kubota, one of the Ministry of Finance officials working on the Japanese side and now in charge of foreign financial institutions at the Ministry, 'we adhere to a more traditional theory. We consider interest rates play a rather important role in the economy. We believe they are still an important policy instrument.' 'We believe,' he told the audience at Oxford, a university that has kept well clear of monetarism, 'that the government is, at any time, in a better position [than the markets] to judge the *status quo* of the economy as well as its desirable course in the future.'

Japan was completely in agreement with the Americans on the need to liberalize its domestic markets. Where it differed was over the pace. The Americans wanted acceleration. The Japanese wanted to work things out more gradually, in line with their economic policies and their different financial system. 'Our liberalization process,' Kubota argued, 'should be a sequence of trials and errors. Hence we are to proceed step by step, carefully ascertaining the effects of each step. This does not imply, however, that we are to go slow. Though there is an opinion to the effect that liberalization should be carried out stride by stride, not step by step, I don't think what is implied by this opinion differs much from our aims in practical terms.'

The interpretation of the difference of approach of the two sides is crucial because it in turn determines the view of those on the one hand who believe that Tokyo is quite naturally emerging as a financial centre the importance of which is commensurate with Japan's economic status in the world, and those on the other who believe that the Japanese financial system, like its industrial system, remains enclosed, protected and resistant to outside forces, giving ground only under pressure and then very slowly.

In a sense the two views are both right and wrong, in that they are based on a misunderstanding of each other's position. Since the agreement the Japanese have pointed out, not without a degree of relish, that most American expectations, at least in so far as they understood them, have been disappointed.

The yen did not strengthen as a result of the agreement. In fact, the opposite occurred. In the year immediately after the agreement it actually fell by 7.5 per cent against the dollar. Beryl Sprinkel and David Mulford argued, rather defensively, that it did not depreciate as much as the Deutschmark or pound sterling. But depreciate it did. And the reason was simple enough. While Japan's trade surplus soared in 1984 to $35 billion, its outward flow of capital soared even faster to well over $40 billion, most of it into dollars. The first effects of the liberalization of exchange flows and swap arrangements were, as the Ministry of Finance and the Bank of Japan had thought they would be, to encourage the flight of capital from the yen into other currencies as pension funds and other institutions rushed to balance their portfolios with the new allowance of 10 per cent in foreign assets, as companies moved to take advantage of easier terms on foreign bond markets and as financial institutions began to ride the current of swaps, convertibles and other debt instruments in the eurocurrency, Swiss and other markets.

The euroyen market certainly got off to a quick start. Every major financial institution in Japan wanted the kudos of being assoc- iated with the issues permitted under the more liberalized terms of December 1984. But within one month, after twenty-two issues worth 479 billion yen – more than the total raised during the previous eight years of the euroyen market's existence, when issuers were limited to sovereign and supranational borrowers only – the market effectively closed, choked in a surplus of issues arranged on terms that may have made them agreeable for the borrower but were hardly appealing to the investor. High though the US Treasury's expectations were, the reality proved to be, in the initial phase at least, a meteor market driven largely by borrowers anxious to take advantage of attractive terms and then to swap the yen for other currency-denominated loans.

Nor, as observers as well as foreign financiers soon pointed out, was the agreement that successful in promoting the entry of foreign firms into Tokyo. At first liberalization forced most of the banks operating in Tokyo into sharp deficit. For a generation most of them had, in fact, enjoyed a cosy, if restricted, position in Tokyo, seeking Ministry sanction for nearly every transaction, including the size of the loans they offered to domestic customers and the interest they charged. In return they were allowed vastly increased limits on swap arrangements, a monopoly position in impact loans (foreign-currency credits, usually over five years, for specific projects) and a protected position on foreign-currency transactions. 'We may not have been able to expand much in seeking deposits or widening our range of activities,' one European banker with a decade's experience admits, 'but we made a very handsome profit from the loans we did make. Japanese banks were even coming to us with the loans organized and the local currency to finance it in order to provide foreign-currency loans to their favoured customers, which they themselves weren't allowed to do.'

The liberalization of foreign currency, pushed by the Europeans and Americans in 1980, effectively ended that game. The further liberalization since then has only increased the foreign competition, as the major international institutions have each sought to gain a position in the third leg of the new world. Nearly all the big commercial banks have set up shop in Tokyo's Marunouchi business quarter of glass and skyscrapers, alongside the old palace gardens of the Edo period. 'You can tell it's international now,' said an American banker in the summer of 1985, pointing to a sprightly, if portly, figure in blue suit and sober tie, 'because the lawyers are starting to come in.'

For some, particularly US securities firms with dealing muscle and a strong line in buying and selling US bonds to Japanese customers and the limited number of foreign firms with securities licences, the pickings were good. Japanese investors were becoming sophisticated, and the institutions wanted to load up with foreign-currency holdings. But for many, including the banks that had been in Tokyo ever since the war, things were less easy. As the Americans and British had suspected, the Japanese authorities were in no hurry to open up the doors of their financial heartland to foreign companies. Claiming, with some sincerity, the rules of the Securities Act, which had been modelled on Glass–Steagall and excluded banks from any underwriting activity, the Ministry refused to allow capital markets or merchant-bank subsidiaries of foreign commercial banks to undertake any underwriting or securities dealing. The sole exception was Vickers da Costa, the British broker bought out by Citicorp in 1983, which continued to be allowed to deal. Others, like Barclays Bank, were refused, while even legitimate securities houses found the wait long before they could get a licence that would allow them a considerable percentage of commissions.

The trust-bank business that had seemed so alluring to foreign institutions also proved less attractive close to. The banks, together with the insurance companies, were the only institutions that were allowed to handle the country's annual $10 billion pension-fund business. But, unlike similar institutions in the USA or Europe, they were also charged with all the administrative costs of arranging the pensions, doing the actuarial calculations and other work. The nine banks applying to join the select band of trust banks were eventually allowed in. Instead of giving them a few years' grace to learn the ropes and establish a profit base, however, the Ministry announced within a few months that it would permit links with virtually un-limited numbers of foreign institutions, whose remit would be to advise trust banks and insurance companies on pension-fund business and, equally lucrative, the new field of investment funds for the surplus cash of corporations.

This was typical of Japanese protectionism, the willingness to go along only at the pace that suited Japan and to allow foreign competition only as far as it was useful to learn from, suggested the critics. Just as they had done with steel and heavy industries in the 1960s and then with automobiles and electronics in the 1970s, so the Japanese were keeping up non-tariff barriers long enough for their domestic financial companies to prepare themselves for international competition. Once they were ready, the barriers would come down to reveal not an unexploited valley ready for the taking but a fully fledged international financial industry ready to launch forth and conquer the world.

Yet the parallel with heavy and consumer industries is not a bad one and not as unfair to the Japanese as might be suggested. In the post-war period they had indeed protected their industries from outside competition and their agriculture from imports. Their economy shattered by the war, they regarded themselves as a developing nation, needing to reorganize through government direction and ever vulnerable to their reliance on imports of raw materials. During the late 1960s a group of younger-minded officials of the powerful Ministry of Trade and Industry (MITI), most of them with experience abroad and particularly in the U S A, developed a programme for liberalizing trade barriers on the grounds that many of Japan's industries were then ready and able to compete. In consultation with the industries concerned the programme started with those (such as the steel industry) that could operate under free-market principles immediately, those (such as microchips) that could do so over a set period and those (such as oil-refining) that would take a long time, or were considered too strategic, to weather exposure to the blasts of foreign competition. By the time that the first oil shock of 1973 shook the Japanese and revived all their old fears of vulnerability to raw-material imports, that programme was already in force, and Japan had already established the basis for prosperity in a post-energy-crisis world.

In a similar way the younger, more internationally educated and minded officials of the Ministry of Finance (or M O F, as it is familiarly and not always politely known in Tokyo's financial circles) were also developing a programme of liberalization some years before President Reagan and Treasury Secretary Regan pushed the ball into the international negotiating court in November 1982.

The Japanese financial system was, and to an extent still is, extraordinarily primitive by the standards of most other industrialized nations. The short-term money market is barely developed and certainly unsophisticated in its range of products. Most deposits have traditionally been held in the banking system; most finance has been through the banks. Interest rates have been heavily controlled, both at the long-term and the short-term end. There was, until recently, virtually no secondary market in government debt. The loans of corporations were, until this decade, subject to detailed supervision by the Ministry of Finance. Great areas of capital markets – the bankers' acceptance market, a Treasury-bill market, futures, options, convertible bonds – simply did not exist when the Yen–Dollar Committee started its discussions.

The system has been finely tuned to the industrial and economic circumstances of the country in the immediate post-war period, however. To the extent that the so-called 'Japanese Miracle' was based on a unique nexus of government and corporations, operating through a complex of interrelated cross-shareholdings in quasi family groupings – *keiretsu*, as the groupings have been called – so the financial system was developed as part of this.

Each grouping has its main bank, which acts as the principle lender to both the central company and the various member companies associated with it. The main bank, either one of the thirteen commercial banks or one of the three long-term credit banks, also acts as commissioned bank, in a type of merchant-bank role, advising and organizing bonds or equity issues for the company. Although formally prohibited from acting as underwriters by the Securities Act, the banks none the less ended up buying and thus effectively guaranteeing many of the bond issues. The role of the banks was further extended by the restructuring that followed the US-directed abolition of the old *keiretsu* industrial groups. A central part of that restructuring took place around the banks, such as Mitsubishi.

This system of main banks, reinforced by the shareholdings held by banks in industrial corporations and the shareholdings of industrial corporations in their main bank, gave the industrial groups a sure access to capital, a freedom from take-over bids and the ability to concentrate on long-term managerial aims without the burden of short-term financial pressures that have been in marked contrast to the freer American and British markets (although it should be remembered that in these countries too there has traditionally been a close relationship between at least the merchant banks and investment houses and their corporate clients).

The main-bank structure was in turn part of a government-influenced, if not directed, financial system that enabled Japan to channel large amounts of savings among consumers into long-term industrial investment throughout the 1950s and 1960s. The system was based on a high degree of specialization, or segmentation, of the banking sector, made possible by, and in turn making possible, the tight control of interest rates.

Deposits were collected throughout the country by a variety of local and central institutions, ranging from the agricultural co-operatives, credit co-operatives and securities companies to the bigger regional and city (commercial) banks and the Post Office, the latter accounting for an extraordinary share of over 20 per cent of all deposits. At the centre of the system was the relatively limited number (by comparison with the USA at least) of twelve city banks and one specialized foreign-exchange bank, the Bank of Tokyo (which acted as a city bank as well), three long-term credit banks and seven trust banks.

The long-term credit banks (the Industrial Bank of Japan, the Nippon Credit Bank and the Long-Term Credit Bank), unique to Japan, were charged with the long-term financing of industry and commerce, backed by a monopoly on the issue of long-term debentures. The city banks held a commanding position with respect to time deposits and normal banking functions. The trust banks, which also acted as city banks, held a monopoly of trust accounts.

It was, in its way, both a tidy and an effective system. The government buttressed its financing needs from Post Office savings, made attractive by tax incentives and a slightly better interest rate on small deposits. Industry gained its long-term funds, aided also by the tendency of the major holders of equities to hold on to them, partly because they too were part of the grouping system. At the one end were the consumers, with one of the highest savings ratios in the world, varying between 18 and 22 per cent (as against the US 5 per cent); at the other end were the restructuring needs of the country. In between was a government that, until the energy crisis of 1973, followed the principles of a balanced budget and an issue of paper limited almost exclusively to the short-term smoothing out of its funding needs through the Bank of Japan and the major banks. There were tensions in the system, as the growth of the uncontrolled consumer-credit companies (the *sarakin*) showed. There was some

competition, fierce at times between the main players in each sector
of the market. But broadly each sector kept itself to itself and out of
others' patches. It was the Japanese corporate way, and M O F was
there to make sure that no one stepped out of line.

It worked throughout the financial system, even in the securities
business, where a natural hierarchy remained intact. The Big Four
securities houses (Nomura, Daiwa, Yamaichi and Nikko), which control about half the total volume of the Tokyo Stock Exchange, led the
underwriting. The middle-ranking securities houses were given co-
management positions on selected issues. The smaller ones were allo-
cated shares. The financial organizations knew their place and stayed
there, not only because it was unwise to risk the disapproval of their
peers but also because that was the way to be sure of a piece of the
profit. It may have been – it still is – a relatively uncompetitive
system of financing, but it ensured a wide distribution of the margin
and oiled the wheels of the Japanese revival.

Even before the U S pressure for reform, however, it was having to
change. One reason was the rapid move by the major Japanese corporations, from the time of the second oil shock in 1979, to slim down
their finances. Investment within Japan was in any case slowing after
a generation of expenditure during the 1960s and 1970s. The larger
corporations were beginning to think more of investment overseas.
Earlier than most of the European and American corporations, they
moved to reduce overheads, reallocate labour and improve their cash
flow. By the mid-1980s, the biggest corporations were recording huge
cash mountains. Toyota, the Nagana motor corporation, was openly
being referred to as the 'Toyota Bank', so great were its earnings
from investing its cash flow. *Zaiteku*, the technology of finance,
became a new buzz word.

The effect of financial management by corporations was sharp.
Estimates by the Bank of Japan showed that 85 per cent of the increase
in large corporate funds was being invested in market-rate assets by
1983, compared with less than 30 per cent only five years before, and
that regulated-asset investments were for the first time being drawn
down in significant quantities. At the same time cash and deposits,
which in the early 1970s had accounted for nearly two-thirds of the
use of surplus corporate funds, by 1983 had slipped to only one-
third, while investment in liquid securities (chiefly bonds) had grown
from only 6 per cent of new funds available to over one-third. The
funds of top corporations, the *tokkein* funds, have become some of
the most sought-after prizes in the trust game, and corporations have

demanded a higher and higher short-term return on this area of business, much of it going abroad.

A similar change in approach was developing among ordinary consumers and particularly institutions such as the pension funds. The question of why the Japanese consumer should continue to save such a high proportion of his or her income is open to endless discussion. Cultural attitudes have certainly made a contribution. More concretely, so has the very high cost of land and housing within the overcrowded main island of Japan. Young people have to save a long time for a deposit on property, and for historical reasons they have tended to save in banks and other deposit institutions rather than in building societies or savings and loans banks. Minimal social security provision, tax advantages with respect to savings and the depletion of financial assets in the aftermath of the war have all played a part.

Consumer saturation may also have contributed, although this can be exaggerated. Certainly, there have been signs recently of greater consumer spending and borrowing, partly for foreign holidays as leisure increases and attitudes among the young change. But the greatest worry to emerge during the late 1970s was the problem of the ageing society, as it was dubbed by the government's planners. Demographic trends suggested that Japan, more than any other country, would move rapidly into a higher and higher ratio of retired to working people from the late 1990s onwards. By the year 2025, the government calculated, 21 per cent of the population would be over sixty-five as opposed to 10 per cent then. The effect of bringing more women into the labour force, and the impact of this on consumer spending, was one implication. The most immediate requirement, however, was to increase the pressure on pension funds and savings institutions to raise returns in preparation. By the late 1970s the institutions were growing both more sophisticated and, in line with corporations, more anxious to diversify their funds into foreign holdings, both as a hedge to a slowing down of the Japanese economy and as a quick route to higher returns.

The greatest pressure for change on the Japanese authorities, however, came from the government's funding problems. The slow-down in the rate of Japanese economic growth from the first and the second oil shocks, and the reduction in the borrowing by corporations (the deficit of the corporate sector fell from 8 per cent of GDP to 4 per cent in the early 1980s, dropping to as low as 1 per cent in the period immediately before the second oil shock), coincided with a dramatic increase in government deficits. After a generation of balanced budgets, the Japanese government – for democratic reasons similar to those of other major industrialized countries at the time – began to move to deficit financing in 1975, and it has continued to gather pace ever since. From being the country with the lowest proportion of government debt as a percentage of GDP and as a percentage of the total state budget, Japan now has the highest. From a figure of some 5 per cent of GNP, central government debt had climbed to nearly 40 per cent by 1984, twice the proportion of West Germany's debt and roughly equivalent to that of the USA. As a proportion of budget, at nearly a quarter in 1985 (although reduced from the beginning of the decade), it was still twice that of the USA.

The increasing size of the Japanese budget deficit posed considerable problems not only for direct funding but also for the refunding of the extensive ten-year bonds that began to be issued in 1975. Ten years later, by the mid-1980s, the cost of servicing Japan's debt had risen to over 10,000 billion yen, the largest single item of government expenditure; the outstanding balance of bonds issued had soared to over 133,000 billion yen; and the government was having to refund over 5,000 billion yen in bonds coming up for redemption each year.

In one sense this huge government financing burden – all the greater when one considers how quickly it had developed – made the Ministry of Finance more chary of tampering with interest rates in a way that might make its own debt-servicing costs greater. In another sense, as the Bank of Japan (the body actually charged with the funding operation in the market) pointed out, it greatly intensified the need for the development of a mature secondary-debt market on American and European lines if the government was to be able to fund the debt at all. A traditional system in which Treasury bills were little more than short-term smoothing instruments, issued by the Bank of Japan to the banks and repurchased within a year, was clearly inadequate to the task.

The combination of all these pressures – the pressure on institutions to cope with the ageing of the population, the move by corporations as well as savers away from controlled-interest-rate bank deposits and the challenge of refunding – were sufficient to launch the Japanese Ministry of Finance on a series of financial reforms well before the Yen-Dollar Agreement talks. As early as 1972, when Japan had seemed destined to accumulate a long-term current-account surplus, the government had been planning a substantial easing of foreign-exchange controls. This had been scotched by the first energy crisis. But as the country coped, with astonishing resilience, with the second oil shock of 1979 and as institutions pressed for change, a Foreign Exchange and Foreign Trade law was introduced in 1980 that suspended limits to the outflow of funds.

Controls remained formally in place, and the Ministry still had the right to supervise swap arrangements and foreign-currency issues by resident companies and to limit the amount of foreign assets held by insurance companies and pension funds. The hand of MOF was not to be withdrawn that easily. But a spirit that had been dominated by the fear of foreign incursions and the take-over of financial institutions was now being replaced by confidence: institutions seemed ready to go out and compete abroad, and Japan was ready to become the world's biggest banker.

At the same time a number of reforms were made to cope with government debt funding. In 1975 the Bank of Japan freed the call-money and bill-discount markets and allowed banks to issue yen CDs in the first move towards free money markets. In 1981 a new banking law allowed banks to sell government bonds directly to the public – the first encroachment of the banks on to the securities houses' territory – while the securities houses in turn were freed to develop money-market funds based on medium-term government bonds. The markets were hardly freed 'at a stroke', but the process was in train.

The impact of the brute force of the American government, assaulting half the financial castle's walls at the same time, was dramatic. It is easy to argue, as some MOF officials in Tokyo and Japanese bankers do, that liberalization was under way, whatever the pressures, and that the Americans did no more than make a lot of noise about their own part in it. In a broad sense this is true. Most of the measures announced as part of the Yen-Dollar Committee's report – further liberalization of interest rates, further removal of foreign-exchange controls, further deregulation of euroyen issues by residents – followed the path that the Ministry was already pursuing and would have continued along anyway, albeit perhaps at a slower and more stately pace. Most of the points at which the Ministry balked – the free entry of foreign institutions into the trust-account market, the rapid deregulation of interest rates on small deposits that would have undermined the Post Office, the early creation of the Treasury-bill market (on which the Bank of Japan, a proponent, and the Ministry, an opponent, were at odds) – were either shelved or hedged about by administrative restrictions.

The euroyen market was formally decontrolled but was un-attractive at first for residents because of the continuance of the withholding tax. Administrative guidance, if less formal, remained for most transactions involving foreign currency or euroyen. The pace of domestic interest rates and euroyen decontrol was kept well reined in by the phasing of controls both on deposits and issues and on time deposits and issues. The American negotiators saw a frame-work of deregulation lasting a few years; the Japanese government officials saw it in terms of a decade. In their own terms that was speedy. It was dreadfully slow by American standards.

'When we started negotiations at the beginning of 1983,' explained Shigemitsu Sugisaki, Assistant Vice-Minister for International Affairs and a member of the ad hoc committee at the time, 'we were well prepared with measures to implement deregulation of short-term interest rates. We have a serious problem of refinancing large volumes of government debt. In addition we have for some time felt that we could not internationalize our industry without inter-nationalizing our finance. What we did not have the consensus for, and what we still do not understand American insistence on, is the promotion of a euroyen market and demands for decompartmentaliza-tion of our internal financial system. That we will have to study further before undertaking change.'

What American pressure did was not only to bring forward the pace of interest deregulation but also to throw the whole Japanese policy debate on financial issues into a different gear. Japan's hesita-tion over the euroyen and its internal financial structure reflected deep divisions with the financial world and the government.

In all the discussion about the Japanese consensus approach to business – its corporate-planning process – it is often forgotten that this consensus is a process of balancing quite marked differences of interest and opinion within the system. Japanese success owes as much to the drive for results and achievement by individual parts of the system as it does to the ability of the country as a whole to co-ordinate its aims. It is not individual drive that Japan's businesses lack. But their drive is constrained by willingness to bow to a com-munity agreement once an agreement is reached.

In the case of many of the issues thrown up by the American negotiators that consensus had yet to be reached. The Bank of Japan, for example, fiercely opposed the idea of an off-shore banking centre on the grounds (similar to those advanced by the Bundesbank in West Germany and the US Fed. over the development of the eurodollar and euromarkets in the 1970s) that it led to a leakage of money out of the system and therefore to a curtailment of its ability to control the money supply. The Ministry of Finance, on the other hand, was much less worried by an off-shore banking centre, seeing it as a means of exercising more direct control of the Japanese players than if they were operating abroad.

Equally, the Bank of Japan and the Ministry of Finance were in disagreement over the creation of a Treasury-bill market.

Even greater differences were recorded within the Ministry of Finance. The Ministry had long been divided into the 'Four bureaux' – tax, banking, securities and international affairs – each of them protecting its own patch and the interests of its particular constituents. The Securities Bureau, perhaps the most regulation-minded, was determined to keep banking and underwriting separated and to maintain tight control of a market that, in the light of experience, could otherwise all too easily let loose some surprisingly anarchic instincts in traders. It was also more worried than other departments by the threat of outside competition in an area that was relatively less developed than the New York and London markets.

The Tax Bureau was equally adamant about withholding tax. It saw no reason to make an exception of residents in the euroyen market when they had to pay tax in the domestic market. Like other revenue authorities, it was driven by a desire for even-handedness and a fear of tax evasion. Divorced from the policy-making parts of the Ministry, it resolutely refused to hear of abolition of the tax.

Not the least virtue of American demands was that they forced the process of consensus within the government and gave extra weight to the arguments of the younger officials, particularly those in Vice-Minister Tomamitsu Oba's International Affairs area. 'For the first time,' recorded one of the officials, 'the heads of all the four bureaux had to sit together, alongside each other, and in front of foreigners. They could not display openly their disagreements.' Pushed on by Prime Minister Naksone's personal commitment to the success of the talks, it was the international affairs officials and the more liberally minded middle-rankers who predominated the regular June reshuffle of official responsibilities that immediately followed the May 1984 agreement.

Outside pressure also enabled the Ministry to twist arms within the financial industry. Deregulation was being pushed, particularly by the big securities houses, such as Nomura, anxious to ride the tide of market-related interest rates and more open competition for deposits. The commercial or city banks too were keen to start to spread their wings into the money and bond markets in order to counter the decline in interest-regulated deposits. It was the trust banks and the long-term credit banks, the previous kings of the system, that felt more threatened. The long-term credit banks in particular had done well out of internationalization, accompanying their clients as they raised foreign-currency loans on the euromarkets and the New York markets. The last thing they wanted now was a sudden undermining of their funding base in a monopoly of debentures; they were in accord with the trust banks, which had recorded fairly feeble returns on their pension and managed funds compared with results in the USA and wanted to face the full force of competition from the Morgan Stanleys, Goldman Sachses and Morgan Guarantys of the world.

The agreement, as negotiated in May 1984, was thus inevitably something of a compromise, giving credence to those who argued that any change in Japan would be slow, at the pace and in the direction of its domestic interests, and very far from allowing Tokyo full entry to the international world of finance until well into the 1990s. And, indeed, there are good reasons for caution in greeting Japan's new mood of liberalization.

The immaturity of many of its most basic markets – the interbank market, the government bond and euroyen markets – and the maintenance of restrictions, both legal and informal, in so many facets of the financial world continue to shock bankers arriving there for the first time or bankers who have spent long enough there to grow used to a centrally directed industry. In the mid-1980s Japan is at least ten years behind the USA in its bond markets and at least a generation behind Europe or the USA in its money markets.

There remain all too many reasons why it should not want to alter this state too fast. 'Japan's problems,' argues Toyoo Gyohten, head of the International Finance Bureau of the Ministry of Finance and a leading light in the push for liberalization within the government, 'is that we have to think while we keep walking. We really cannot stop, but we have to keep thinking about what we are doing. You can't remove competitive demarcation without doing anything about the structural framework of the industry. Nor do you want to produce a situation in which you risk failures of businesses, with real social problems and problems of confidence. Some of our system stems from our experience of bank failures in the 1930s. Now everyone is forgetting that, as the voices grow louder for the complete removal of barriers.'

The Japanese caution about ill-discipline in the market is a real one, based partly on cultural attitudes (failure bringing shame and harm to the whole community) but partly also on very real experience. The collapse of several of the poorly supervised consumer credit organizations, the *sarakin*, in the early 1980s and public scandals, such as the fraudulent gold-fund company, Toyota Shoji, which ended with its chairman, Kazuo Nagano, being hacked to pieces in his home by *samurai*-sword-wielding clients in front of door-stepping ranks of television cameras, are signs of the volatility and vulnerability beneath the surface of Japanese calm.

When the Ministry of Finance, in its traditional way, sent teams of officials and industry-consultative groups around Europe and the USA to study foreign examples in the early 1980s before coming to their own decisions, they came back with three firm conclusions: one was that liberalization was inevitable; the second was that it need not overwhelm the Japanese institutions; and the third was that the process needed far more care than the Americans were giving it if a disaster such as the collapse of the Continental Illinois Bank were to be avoided. As long as this is so, 'administrative guidance' will be continued in one form or another, and the Ministry will hold on to its Glass–Steagall divisions. The Japanese think that nanny is still needed.

At the same time, Japan will not abandon lightly either its peculiar system of groupings and specialized banks. It accepts now that those banks and institutions will become more and more like each other, straying into each other's patches and eventually enjoying no distinction at all between sizes or terms of deposits as far as the limits of activity are concerned. There are even those in the Ministry who believe that the Glass–Steagall provisions will be progressively blurred and that should the USA cancel them, Japan might follow. In the USA too there is a growing acceptance that the dismantling of fences between territories, and the greater competition and lower margins that this implies, will force at least mergers and perhaps some closures of the weaker banks, particularly in the local areas. It is not the Japanese way to allow companies to go to the wall, but mergers such as that of the two big city banks, Daichi and Kangyo, in the 1970s, and among smaller banks, will occur.

But the system of main banks will not disappear quickly, for reasons both of tradition and the cross-holdings of shares. Corporations that owe a great deal of their prosperity to particular banks will tend to continue to use them as 'main banks' even if they grow more adventurous in the investment of their cash flow and surplus funds. The nexus of interrelations will continue to mean that one bank will support another, or the associated securities houses, in their allocation of underwriting shares and financial services.

The government for its part will slow down, although not necessarily stop altogether, the deregulation of long-term debenture issues, for example, and the growth in capacity to raise long-term money on the euroyen market in order to portect the position of the long-term credit banks, the most vulnerable sector of the trust banks, whose relatively low rates of return, after all, owe much to their adherence to investments wished on them by government. Even so liberal a figure as Gyohten could argue after the Yen-Dollar Agreement, 'The euroyen market is our bastard child. The domestic market is our legitimate son. Naturally we want to look after our own child first and see that his future is assured before that of his bastard brother.'

On the other side of the coin, however, is Japan's ability to move with extraordinary speed once its mind is made up. This has been seen in its response to the energy crisis, in its move into microchips and computer electronics, in its investment in space; it will no doubt be seen in its financial aggression as well. 'Before consensus is achieved,' said a slightly aggrieved senior banker in Tokyo in the summer of 1985, after vainly attempting to convert a parliamentary group to his view that conservatism should prevail, 'nothing seems to move. But once it is achieved, then no one wants to hear from the objectors. Their view has been heard. Now it is our job simply to accept.'

The point is the more valid for finance. Money never moves faster than when barriers start to come down. Like water, it finds the cracks and forces them open. So with Japanese finance. Within a year of the May 1984 agreement, the two sides were meeting again in Tokyo to record that Japan had fulfilled all its assurances and had actually progressed much faster than expected. The Japanese Diet, after prolonged wrangling within the M O F, had, under intense American pressure, agreed to abolish the withholding tax, a major step forward for the euroyen market. The schedule of deregulation in the euroyen market had in turn accelerated the pace of deregulation within the Japanese market and led to the *de facto* collapse of the collateral principle for borrowing – the principle under which banks were limited in their borrowing in yen by their ability to repay on set criteria (virtually preventing corporations from borrowing in certain markets unless they were of double- or triple-A standing).

The Ministry of Finance approved the issuance of money-market certificates (MMCs) in March 1985; the minimum denomination of CDs was reduced in April 1985; a yen-denominated bankers' acceptance market (bills guaranteed by banks to finance trade) came into being in June 1985; interest rates on large deposits began the process of a three-year deregulation. All of these were small steps in the eyes of Western bankers but giant leaps by the standards of Japan. And so with foreign entry to the market. Nine foreign banks were allowed into the trust-bank market by the summer of 1985 and, more important, foreign institutions were also allowed to establish joint deals with Japanese institutions and to go it alone in advising pensions funds and corporations on their investments. For the Americans, if not for the British (who were still involved in arguments over the provision of banking licences to Japanese securities houses operating in London), there was some movement in the queue for branch status for banks and dealing licences for securities houses. Foreign institutions with ten years' experience were allowed to distribute government bonds.

By the summer of 1985 an advisory committee of the industry (a traditional means for the Japanese government to gain not just consensus but also the support of industry), the committee for Financial System Research under the chairmanship of Mr Tokuda, a former head of the MOF banking bureau and now head of Nomura Research Institute, could conclude that the liberalization of short-term interest rates should actually be speeded up and that the price of this might well be failures among banking institutions. Instead of slowing the pace of deregulation to protect the weak, it instead suggested the imposition of tougher guidelines on asset ratios and reserves and on mergers and acquisitions to prop up the weaker. Other ways too, such as the creation of special MMCs, should be found for preserving the position of Post Office savings.

At the same time, the idea of an off-shore banking centre, which seemed to have been shelved indefinitely, re-emerged despite the opposition of the Bank of Japan. 'It would be like,' argued a Bank of Japan executive, 'bringing home a mistress to live with a dowdy wife. One would be bound to outshine the other and cause endless trouble.'

As it was, the relaxation of rules in the euroyen market deprived the Bank of Japan of its main argument that this would encourage too much leakage from the monetary system. That would happen anyhow. The advantages, promoted by the Ministry of Finance, were

that it would both allow for greater control and that it would meet the
growing demands of the middle-sized and smaller Japanese financial
institutions, which now needed ready access to international eurocurrency finance but did not have the resources to set up branches
in London, New York and elsewhere.

The creation of an off-shore banking centre and deregulation of
the euroyen markets will not, of course, of themselves internationalize
either the yen or Tokyo as a financial centre. For a long time to come
Tokyo will remain an expensive centre in which to operate, circum-
scribed by language and cultural differences, M O F guidance and the
natural tendency of Japanese institutions to support each other in the
face of foreign competition, even if that competition is openly allowed.
'There won't be many pensions funds handing over their main
portfolios to Americans or Europeans' is a typical comment in
financial circles.

There remain powerful constraints on the use of the yen as an
international currency. Only 3 per cent of Japan's imports and only
40 per cent of its exports are denominated in the domestic currency,
compared with 38 and 76 per cent respectively for U K imports and
exports and 43 and 82 per cent for West German imports and exports.
Since so many of its imports are raw materials and most of these are
dollar-priced commodities, this position can change only as fast as,
for example, the oil exporters are willing to accept it and as fast as
Japan is willing or able to increase its imports of foreign manufactures
(both processes will tend to be very slow). Japan's export of capital
has been huge, as great as Britain's in the nineteenth century and the
U S A's just after the war. But, unlike those two experiences,
Japanese capital is an export that has so far gone largely into short-
term dollar instruments.

This is changing, as the dollar weakens and Japanese corporations
seek to diversify their holdings. But it is, again, a gradual change
rather than a rapid one. Finance is the servant of basic economic
facts, not yet its master.

Yet there is no doubt, as the American negotiatiors argued from
the start, that deregulated finance can smooth the way to change. The
astonishing thing about Japan is, in many ways, not how slowly it has
changed but how fast. Beneath the surface it has already emerged as
second only to the U S A in terms of the foreign participation in its
stock and bond markets, both absolutely and in relation to market
capitalization and G N P. The amount raised in yen by foreign borrowers, at a total of around $10 billion in 1984, was three times the

figures of 1980 and ten times the figure of a decade before. Issues in
the foreign bond market amounted to almost $4 billion (about $8.5
billion if long-term yen loans are included), next in size to the Swiss
market. Japanese banks have now taken seven of the top twenty
positions among lead-manager banks in euroloans. Japanese banks
have nearly three hundred representative banks abroad; Japanese
securities companies have nearly a hundred subsidiaries and representative offices abroad.

Not the least reason for the acceleration in Japan's financial liberalization is the growing competitive confidence of its major financial
institutions. It is easy enough – looking at the unbalanced start of the
euroyen market in late 1984, the over-enthusiastic beginnings to the
futures market in Tokyo and the expressions of diffidence among
the firms themselves – to underestimate the learning capacity of Japanese banks and securities houses, just as Europe and the USA did in
the case of Japanese electronics and industrial companies in the 1960s
and 1970s. But if dealing is not a natural skill in a co-operative
society, trading is. And the sheer size of the funds at their disposal,
their placing power, give the Japanese considerable international
advantages.

From a back-of-the-room position even five years ago, when most
Japanese institutions preferred to be sub-underwriters or co-lead
managers rather than lead managers, they have emerged as considerable bond and syndicated-loan 'bookrunners', in their own right.
In the first half of 1983 the Japanese securities houses (Nomura,
Daiwa and Yamaichi) claimed three of the positions among the top
twenty lead managers of eurobond issues and eight of the top fifty,
according to a *Euromoney* survey. Japanese houses accounted, in the
same period, for five of the top ten positions among managers of
convertibles issues and three of the top twenty positions for lead
managers of dollar eurobond issues.

Most of the banks have cross-shareholding with securities houses
in anticipation of the moment when the barriers come down. Indeed,
Sumitomo is already using its Banca del Gottardo majority share to
take it into securities underwriting. Others, like the Industrial Bank
of Japan with New Japan Securities, Sanwa Bank with Towa Securities and Sumitomo with Meiko, are using minority holdings to teach
younger staff the art of dealing. All the large institutions have a
strong presence in the major financial centres, and a number of them
have made direct acquisitions – the Industrial Bank of Japan bought
75 per cent of J. Henry Schroder Bank and Trust in New York in

June 1985, for example. All are training up their staff, and all have ambition to be as big and as good as the American banks.

The difficulty, and the criticism, is essentially one of balance. Japan's welcome to competition at home is not as ardent as its aggression towards competition abroad. Japanese foreign investment is not matched by equivalent inflows of investment (although this may change with the growth of a secondary government-bond market in Tokyo). Its outflow of funds tends to go in short-term paper rather than long-term assets, thus contributing to the volatility of the world's financial system. 'The yen,' Yoh Kurosawa, deputy president of the Industrial Bank of Japan, said at a conference in early 1985, 'is fairly important as a borrowing currency, but it remains rather insignificant as yet as a settlement currency, as a reserve currency and also as an asset-holding or investment currency.'

Global integration of the country's capital market, on the other hand, was moving apace. By the time the Yen–Dollar Committee came to review progress in mid-1975 it was no longer a question of whether Japan was ready to accept its role as the third leg of the world's financial stool but of how far and how fast. And the answer was a lot faster than anyone had believed possible a year before.

EIGHT

WHITHER THE REST?

When the Australian Labor Party was elected to power in February 1983 one of its first acts was to set up a committee, the Martin Review Group, to reconsider the previous government's plans for radical financial liberalization, as recommended by the Campbell Report on the country's financial system. Campbell's committee, which had reported in late 1981, had recommended sweeping changes to bring Australia into line with the rest of the world, including deregulating domestic interest rates and opening up the market, for the first time, to direct entry by foreign financial groups.

Many expected that Martin would conclude that the time was not yet ripe for such decontrol, especially under a Labor government. Just the opposite happened. Martin did indeed suggest slowing down the pace of change. But he supported completely the thrust of the Campbell Report. So did the new young Australian Treasury secretary, Paul Keating, who had even fewer qualms about the pace of change. Far from putting the brakes on reform, he actually pushed them ahead faster than his predecessor had been suggesting. Exchange controls went within six months. Interest-rate controls went next. The banks and merchant banks were allowed into each other's territory of exchange and deposit-taking. And, to the surprise of most of the Australian banking community, he opened up the country to foreign banks, accepting not just half a dozen new foreign entrants (his original number) but over ten.

Of course, there remained subtle restrictions – requirements for local equity-holding and continuing reserve powers to replace controls. But the simple point was that Australia was suddenly off and running in the international financial race to deregulate. The vacuum apparently being left by Hong Kong as it negotiated its return to Peking rule, Australia's desire to promote services to replace its declining raw-material trade and its rising industrial lay-off: these certainly played a part in Keating's thinking. But the overriding reason was the same as that which was making itself felt in every financial centre from Frankfurt to the Philippines and from Singapore to San

Francisco. The tide of financial change was irresistible. Once you were caught by it, you had to swim or be sucked under.

The suction is now sufficiently strong to draw in most, and eventually all perhaps, of the free world's markets. The mid-1980s have seen a steady stream of announcements releasing various countries from financial regulations and controls that have been in place for generations. In 1984, after a persistent resistance ever since the Second World War to any real internationalization of the Deutschmark, the West German government announced the abolition of withholding tax for foreign buyers of domestic as well as foreign issues of Deutschmark bonds, thus effectively opening the gates for a radical increase in Deutschmark borrowings by foreign institutions and ending the distinction between domestic and international securities. The formal reason given was that the US decision to abolish withholding tax earlier in the same year made it impossible for West Germany to retain the tax. The broader reasons, as expressed by the head of the Bundesbank, Karl Otto Poehl, was that deregulation was a good and necessary spur to West German institutions.

Simultaneously Sweden and Norway announced that, for the first time, they would be allowing the entry of foreign banks into their domestic markets. This left Portugal the only member of the Organization for Economic Co-operation and Development (OECD) that was still refusing entry to foreign banks. And even Portugal, in the summer of 1984, declared its intention to let two American banks in as the first move towards freer entry to its markets.

Singapore, which had been tightening its banking controls after a rash of failures among local banks, at the same time introduced tax incentives to attract international fund managers to the island and to give banks added inducements to lead-manage international issues from Singapore. Nor were changes limited to bond markets. The West Germans started the first moves to co-ordinate their provincial stock exchanges, previously too small to encourage international activity. So too did the Swiss, who 1985 set in motion a committee to discuss bringing the Zurich, Basle and Geneva exchanges closer together, express their determination to bring down commission rates and to consider the trading options on the shares and bond indices. (For the comparative sizes of the world's stock exchanges, see Table 14.)

In this rash of pronouncements there has been, inevitably, a strong element of fear of being left behind. Central bank authorities, like the

Table 14 The world's stock exchanges, 1984 (£ million)

		Market value of shares listed	Equity turnover	No. of domestic companies listed	No. of foreign companies listed
I	New York	1,320,840	660,428	1,490	53
2	Tokyo	535,357	225,201	1,444	11
3	UK	204,418	36,560	2,171	505
4	Toronto	116,253	17,445	878	55
5	Germany (association of exchanges)	67,497	27,779	449	180
6	Johannesburg	48,495	13,124	470	25
7	Australia (association of exchanges)	42,968	8,744	1,009	18
8	American Exchange	38,702	16,166	743	49
9	Paris	36,852	8,221	550	182
10	Zurich	34,248	n.a.	121	175
11	Geneva	33,154	n.a.	268	510
12	Basle	31,512	n.a.	322	475
13	Amsterdam	30,498	9,730	263	300
14	Singapore	25,925	2,650	121	187
15	Milan	22,130	3,175	143	—
16	Stockholm	22,099	6,750	159	6
17	Hong Kong (all exchanges)	20,104	n.a.	247	22

Source: London Stock Exchange Companion, 1985.

Monetary Authority of Singapore (MAS), might feel that now was the time for tightening regulations, not loosening them. Socialist governments in Australia and France might believe that world recession and industrial restructuring signalled the need for greater direct control of banks in the interests of domestic markets. But once exchange controls on most of the major currencies had been abolished in the 1970s and once the big financial centres started to deregulate in earnest in the 1980s, it became impossible for individual countries to stand out against change. West Germany, despite its worries over monetary control, found that it had to follow the USA's lead in abolishing withholding tax on foreign buyers of domestic gilts if it was to attract any international capital at all into its bond market. If it had not, the money would all have moved to the other side of the

Atlantic. The MAS had to follow up its banking-rule changes by a move towards greater liberalization of the international syndication market and bond management, otherwise it was in danger of losing its position entirely as an Asian financial centre. Even Switzerland, which had always regarded its market as a particularly privileged one because of its probity, its discretion and its ready availability of private funds, by the mid-1980s was finding itself left behind by the variety of new financial instruments being developed in the eurobond and US markets.

The jostling for position has been seen most clearly in Asia, where Singapore and Hong Kong have long competed for financial pre-eminence in the world's fastest-growing economic region. Both have had some domestic base for their bids. Singapore, under the centrally directed economy of Lee Kuan Yew, during the 1960s and early 1970s achieved remarkable success in building up a cheap labour centre and a vigorous local equity market and banking system. Very deliberately, in the late 1960s, it sought to add to this a regional international financial centre, encouraging foreign banks and fund managers to set up shop, and had considerable success in establishing itself as a major centre for syndicated Asian loans. By the early 1980s more than a hundred and twenty banks of all nationalities were represented on the island, as well as over fifty merchant banks. The island had over $100 billion in assets, while bank estimates suggested that between $5 billion and $10 billion in foreign capital flowed through Singapore each year.

Hong Kong's success has been even greater. With a regime that was the very opposite of Singapore's centrally controlled economy, it made itself an entrepot of astonishing vigour, becoming China's largest foreign-currency earner and port as well as Asia's most flexible low-cost manufacturing centre. The Chinese refugees from the mainland ensured a remarkable entrepreneurial and hard-working drive that bore fruit to a remarkable extent in a domestic economy able to switch with rapidity from watches to tape recorders and from leisure wear to furs. Its position off the coast of Canton in mainland China gave it, of course, a special position as China's contact point with the West and its foreign-currency window, even during the most intro-verted days of the Cultural Revolution. But its real success in becoming, during the 1970s, the third largest banking centre in the world after New York and London owed much less to the vitality of the local economy, its volatile local exchanges (it has traditionally had three) or its position in relation to China than to its attractions as a secure and discreetly run centre, where expatriate life was comfortable and untaxed, where finance was largely unregulated (Hong Kong has no central bank) and where the ultimate appeal to English law and the higher courts of London gave it a stable framework in which to deal. Chinese money flowed into Hong Kong from all over Asia. Most of the world's major banks set up their regional headquarters there. Through most of the post-war Asian miracle Hong Kong was the unchallenged financial head.

Yet the financial position of both Singapore and Hong Kong owed as much to Tokyo's controls as to their own lack of them. So long as Tokyo, the natural financial and economic capital of Asia, determinedly controlled the entry of foreign institutions to its markets and, like the West Germans, resisted any effort to internationalize the use of its national currency, international capital tended to flow through Hong Kong and Singapore. And it was these islands that the Japanese themselves tended to use as a booking centre for the syndicated loans that enveloped the banking world during the 1970s.

The opening up of Tokyo as an international capital market, and the discussion now about developing an off-shore banking centre there, must curb the ambitions of other centres. The size of the Tokyo debt market, the depth of the market and the strength of its institutions make it the natural point of concentration for any operator in the capital market. And as Tokyo is opening up, its rivals have been undermined by other developments. One has been the decline in the syndicated loans business on which Singapore particularly founded its role as an international centre. The market is far from dead in Asia, especially for project loans such as that for the Rapid Transit Authority of Singapore. And there are always the beckoning glimmers of hope that China may come into the market more readily to finance some of its huge infrastructural schemes. But syndicated loans are, and are likely to remain, a shadow of their former selves at a time when every major bank worth its international salt put all its effort into this market.

The role of Singapore and Hong Kong as freewheeling entrepreneurial centres, at least as far as finance is concerned, has been further undermined by the scandals and collapses of 1983–5 – the Hang Seng index's collapse in 1983, the Overseas Trust Bank scandal of 1985 in Hong Kong and the ramifications in Malaysia and Singapore. In both cases fear that the troubles would spread and anxiety to present a consistently responsible and well regulated face to the international community (especially in the case of Hong Kong, with the shadow of the Chinese take-over of the island in 1997 hanging over it) have forced the authorities to take action to preserve probity. In the case of Singapore that action took the form of revisions to the Banking Act, tightening up the regulations for liquidity of reserves and reporting procedures, and in Hong Kong, following the appointment of a banking commissioner seconded from the Bank of England, there was discussion about the introduction of new controls.

On top of this have been the uncertainties over the future of Hong Kong during the 1983–4 negotiations for an eventual take-over by Peking after the lease on the New Territories runs out in 1997. The negotiations, which started off in an atmosphere of confrontation, intensified by statements by the British Prime Minister, Mrs Margaret Thatcher, not only caused a savage short-term collapse of confidence on the local stock exchanges and a run on a number of local banks but also prompted the major financial institutions to reconsider their position. Nor were others slow to see advantage. Although Singapore seemed intent on not taking up where Hong Kong was leaving off – the Hong Kong renegotiations coincided with a vigorous review of capitalization and procedures among the financial institutions of Singapore, including the subsidiaries of Citicorp and other major international banks – Hong Kong's dilemma did much to encourage the Australians to contemplate the possibilities of attracting the international banks from Hong Kong to Sydney, Melbourne and Perth. Even when the issue between China and Hong Kong seemed satisfactorily resolved in October 1984, and the local stock markets went surging up again, there remained long-term questions in the minds of many financial groups. The Peking government might well be prepared to protect the local industry and manufacturing base. The Chinese who made up the local economy had nowhere else to go anyway, as one of the colonial officials put it tersely at the time of the agreement as sounds of complaint were heard among the population, which felt itself deserted by the British government. It was only the big shipping magnates and the traders who were sure of an exit route. But the ability of the ordinary Hong Kong Chinese to ensure that conditions would remain attractive for international capital once they took over was much less certain. The lack of clear commercial law, the whims of local officials in a country that remains decentralized in most of its administration, the sudden about-turns of policy that have long characterized China – all these raise question marks over the willingness of Chinese families throughout Asia to centre their money in Hong Kong and of the international financial institutions to centre their Asian operations there.

Yet Hong Kong has survived the wobbles of 1983–4. Commercial rents in the financial district were on the rise again by 1985. A number of US financial institutions were setting up their regional headquarters, if not their dealing-rooms, in Hong Kong. There was little sign of withdrawal by the Japanese banks from their offices.

Part of the answer must lie in the opening up of China. By any logical standards China now looms as potentially the greatest unexploited economy in the world in terms of size, number of people, resources and possibilities. The swing of Peking from extreme economic constraint to dramatic liberalism has been one of the most dramatic developments of the last decade. In October 1985 the first broker even started business in Shanghai to deal in shares of local companies. How far this conversion to capitalism will go is still uncertain and will probably remain uncertain until the end of the century. But a whole range of market possibilities thought unmentionable a few years ago are now being mooted. The great long-term question will be the extent to which Peking is prepared to consider a substantial international debt to fund the country's development. So far it has proved highly conservative in its view on debt, but it may eventually be forced to change this approach if it is to gain the kind of lift-off and rapid infrastructural investment that it needs. In the meantime, however, it is a market of considerable potential for old-fashioned trade and project finance, well served for the time being, and apparently with the willing consent of China, by Hong Kong.

Hong Kong also maintains, to the surprise perhaps of some of the pessimists on the island, a continuing attraction on its own account as a financial base. It has the infrastructure. It has the skills. Its rents are now set at more acceptable levels. Despite Tokyo's flowering as a more open capital market, the Japanese authorities still follow a basic policy of supervising their own institutions. It is the medium-sized and smaller Japanese financial groups that would take advantage of an off-shore market in Tokyo because they cannot afford to go abroad. For the larger banks and securities houses the benefits of maintaining a presence in other regional capitals as booking centres for deals remain, the more so in Hong Kong because of the Chinese connection. Nomura, for example, is one of half a dozen institutions with offices in China itself, merely in preparation for the opportunities of the future.

The real competition in Asia may well be between Australia and

Singapore, rather than between either of these and Hong Kong. Australia's distrust of foreign entry into its industries and its finance must serve to inhibit its development as an international centre. It has the equity markets and, by the standards of the region, sophisticated debt and insurance and commodity markets. It is now intent on developing additional markets in futures and in international bonds. Judging by the rise in property prices in Sydney and Melbourne and the sudden surge in foreign investments in key investment industries, Australia is attracting the 'hot money' of Asia, the money of Chinese families and part of the vast capital outflow of Japan. But its pace of development will always be controlled ultimately by the same factors that have held back its development as a major industrial nation of the Pacific – the size of its population, its restrictions on immigration, its dependence on raw-material exports and a degree of xenophobia in its politics.

Singapore's efforts to become South-East Asia's natural financial centre is similarly constrained by its willingness to sacrifice domestic control in the interests of international freedom. The domestic economy, of course, has for over two decades been a controlled one. Enforced savings by all employees, state or private, have been directed towards particular investments. The government itself has been the main provider of capital and support, the major owner of industry and the main balancer of economic demands and pressures. Alongside a tightly controlled domestic economy, however, the government of Lee Kuan Yew has traditionally managed to maintain a flexible stock exchange and an international financial presence for Singapore as a centre for the gold market, for international syndicated loans and for international fund management through tax concessions. Yet at the very moment when Hong Kong's position as Asia's main financial centre seemed most threatened, during the delicate negotiations over its future return to the Chinese mainland government, Singapore chose to tighten its control of foreign financial operators. 'It has shot itself in the foot,' declared a wondering but delighted Hong Kong banker.

Singapore's puritanism and Hong Kong's troubles were not unconnected. The sudden loss of confidence in Hong Kong's future that struck it in late 1983, following remarks by Prime Minister Mrs Thatcher suggesting that Britain would never compromise the island's independence in talks with the Chinese, hit the stock market hard. The Hang Seng index fell by 30 per cent in a single week. Local banks and property companies, heavily mortgaged, suddenly found themselves under heavy pressure. Even without the troubles over the 1997 take-over the property market would have been over-extended. Building costs had soared; the number of potential users of space had not. A plummeting stock market and you had the makings of a sharp financial crisis that would spread throughout Asia. It did; local Malaysian and Singapore banks that had lent heavily to Hong Kong property developers suddenly faced cash crises of their own. And to top it all, even when Singapore appeared to be getting over the worst of its problem in 1985, and the Stock Exchange was forced to suspend dealings indefinitely in the wake of the collapse of a local group. Pan-Electric, which had been the object of extensive forward share dealing.

The response of the Singapore authorities has been to step in to restore confidence and to impose new controls on liquidity and assets among local companies. In one sense the controls were intended to reassure the international financial community that Singapore would remain a safe haven for finance. 'Our aim is to be Zurich, not Hong Kong,' declared a senior official of MAS. But in another sense the controls had the opposite effect. The spectre of Singapore's Monetary Authority looking over the books of their subsidiaries, be they Citicorp or a local bank of ill repute, and the powers being given to that authority, were enough to frighten many away. And the worst fears of political abuse of power seemed to be realized when, in October 1984, MAS expelled Jardine Fleming, a joint venture between Jardine Matheson, one of the great 'white' trading houses of Hong Kong, the *Tai Pei*, and Robert Fleming, one of London's most prestigious merchant banks. The bank, said MAS, had 'failed to meet the high standards of professional competence and care expected of a merchant bank'. The feeling in the expatriate community was that Jardine Fleming was being made a scapegoat for the embarrassingly over-priced state take-over of Straits Steamship, a scandal involving a number of prominent local politicians. Nor were sensitivities assuaged by MAS's decision to publish secret documents, a breach of confidence by the Authority that had unsettling implications for every financier on the island. The Jardine Matheson incident has been an awkward one for Singapore. It came just as the authorities were attempting to promote the island as an international centre following the collapses of the previous two years and the decline of syndicated loans. New tax regulations had been introduced specifically to encourage international fund managers to operate out of the island.

At the same time Singapore has also pioneered an ambitious link with Chicago to create a new futures market, Simex, and to move forward from the troubles of the gold market. The association with the International Monetary Market (IMM), the financial futures divisions of the Chicago Mercantile Exchange, is designed to develop a twenty-four-hour trading market. Under the terms of the deal with Chicago, Asian traders can establish a position in Singapore and liquidate it on the IMM and the other way around. For Chicago it seemed an opportunity to expand and to gain the edge on its New York rival. For Singapore it was a brilliant, if brave, effort to launch a market with immediate liquidity, using the depth and prestige of IMM, starting with gold and going on to eurodollar time-deposit contracts.

The futures market is intended to give Singapore a strong corner of its own in the Asian financial market. The history of this kind of exchange is that those first in tend to be in the best position to hold a market because it soon attracts the players, and hence the funds, to give it depth. Although Tokyo is talking of setting up a futures market of its own and Hong Kong has also shown interest, Singapore has a head start. It also remains relatively well placed to handle the international flows in the South-East Asian region of the Philippines, Malaysia and Indonesia, all of which are now beginning to unfreeze their local financial markets. But, given its instinctive and perhaps justified tendency to control, it will be a niche and not the position of Zurich that Singapore will occupy.

Exactly the same issues are being raised in the Middle East. For much of the last decade the Middle East oil producers have been the greatest source of international capital in the world. On the whole they have preferred to move it into Western financial institutions, particularly the international banks, but as wealth has seeped down to a new middle class, so local market have begun to develop and Bahrein to emerge as the regional financial centre.

However, reduction in the demand for oil, the erosion of oil prices, the plunge in oil revenues have swept away the dreams, and the lifestyle, of much of the Middle East. A series of scandals climaxed in the collapse of the unofficial stock exchange in Kuwait, the Souk al Manakh; the enforced rescue by the Dubai government of the Union Bank of the Middle East after its founder, Abdul-Wahab Galaderi, had gone under in a welter of bad debts and unsuccessful gold speculation; and the troubles of some of Saudi Arabia's biggest contracting firms during 1983–4. Suddenly the vision of a Middle East clambering to success as a major international financial centre on the back of a huge oil income seemed to be evaporating.

The reponse has been, as it was in Singapore and Hong Kong, to draw in the horns and to search for respectability and conservatism. The Saudi Arabian Monetary Authority has moved to license exchange dealers and to tighten its control of foreign use of the local currency, the riyal; in the United Arab Emirates the Central Bank took over the Union Bank of the Middle East in 1984, restructuring it and trying to fill the vacuum caused by a legal system that had no rules governing bankruptcy. In Kuwait a new exchange was established to replace the old Souk al Manakh. And in Bahrein a law was introduced to establish the sultanate's first stock exchange.

As Singapore, discovered, however, the modern world of finance does not make the choice between conservatism and chaos that simple. What the series of collapses and scandals of the mid-1980s has shown is how rudimentary the domestic markets are in the Middle East. Most of the money accumulated during the golden days of oil wealth tended to go abroad, either into private accounts in Switzerland and into dollars or, through the banking system, into syndicated loans. Arab banks were certainly set up and grew with this capital outflow. But they tended to go with it to the international capital centres of Europe, particularly London and Paris, where they became participants in the loans and, occasionally, lead managers.

'In the past,' said one Arab banker in London, surveying the failure of the Middle East to meet expectations, 'the small Arab international banks used to line up with their mouths open to take bits of syndicated deals fed to them by people like us. But now their mouths stay open, and nobody is spooning them in.' In the world of syndicated loans the bigger and most internationally minded Arab banks forged their links with the Americans, Japanese and Europeans, for that was their route into international lending. The object was to get into the outside network, not to build a new network of Arab banks.

The domestic markets, meanwhile, developed only haltingly, and then very much in the traditions of trading, just as in the past. The Souk al Manakh, literally placed beneath the main *souk*, or alley, was a place dominated by the big dealers and talk. The dealers, maybe a dozen with real weight, would stroll in, stop, chat a bit over coffee, buy perhaps, sell perhaps. The rest would take their cue from them. The new Kuwait exchange, opened in September 1984, has all the accoutrements of a modern exchange – a dealing floor larger than London's, a computer system more expensive than Frankfurt's, a system of marking up bids and offers modelled on Hong Kong's and regulation of what the dealer and the broker can do that is aimed at ensuring what every other centre strives for – fairness and openness. The trouble is that it does not provide what the modern financial centre really demands: the ability to deal in depth and at risk.

The collapse of the old Souk al Manakh had a cataclysmic effect on the still tender flower of local markets. It ruined confidence and brought with it a chain reaction throughout local banks in the surrounding countries and some of the biggest trading houses of the area. More, by impelling the Kuwaiti government to intervene with some $50 billion of support, half of it in share-price support and half of it in direct payment to creditors, it divided the country. There seemed to be one law for the rich and one for the poor.

The 'retreat to quality', as it is called throughout the world's financial markets, has meant in the case of the Middle East the triumph of old money over new or of the old families over the new middle class. From the general banking view, the new conservatism can only be for the good. Tighter control by the financial authorities and more regulated markets will reassure investors. The days of big spending are over, probably for good. And there are many who would argue that retrenchment can only be of benefit to the area. Unsolicited oil wealth was bringing to bear pressures with which some societies, such as Iran, could not cope without slowing down. The collapse of the Souk al Manakh, in that sense, was the bubble bursting. If it had not burst there, it would have grown and burst all the more dramatically elsewhere in the Middle East.

Yet the Souk al Manakh was always the point at which new money and new trading habits were being developed. Without something of that sort, the Middle East will find it difficult to develop a domestic financial market of its own, in its own style. The tendency has been for the brightest to go into banks via long years of study, not years in a commodity pit. It was fine in the days of syndicated lending, less good in the days of bond trading.

The question mark must lie particularly over Bahrein, which has developed in the last two decades largely as the financial centre for the region, the point at which Saudi contractors and trading houses in particular have sought to raise funds through syndicated loans in the local Saudi currency and in which international banks have established regional headquarters. The more restrictive policies of the Saudi authorities, aimed in part to protect the position of the domestic Saudi banks, has been a blow to this. So has the collapse of loan demand from local contractors and merchants.

Bahrein can survive. At least two of its banks, the Arab Banking Corporation and the Gulf International Bank, are now probably strong enough to hold their own as international players. The Bahreini economy itself is less dependent on oil than any of its neighbours'. It remains the regional centre because of its lenient tax laws and treatment of expatriates. It still has a part to play in providing the foreign-currency component of syndicated loans by the Saudi companies and others. Furthermore, its geographical location, between the European and Asian times zones, has aroused the interest of Japanese as well as European banks. But to develop it needs a free and growing regional financial market. And this has been put well back by recent events.

The same problems do not apply to Europe. There it has been more a question of national rivalry for financial pre-eminence, as in Asia. Yet, just like the Middle East and Asia, Europe has also to mediate the tension between regulation and licence in order to allow a truly regional domestic market to develop. Tokyo, New York and London may dominate a universe in which international funds fly between them at ever-increasing velocity. Beneath them, however, are the points where money is collected, invested and lent and where traditionally localized finance is being forced to develop by the same pressures as those evident in the Middle East.

France, despite the nationalization of its remaining private banks and its innate prejudice against money of the socialist regime under President Mitterrand, was by 1985 talking of easing foreign exchanges, lengthening the hours of the Bourse and easing controls on the bond markets. Sweden, Norway and Finland, traditionally the most thoroughly protected and the most highly regulated financial markets in Europe, were all opening their markets to greater foreign presence and easier control of the direction and the allocation of funds. The reasons have been the same. Within the markets the need to fund greater entrepreneurial activity and to lessen the cost of public finance require more fluid financial markets. Externally the major financial banks in each of these countries have been calling for wider opportunities at home if they are not to shift their activities more and more abroad. France, after all, had set itself to rival London as an international bond centre in the 1960s. Institutions such as the Banque Paribas were, and still are, among the top twenty bond underwriters in the world. Nationalization and restriction at home have threatened to sweep it from the top league overnight.

Nowhere was the sense of losing out more obvious than in West

Germany and Switzerland, traditionally the two safest, best-run and most lucrative financial markets in Europe. West Germany was by far the wealthiest country in Europe, with by far the largest pool of domestic funds at its disposal. Switzerland had long enjoyed its reputation as the haven of international private funds: it had been banker to half the heads of state in Europe since the end of the seventeenth century and the repository of private funds from half the heads of the Middle and Far East in the twentieth century. The portfolio management of its banks has made it a major bond market for foreign corporations and institutions who raise more than 100 billion Swiss francs there, particularly Japanese ones. Both West Germany and Switzerland too could claim to have an experience, unequalled elsewhere, of financial supermarkets. The 'universal banks' of the two countries – the Big Three of Germany (Deutsche, Dresdner and Commerzbank) and the Big Three of Switzerland (Crédit Suisse, the Swiss Bank Corporation and Union Bank of Switzerland) have always acted both as commercial and as investment banks, handling portfolios for clients, dealing in stocks and shares and, in the case of the West German banks, holding sizeable equity interests themselves in companies and institutions.

Yet the complacency of the authorities was rudely shattered when, in 1985, Deutsche Bank, one of the biggest banks in West Germany, declared that it was moving its eurobond dealing team from Frankfurt to London and the Union Bank of Switzerland moved into London's liberalizing Stock Exchange with the purchase of a major stake in brokers Phillips and Drew. The implicit assumption of both moves seemed to be that London was to be regarded as the financial centre of Europe and that European financial institutions would have to concentrate much of their capital-market activities there rather than at home. Announcing his bank's decision to take a share in brokers Phillips and Drew with the eventual aim of taking it over, the Union Bank of Switzerland's management chairman, Dr Nikolaus Senn, baldly stated his view that there was 'a marked loss of competitive ability of Switzerland as a financial centre'.

The immediate complaint in Switzerland's case was that of taxation. Switzerland may have developed as a financial centre through a combination of the secrecy surrounding deposits and the ease with which banks could be established (it was, so the saying went, easier to set up a bank than a bar), but financial transactions had become the target of a number of taxes, including an impost on new bond issues, a 'stamp', or transaction tax, on securities trading and a 6.2 per cent tax on individual gold purchases. The duties were not huge – indeed, there has long been something of the banker's bleat in Swiss complaints about tax. On average Swiss banks have been, and remain, the most profitable in the world, blessed with an effective deposit system and large sums for discretionary investment.

So long as Switzerland enjoyed a secure role in European finance, it had little to concern it. But over recent years it has experienced some worrying trends. Its share of new international bond issues has declined rapidly in the mid-1980s. In 1984 only 12 per cent of international issues were underwritten in Switzerland, compared with 80 per cent in London. Banks had also begun to look seriously at their relative inexperience where institutional finance was concerned. The strength of Swiss banks has always lain in their management of the funds of private investors and their unequalled capacity to make in their own country private placements of Swiss franc or even foreign-currency bonds. Of the 20 billion Swiss francs' worth of new issues in 1984, nearly half were private placements (bonds taken up by clients directly without the formalities of issue documents and public offer). The importance of that private-fund muscle has not evaporated. But the new world of finance demands an ability to trade and close relationships between banks, pension funds and other institutions. The major Swiss banks, and even more their smaller brethren, the private banks of Switzerland, were beginning to feel the lack of it.

Where once Swiss bankers talked grandly of their neutral country as the natural haven of safe money for the world, the home of 'Swiss gnomes' and the progenitor of the numbered bank account, they are now talking the language of New York and London. Seriously concerned that their hold even on the largest gold centre in the world was being eroded by new commodity centres, the Swiss are now talking of establishing markets for futures and options, instruments in which their commercial banks trade independently, but not in an open market. At the same time, since the banking scandal in Chiasso in 1977 the Swiss authorities have also been wrestling with wide-ranging reforms of banking regulations that are designed to insure deposits, publicize 'hidden reserves' and ensure more open accounting and, finally (and partly in answer to American pressures), to reduce some of the famous secrecy covering depositors in Swiss accounts.

It is at the last point that the Swiss community has balked. To the authorities of other countries attempting to attack the drug trade or to capture assorted fraudsters, crooks, debtors and gangsters, the escape hole of a Swiss bank account and the closed doors and sealed lips of the banks of Zurich, Geneva and Lugano are infuriating and insupportable. Secrecy is the stuff of the popular press and of political calls for action. It is also still the foundation of the Swiss financial system. Proposals to change Switzerland's banking law root and branch and to open its books to foreign review were soundly defeated by an overwhelming 73 per cent majority in the May 1984 referendum on 'Initiatives against abuse of bank secrecy and the power of the banks'. In its place more gradualist revisions of existing banking laws are being introduced, formalizing some of the informal agreements about the sharing of information between the Swiss National Bank and the lesser banks. The story is not over – Swiss bank secrecy is not all-embracing. It does not protect clients under investigation, in Switzerland or abroad, for criminal offences, and it is being steadily chipped away by international agreements such as bilateral treaties on double taxation, which generally include a clause covering the exchange of information. But Swiss reluctance to question the rights to secrecy is an example of the old double standards: what is shameful financial behaviour in a company is acceptable in the case of an individual.

West Germany's moves towards deregulation meanwhile have found the regionalism of the country its greatest obstacle. Although Frankfurt is generally regarded as the financial capital of West Germany, at least outside the country Düsseldorf and Munich both claim to be important centres in their own right, while the regional banks throughout West Germany and regional pride remain strong. In the summer of 1985 the presidents of West Germany's eight regional exchanges (Frankfurt accounting for around half the total turnover, Düsseldorf for about a quarter, Hamburg and Munich for about 7 per cent each and Stuttgart, Bremen, Hanover and Berlin sharing the remaining 10 per cent) began meeting to see what could be gained from greater co-operation and the sharing of computer-clearing facilities. At the same time the German government also introduced legislation to allow the development, as in London and Tokyo, of an unlisted securities market between the fully regulated markets and the OTC markets in order to aid the financing of small companies.

Parallel with this the West German government, largely at the prodding of the Bundesbank, has also acted rapidly to open up the capital markets of the country. The West German withholding, or coupon, tax on dividends paid to foreign holders of domestic bonds was repealed in response to the US move in the same direction in 1984. Shortly after, in the summer of 1985, the Bundesbank in Frankfurt made the first moves towards allowing foreign banks to issue Deutschmark-denominated bonds in competition with the German banks, whose territory this had been exclusively. After years of opposing anything that might internationalize the West German currency and thus lessen its control over money, the Bundesbank also began to talk openly of allowing banks to issue Deutschmark certificates. The aim was to incite greater competition within West Germany as well as to develop more international capital markets in competition with other centres.

As in Japan, the West German banking community will not easily give up control. While pursuing greater liberalization, it is also introducing tighter rules for reserves and disclosure. It continues to sit as an observer on the bond committees, and it remains suspicious of any proposals to create an off-shore banking centre in West Germany along the lines suggested by Walter Seipp, chief executive of the Commerzbank. Nor will the West German banks, which dominated bond issues through a committee of the top six banks, easily give up their lead-management role; considering their patronage and influence within the country, it would be a brave institution that challenged them straight on.

The same dilemma is seen even more clearly in Canada. In finance, as in other fields, Canada has found itself drawn increasingly into the American fold. More and more of the dealing in major Canadian shares has been siphoned off by New York and Chicago. The more the Canadian authorities have tried to protect their financial institutions from foreign ownership, the more they have seen the growth of those institutions threatened by developments south of the border.

With a new Conservative government in power, the Canadian Financial Ministry proposed in April 1985 a major relaxation of controls on the expansion of non-bank financial conglomerates to increase competition and to give Canadian institutions a chance to develop along American lines. The stock exchanges of Vancouver, Toronto and Montreal, which had been bitter rivals, also discussed plans to co-operate more, to allow each to develop separate specialities and to promote links with the Chicago and New York exchanges. Yet at the same time a series of failures and scandals, including the first bank failure in sixty-two years (that of the Canadian Commerical Bank of Alberta) and accusations of share manipulation on the Vancouver Stock Exchange, prompted the regulatory authorities in a number of provinces to propose tightening rather than loosening controls over the securities, trust and insurance industries.

The two objectives cannot easily be reconciled. The internationalization of the stock exchanges is likely to proceed. Toronto has now formed a fully reciprocal link with the American Stock Exchange, which will enable dealing in a limited number of major stocks to be carried out by either and closed wherever the best price is offered. Montreal, which has tried to promote a special expertise in options, is planning to quote French stocks on its board and is connected with Boston. Internationalization has become the only means of expanding and of retaining market shares even in Canadian stocks. Implementation of the changes to banking law, on the other hand, has been hampered by worries over the bank failure in Alberta, opposition from the banks and concern even among the financial conglomerates that might have most to gain from the changes. The reforms could be abandoned altogether.

That, indeed, may be the balance of change in a number of countries – internationalization in so far as it is necessary but very cautious change within domestic financial structures. The problem for Canada, and even more for Europe and for much of Asia, is that theirs has always been such a different background from the free-wheeling world of trade today. Finance has been part of a web of interlocking interests, adjustments and instinctive trade-offs in which governments have always been present and the limits to behaviour understood. The pressures of change are forcing countries out into the open plains. But few of them yet understand what it is that they are doing. It is too late for them to go back but still too soon for them to keep pace with the new world, fully prepared for what it may bring.

PART THREE

£ $ ¥ £ $ ¥ £ $ ¥ £ $ ¥ £

BOOM OR BUST?

NINE

THE SUPERVISORS

In early September 1985 the heads of the central banks of the ten major industrial nations of the world (the Group of Ten, as they are called) met in Basle for their regular monthly meeting to discuss the state of the banking world. It is a meeting that the top men like to attend themselves: Paul Volcker, the rigorous, tetchy and always forthright head of the US Federal Reserve; Karl Otto Pohl, the former journalist and apostle of the free market and occasional intervention to bloody the nose of speculators, who heads the West German Bundesbank; Robin Leigh Pemberton, Mrs Thatcher's appointee as Governor of the Bank of England, a country gentleman who had formerly pursued a career in retail banking with National Westminster; the Bank of Japan's Satoshi Sumita, an experienced operator in the Japanese Civil Service, who had just stepped up a rung to take over from the formidable Haruo Mayekawa; and their colleagues from Italy, Belgium, Canada, France, the Netherlands, Sweden and, as an observing, non-participating member of the group, Switzerland.

Central bankers are, by their office, people who regard themselves as men apart. They see their role as guardians of order and prudence, often in direct conflict with their finance ministries and always at one remove from their political masters. Their offices are grand; the machinery of central banking bureaucracy is directed towards sustaining their role and their authority. There could be no greater contrast than that between the chaos and fustiness of Tokyo's Ministry of Finance building (feared though M O F is by the financial community) and the grandeur and quiet of the Bank of Japan's headquarters on the other side of the Imperial Palace gardens; or that between the atmosphere of dignity and calm of the Bank of England, with its high-windowed offices overlooking a court and its pink-liveried doormen, and the cigarette stubs and linoleum-covered corridors of the Treasury, enlivened though they may be by the twinkling bust of that reprobate, gambler and warm-hearted debtor, Charles James Fox, half-way up the main staircase.

There is an ambivalence at the heart of central bankers that keeps bursting out in conflict with their political masters. Are they there to preserve the integrity of the currency and to control the money supply, or are they there as the patriarchs and representatives of the banking industry, which they license? The issue re-emerges every time there is a question of a bank going under or a regulation is challenged, and it is one that no central banker or finance minister has yet resolved.

On this occasion in Basle, however, there was no ambivalence. Top of the formal agenda for the Group of Ten meeting was a discussion of what to do about the avalanche of new instruments coming on to the market, the swaps, the options, the N I Fs and the R U Fs, which crossed all previous national and market boundaries and which no one seemed even to know how to calculate, let alone how to subject to reserve requirements. The banking supervisors had been caught out once before in the early days of floating exchange rates, when the Herstatt Bank collapse had shown just how quickly trouble as well as funds can move across the banking system. They did not want that to happen again.

Off the agenda but very much on the minds of the central banks of the five major countries – the U S A, Japan, West Germany, France and Italy (the Group of Five) and, informally, their colleagues was the question of currency intervention now that the new U S Treasury Secretary, James Baker, had called in secret an urgent meeting of finance ministers of the Group of Five to discuss what to do about the rebounding dollar. Contrary to all expectations, the dollar was now edging up again. Contrary to its previous statements suggesting American dislike of concerted intervention in the currency markets to do anything other than temper sharp fluctuations, the U S administration was now sufficiently concerned about the rising tide and protectionism in the country and in Congress to see currency manipulation as an answer.

The results of the Basle meeting were not long in coming. Within a week of their return home the central-bank governors were writing publicly to all their banks, and calling them in privately, to express their concern about the residual risk involved in these new instruments and their desire to see imposed on them more sophisticated and stringent management controls. In a series of public statements Paul Volcker called for much higher reserve requirements for U S banks. In a series of consultative papers the Bank of England proposed new criteria for judging the risks involved.

Ten days after the Basle meeting the finance ministers of the Group of Five met in New York, ahead of the annual jamboree of the International Monetary Fund in Seoul, South Korea, to declare their view that the dollar should be depreciated and their decision to intervene in the markets if necessary to get it down. It was the strongest international statement on currencies since the Americans had been overwhelmed by the opposite problem, the collapse of the dollar, in the late 1970s. And it was the most concerted international action on banking supervision since the wave of bank failures following the energy crisis over a decade before.

The two issues are part of the same problem posed by the sweep of deregulation around the markets of the world. When the major currencies were allowed to float in 1971, and when the UK in 1979 and Japan in 1980 decided to abolish exchange controls, bringing most other countries, with the exception of France, in their wake, the theory was that exchange rates would find their own level by reference to the so-called 'fundamentals' – comparative inflation rates, relative productivity, balance-of-payments surpluses and deficits and general market confidence. This theory has not been disproved, but things have not turned out as predicted to date.

The abolition of exchange controls and the easing of regulations on institutional investment abroad, particularly in Japan, have released a surge of pent-up portfolio investment money seeking higher returns abroad. Instead of the USA's huge balance-of-trade deficit with Japan – some $40 billion in 1984 – leading to a rise in the value of the yen and hence to a rise in the price of Japanese imports into America, the current account was more than matched by an even greater flow of capital out of Japan into the dollar. This actually lowered the value of the yen. Although there were many who suspected that this apparently illogical development owed at least something to Japan's manipulation of its currency, there is little doubt that this explanation is inadequate.

The irony for the USA has been that its own efforts to enforce liberalization of the Japanese markets has only made matters worse. The more the US negotiators on the Yen–Dollar Committee have insisted on a freeing of controls to allow the yen to become a more widely used currency in trade, and thus to share the burden of the dollar, the more this has had the opposite effect. Japanese companies have kept their export earnings in dollars. Ever greater volumes of investment yen have flowed out into the dollar. And the same has been true of the dollar's relationship with the stronger

European currencies, the Deutschmark and the Swiss franc.

This perversity of exchange logic has been immeasurably exaggerated by the workings of an unregulated exchange and international investment market. Finance officials of the non-interventionist governments now in power in Washington, London and most other European capitals have always tended to view the marketplace over-idealistically or at least too theoretically. Ideally, free markets should lead to a much closer relationship between price and underlying principles of supply and demand. Perhaps over time, in laboratory conditions of total non-intervention, they will.

In practice, financial markets do not work as evenly as this – not given the behaviour of the dealers at any rate. With the speed of international communication and with dealing in the exchanges carried out on screens that blip the same message to all operators in an atmosphere of constant movement, the dealers are much less concerned to get it right than to get in first. They make their money by understanding not where a currency will end up eventually – whether the sterling of $2.40 of 1980 will be the sterling of $1.05 of early 1985 and $1.40 of mid-1985 – but whether it will go to $2.43 or $1.02 over the next few hours. Screen trading allows them to trade in and out extremely fast. Indeed, it impels them to do so. As the figures keyed in by the market-makers begin to show that something is happening to prices, the dealers' job is to move that little bit faster, buying and selling all the time to ensure that their exposure is never long-lasting ('pyramidding' this is sometimes called). They see a currency starting to move down. They sell 10 or 20 million units. They buy them back a few minutes later as the trend seems to be firming, sell again, buy again and so on until they sense bottom.

The result is that even the most unsubstantiated rumour flashing across a dealer's screen can set off a run on a currency or share. A rumour that Sheikh Yamani, Saudi Arabia's peripatetic oil minister, had been shot dead in a European city in September 1985 caused the pound to fall more than 3 cents in half an hour before the Sheikh was reported to be hale and hearty and in another city altogether. Once the dealers do move into action, there is little that can stop them as they drive a price onwards by pyramidding until it reaches levels where the markets, or the chartists, put a stop to it. And this curious tendency for prices in today's markets to leap to artificial but somehow agreed-on break-points has become all the more exaggerated by the eruption of options trading in the last few years. Investors in the market tend to work on certain trigger figures that, when reached, induce them to exercise their option to buy or sell a currency or share or bond, especially in the U S A, where options can be exercised at any time within the due date.

The changed style of trading and the huge stocks of institutional funds moving between currencies do much to explain why the exchange markets in particular should lurch in quite such a volatile fashion towards key levels, be it $1 per pound or 200 yen per dollar. Once the market goes through a break-point it tends to go straight on to the next assumed point, wherever that may be. Equally, it can reverse itself very rapidly if it goes too far beyond a perceived limit, inducing dealers to take their profits. This also helps to explain the jerky manner in which markets move at certain periods – a sudden burst of buying or selling through the market towards the end of a month indicates the banks tidying up their books, for example, or the contractual date when a large number of futures mature.

New trading styles, however, make it all the more difficult for central banks to influence the market, whether to smooth their gyrations or to influence their direction more positively. Once a market as big as the exchange market begins to move, its sheer size and momentum make it virtually impossible to stop. Successive failures by the U S Fed. in the late 1970s and by the Japanese and West Germans in the 1980s have made countries wary of spending huge sums on trying to stem the tide. In full flood the exchange markets, or any of the money markets, can easily absorb several billions of dollars without exhausting themselves. Worse, as soon as it becomes apparent that the authorities are taking a view of the market, that in itself becomes part of the game. If dealers feel that the will of the central banks or government can be broken or that the authorities do not have the resources to pit themselves for long against the movement of prices, they set about assaulting the position. It was that which finally made it impossible for the British (or the French, or the Italians, or anyone else whose currency came under attack) to sustain exchange-rate bands. Resistance merely tends to delay the evil hour and to give the speculator an easy profit.

Once the market senses that a price is going to alter (market sentiment, as it is termed), the pressure builds up, increasing as a government denies that there will be any change to interest rates or exchange rates. When it breaks through, it does so with greater force. During the run on the Deutschmark in the early 1970s the only way that the West German authorities could exercise any control was to

stop all international calls. The banks simply could not get through
to deal. Now, with Reuters' dealing systems and in-house communication networks, such a move would be useless. The closure of
the Italian markets in July 1985 was caused by a single deal with $200
million. Pressure on the lira had been building up for months, and on
Thursday, 18 July, the Italian Cabinet decided that it would have to
devalue. Word leaked to the state oil company, E N I, which promptly
brought forward a foreign-exchange requirement for dollars. It could
not find a buyer for lira in the whole international market. Within an
hour the lira had fallen 20 per cent, and it might well have had to fall
by a third or more to find a level at which the E N I could trade if the
authorities had not closed the market altogether, effecting an eventual
devaluation of nearer 8 per cent.

The central banks are not powerless. They can, and do, intervene,
although of all the central banks only the West German Bundesbank
has followed a consistent line of taking the market on at regular
intervals to 'burn' the speculators. The Japanese have intervened
heavily but are not, by tradition, well versed in the tactics of the
market, nor, in view of the size of the outward flow of capital, are
they in a very strong position. The British and the Americans have
followed a more uneven route, partly because of political doubts
about the effectiveness of intervention and partly because, after the
experience of the late 1970s, neither has much left to spend on sustained intervention. The U K went to the markets for an extra $2.5
billion in the run-up to the concerted intervention announcements of
the Group of Five in New York on 22 September. Revealingly, it
raised the money on the euromarkets with a huge floating-rate issue.
The previous time the U K had had to raise such funds, in 1976–8, it
had been forced to go to the I M F, with sour political consequences.

The trick in tactical intervention is to seize the moment, as the
major European banks, with a little help from the U S A, did in
February 1985. When the impetus of a market is exhausted, intervention can force a trend into reverse with powerful effect. When a
market is at full impetus, however, there is little that individual intervention can do. If governments really wish to determine the course of
the markets, they can do so only by international agreement –
agreement to co-ordinate intervention on a massive scale or to impose
some kind of exchange-rate structure on the markets. This is what
the E E C does with the European 'snake', the European Monetary
System (E M S), which includes all member states except Britain,
which remains a passive onlooker for the moment. Concerted inter-

vention is a half-step towards a system of bands between the dominant currencies, which by the end of 1985 the major industrial countries, including the USA, seemed to be taking.

The same dilemma applies to the central bank's old-fashioned role as supervisor of the financial system in order to protect the investor, prevent fraud and preserve the integrity of a country's financial system and the reliability of its institutions. Whatever the other parallels between airlines, electronics, energy and the finance industry, the latter has always held a special place in government regulatory systems because it deals with money and people's deposits. Confidence is all. A crisis spreads everywhere. For this reason governments have always regulated the financial sections of the community. The degree of regulation tends to rise and fall with time, relaxing during periods of rapid expansion, tightening when recession and failures cause public alarm. For fifty years the world has lived under the shadow of the bank failures and stock-exchange collapses of the Great Depression. Now the financial institutions everywhere are trying to start anew.

The mode of regulation equally tends to vary from place to place. The USA has always preferred legal controls of each market through a specific body, be it the SEC or the Commodity Exchange Authority. The Europeans have tended towards a more informal system of control through networks of self-regulating bodies in the exchanges, futures markets and money markets. In the UK the City has traditionally been run, through a system of 'nods and winks', by the Bank of England. In West Germany there has been much stronger regional regulation. Switzerland does not even have a state bank. The Bank of Switzerland is a private bank without direct supervisory powers. Hong Kong has no central bank at all. Singapore has tight central control through the MAS. Japan is a hybrid. The Ministry of Finance exercises powerful informal control through a system of 'administrative guidance' and a business culture that ensures that each party tends to observe certain codes for fear of being singled out as a maverick. ('The nail that sticks up is the nail that is hammered down,' as the saying goes.) But Japan's formal legal control is based on American law, imposed by the US occupying forces after the war, and on the Glass–Steagall distinction between banks, institutions that take deposits and make loans and the underwriting of stocks or bonds.

The financial revolution has increased fearsomely the strains on the system. The Continental Illinois crisis of 1984 and the widespread failures among the thrifts of Maryland, California and Ohio in the last few years in the USA; the much-debated Johnson Matthey Bankers (JMB) insolvency, which led to the rescue by the Bank of England in 1984; the collapse of the Canadian Commercial Bank and the rescue of Northland in Alberta in 1985; the Hong Kong government's take-over of the Overseas Trust Bank in June of 1985 and the consequent run on other banks in Malaysia and Hong Kong – these are all symptoms of the financial world under pressure. The number of bank failures in the USA, where deregulation has been most extensive and the strains the greatest, has increased eightfold, from ten in 1981 to eighty in 1984.

To a surprising degree many of these failures have been the result of breaches in the old-fashioned banking rules of prudence rather than deregulation as such or the growth of capital markets. The problems of Continental Illinois, the seventh largest bank in America, began with excessive lending to the failed Penn Square Bank of Oklahoma and to other small banks, which had grown too fast on the back of lending to the troubled oil and real-estate industries. Northland and the Canadian Commercial Bank became unstuck because of imprudent lending to the booming oil industry of Alberta in the late 1970s and early 1980s. In the case of JMB, which had buckled under the weight of nearly £250 million in bad loans, the bank's directors had allowed a disproportionate amount of their lending to go to just three individuals, quite aside from the question of fraud that was hinted at by the Bank of England after its rescue. Fraud, on the other hand, was quite clearly alleged by investors to be at the root of the problems in the collapse of the Overseas Trust Bank in Hong Kong, which had to be rescued by the Hong Kong authorities at the cost of some $250 million. Fraud too has been alleged in the case of some of the mortgage-backed securities which caused the Bank of America serious losses in 1984–5.

The problems experienced by much of the American banking world are due largely to an over-enthusiastic pursuit of certain types of lending during the days of expansion in the last decade. Commercial banks, like oil companies and chemical groups, tend to act in herds, and this tendency has been intensified by the growth of syndicate lending. In theory syndicated lending, where one bank agrees to manage a loan and then invites a group of other banks to co-manage it, is supposed to spread the risk. In practice it has had a tendency to do the opposite. A single loan blossoms into big business with further loans, and banks develop increasingly close ties with their fellow underwriters, guaranteeing certain banks a share in each new issue as a matter of course. When trouble develops in a broad area of loans, it is the same group of banks that is generally afflicted.

This is what happened with sovereign debt. Individual countries in financial difficulty sucked in a small number of soon to be highly exposed banks – the Poles borrowed from German banks, the Mexicans from the American banks. Even the largest and most experienced commercial banks failed to exercise caution over their individual country and region exposure. The smaller regional banks of the USA followed, lured by confidence in the big banks' names without bothering to assess their own exposure. The same was true of oil and energy loans in the case of the regional banks of the Midwest and Texas and of real estate in California. Everything was fine so long as business was expanding. As soon as the oil market went the other way, even some of the largest banks found themselves at risk. This is now happening with farm loans. The shake-out of the oil industry started in 1983 and is reaching its peak in 1986. The shake-out of the farm industry is only just beginning in the USA and is likely to have just as dramatic an effect on the banking industry. By the end of 1985 the US Federal Farm Credit System was talking of nearly $20 billion in bad debts, an increase of nearly $10 billion on the $10.9 billion recorded only six months before. The figure represented over a quarter of the Federal Farm Credit System's total lending portfolio, and the System's loss for that year, at nearly $400 million, was the first since the Great Depression. As the stones were turned over in the investigations that followed, all sorts of poor credit-control practices were revealed, just as they were in the oil-loan sector.

It is easy enough to deride the banking industry after the event, although in this case there were plenty of people within the industry who warned of the difficulties at the time and were termed old-fashioned and out-of-date for their pains. But then many of the great banking names of today were founded on, and thrived originally on, just such specialization. J. P. Morgan developed his father's house of Drexel Morgan on the growth of American railroads; the growth of Citibank was intimately connected with the rise of the Standard Oil Company; the Mellon Bank grew with Gulf Oil; and the Antony Gibbs merchant bank in London was founded on a fortune made out of guano ('selling turds of foreign birds', as a Victorian rhyme recorded by Anthony Sampson in The Money Lenders has it). But as a presage of what is happening today Barings, the greatest merchant bank of nineteenth-century London, had to be rescued in 1890 by a group of its fellow banks in an operation launched by the Bank of England after bad debts to Argentina had caused it to totter under liabilities of £21 million.

The difference now is that banks are no longer having to cope with cyclical problems in industry; they are having to cope with long-term structural adjustments that are changing for ever some of their main client industries. First it was automobiles, steel and the 'smokestack' industries, then oil, chemicals and consumer electronics. More recently it has been computers and farming. And these industries are now so international that the problems tend to spread more widely than before. The difficulties caused by energy loans were born of the dramatic investment boom in the industry after the two oil shocks of the 1970s on the one hand and of the fall in prices and the collapse of demand during the 1980s on the other. The problems experienced by lenders in Texas, Alberta and Australia then spread, to the detriment of oil-producing countries such as Mexico and Venezuela. They may yet extend to the loans made by banks to oil producers in the North Sea. Similar difficulties are affecting agricultural lending in the USA because of the greater intensity of the investment cycle there. But they could yet spread to Europe and the agricultural exporters of the Third World. The supervisors' remedy can only be the old-fashioned one – greater prudence, stricter adherence to lending guidelines and the imposition of tighter capital ratios.

Part of the problem of the finance industry today, however, is that it is not only its customers that are going through a process of fundamental and painful long-term adjustment but the industry itself. The dismantling of the old regulations covering deposits and interest rates and aimed at preserving the different deposit-taking sectors of the banking community – the commercial banks, the thrifts or building societies, the regional banks – has exposed these institutions to competition that all cannot possibly survive. In the USA in 1982 more than 90,000 companies were involved in the financial services industry (contributing, it should be added, over $100 billion, or 5 per cent of the US national income on 1980 figures). These included 15,000 commercial banks, 4,000 savings and loans associations, 1,000 mutual savings banks, 22,000 credit unions, 1,000 investment banks, 5,000 broker/dealers, 1,000 mutual funds, 1,000 mortgage banks, 3,000 pension funds, 2,000 life and health insurance companies, 3,000 property and casualty insurance companies and more than 33,000 insurance brokerage companies, quite aside from finance, credit-card and leasing companies. Other countries may be less fragmented. In

Britain there are more than 200 building societies, while Japan has only 86 commercial banks, including 63 regional banks, but it has well over 4,300 agricultural co-operatives, 468 credit co-operatives, 456 credit associations and 71 mutual banks.

This number of small institutions could survive only under a highly regulated regime in the era of the car and telecommunications. Now that the props are being removed, the strains are immediately being felt. In the five years to 1985 about a thousand US thrifts, nearly a quarter of the total, disappeared or were merged in response to the pressure of trying to finance fixed-rate loans out of floating-rate, deregulated deposits. Even in 1985, when some of the financial pressure on the thrifts seemed to have eased, a succession of failures among the state or privately insured thrifts caused a run on deposits in both Maryland and Ohio. In mid-1985 the Federal Deposit Insurance Corporation (FDIC), which insures 14,880 US banks, had 947 on its problem list, while the US Federal Home Loan Board was talking of borrowing an extra $20 billion to bolster the Board's Federal Savings and Loan Insurance Corporation, in the face of the problems of the thrift institutions insured by the Corporation.

There is little doubt that the whole structure of US banking will have to undergo severe rationalization. Predictions of the numbers of thrifts and local banks likely to disappear range from 10 to 50 per cent. In Britain observers believe a similar proportion of building societies to be under threat, while in Japan an advisory committee, set up by the Ministry of Finance to look into the pace of deregulation and including senior figures from most of the sectors of the Japanese finance industry, took the unusual step of concluding publicly that a shake-out among local co-operatives was inevitable. The question is, how is this to happen? Through centrally assisted mergers or through collapses caused by the cold winds of competition? The Japanese will certainly attempt to make the best of the shake-out by combining the forces of many of the local banks into the bigger regional bank groups. Building societies in Britain will be encouraged to merge into larger groups. In the USA, where local interests have a stronger voice in Congress than their equivalents in Europe and where the dislike of larger combinations is much greater, the choices will be much more difficult to make. The temptation so far has been to preserve the individual institutions through loans, some manipulation by the US Federal Reserve of the funds available in the system and legislative blocks to take-overs by the commercial banks. The fear, though, is that the forces of rationalization are too strong and that the result will be the same, only with a bigger bang when the shake-out comes.

The experience of the Bank of England and the JMB rescue has been a salutory one. Johnson Matthey are bullion dealers, one of the select group of five dealers who decide twice daily the prices on London's gold market. Founded in the 1960s, the group's bank, JMB, expanded its commercial banking business rapidly in the early 1980s, increasing its volume of lending ninefold to £300 million in 1984. As a subsidiary of a highly reputable bullion firm, JMB was categorized as a recognized bank, requiring relatively little detailed supervision, as opposed to a licensed deposit-taker (that is, one of the smaller banks) that came under closer scrutiny after the secondary banking crisis of 1974. Almost unnoticed apparently either by its own parent company or by the Bank of England, the bank lent a disproportionate amount of its total assets to two customers. In spite of the fact that the general guidelines for UK banking indicated that it would be imprudent for a bank to lend more than 10 per cent of its capital to one customer, by 1984 the loans to these two totalled more than 100 per cent of JMB's capital base, although the figures on the book suggested rather less than this. After a series of delays and some confusion while the Bank of England supervisors belatedly asked for an explanation, it became apparent that the bank was in serious difficulties, with losses of £248 million on a total loan portfolio of £400 million. Over the weekend of 28–29 September the Bank of England called in the other bullion dealers and the major banks, desperately seeking a discreet rescue by a foreign bank. It failed and was eventually forced into taking over the bank itself, at a cost of £100 million. The Bank's attitude from the start was that JMB had to be rescued if its problems were not to spill over into the all-important gold bullion market and threaten others, including the strained Midland Bank. The government's and Parliament's concern was that the Bank of England should have seen the problems much earlier. Some of those involved in the rescue and other observers wondered whether it had been necessary to save the bank at all and suggested that the bullion dealers alone should have been rescued.

The same kinds of question were asked in Hong Kong in May 1985, when the Hong Kong government stepped in over a weekend to take over the Overseas Trust Bank. The attitude of the government was that a rescue was crucial to maintaining confidence in the Hong Kong financial system, the more so now that the colony is living under the shadow of 1997, when the Chinese mainland government will take it back under its control. The attitude of observers in the colony and of some of the bankers involved in the rescue was that there was no need to spend more than $200 million to rescue a bank that appeared to have been used for personal gain by its principal shareholders. Better, it was argued, to let the bank fail and protect the smaller depositors.

It is an issue that is likely to come to the fore increasingly as the volatility of markets throws up problems. How far can the supervisory authorities afford to prop up every financial institution that comes under pressure? Do they indeed, in the light of the JMB affair, have the ability to identify the problems? Yet can they afford *not* to keep plastering over the cracks in a structure that is under such strain?

Once the process of deregulation starts, it is extremely difficult to prevent financial institutions from moving rapidly to take advantage of it. In 1985 the US thrift industry was hit by a series of failures among government security dealers, most notably ESM Government Securities in March and Bevill, Bresler and Schulman in April. The failure of Bevill Bresler threatened some seventy-five thrifts with losses of up to $200 million, jeopardizing the solvency of several, according to reports at the time. The problems stemmed from the thrifts' heavy buying of repurchase agreements, or 'repos', from the firm. With these instruments, the seller – in this case Bevill Bresler – agrees to sell government securities to an institution and to buy them back at a fixed date in the future, giving the initial buyer an apparently certain return in the difference between the purchase and the re-purchase price. For the thrifts it seemed a safe form of investment because it involved government securities and thus came within the new definition of acceptable investments for them. For the dealing firm it freed cash for further investment during the period before repurchase. The only trouble was that, in this case, the freed cash was lost in speculative deals. Some of the thrifts had never taken possession of the security for the repo deals, the government secur-ities, because of the administrative burden. When it came to re-purchasing time the dealers were unable either to fulfil their obli-gation to repurchase or even, in many cases, to provide the underlying security. Yet repos are not some weird form of financial instrument. In the USA they are the essential means to ease the sale and trading of government debt, 'the cornerstone of the US economy', as Peter Sternlight, executive vice-president of the Federal Research Bank of New York told a House of Representatives subcommittee. Without them the thirty-six primary dealers in the US government securities

market would not be able to handle such large volumes of new issues
in the market, as far too much of their cash would be tied up.

When trouble does develop in a deregulated, electronic market, it
spreads very quickly. In the old days a bank crisis was seen in the
queues of depositors lining up outside a bank's doors, from early in
the morning, to withdraw their money. To judge from the lines
outside the Maryland and Ohio thrifts in early 1985, the picture has
not altered much since the bank failures of the Great Depression.
The Penn Square Bank collapse of 1982 was originally started by a
run at its drive-in window one Saturday. The failures of the
Greenwich Savings Bank in 1982 and the First National Bank of
Midland, Texas, in the following year both started with a classic
withdrawal of deposits as rumours of problems in the bank began to
spread. They marked the first major bank runs – with the single
exception of the Franklin National Bank in 1974 – since the Great
Depression. Then over 10,000 banks failed within three years. The
difference now was that government insurance through the FDIC
(founded in 1933), by guaranteeing deposits of $100,000 and under,
ensured that the small investors at least were secured and hence,
presumably, calmer in the face of a rumour.

In 1984, however, the collapse of the Continental Illinois Bank and
Trust Company in Chicago, which led to the biggest bank bail-out in
American history, showed that it was no longer just the small
depositors who were the source of the run, as they had been in the
1930s. It was the big depositors, the institutions, corporations
and other banks, who were fuelling the run. Their deposits ran to
billions of dollars in total. They were not covered by Federal insurance, and Penn Square had made them extremely nervous. What
was more, in an age of electronic wholesale markets, they did not
need to queue up at a window to get their money out.

In Penn Square's case the bank failed because it did not have the
capital to repay all its depositors once its oil loans went bad – in
banking terminology it had 'negative net equity'. In Continental
Illinois's case things never reached this stage, but the run was far
worse. Rumours of trouble sparked off a mounting withdrawal of
deposits, starting in Japan, spreading to Europe and eventually extending to the USA. Worse, banks in the $1.5 trillion per annum
interbank market started to mark down Continental's credit and, in
some cases, to refuse it credit altogether. Suddenly the bank could
not fund itself. Statements of support from the FDIC had no effect.
Neither did a hastily arranged standby credit of $4.5 billion from

other major US banks. It was simply swamped by a run that, over
three weeks, saw $8 billion of deposits withdrawn, the share price of
the bank collapse and its source of wholesale funds in the interbank
market dry up. Eventually it got an injection of $2 billion in new
capital from the FDIC, accepted a $5.5 billion line of credit from
twenty-eight banks and received the promise of unlimited Federal
Reserve Board funds from its discount window. Effectively the bank
had to be nationalized before the run stopped.

Even that was not enough to calm the nerves in the international
wholesale markets. Within a week of the outbreak of the Continental
Illinois crisis Manufacturers Hanover came under pressure from a
rumour-ridden interbank market. Within two months of the Continental Illinois rescue a new crisis developed in the USA's financial
system, this time around the Financial Corporation of America
(FCA) and its subsidiary, the American Savings and Loan Association. An over-ambitious drive to increase its loan portfolio was again
the cause of the institution's difficulties, complicated on this occasion
by involvement in the funding of take-over bids. The point of
weakness was FCA's heavy dependence on institutional deposits.
During July that was a net withdrawal of nearly $800 million. It took
a change in management imposed by the Federal authorities, and the
undertaking that large deposits as well as small would be protected,
to stop the flight of capital.

The instinctive response of legislators has been talk of re-regulating
the markets and limiting by law the activities of thrifts and deposit-
taking institutions. The instinctive response of central banks and
financial supervisors has been to seek a raising of the capital–asset
ratio of banks to ensure greater coverage of poor loans and bad investments. The Continental Illinois crisis had a profound effect on the
thinking of supervisory bodies in every country. Since then nearly all
have moved to impose higher capital ratios on their banks and to
institute tighter reporting systems. If it had not been for Continental
Illinois, the Bank of England might not have taken such a protective
view of the problems of JMB four months later.

Re-regulation in these conditions is a great deal more difficult than
deregulation. The reason for allowing the thrifts in the USA or the
building societies in Britain to go into new forms of borrowing and
lending has not been simple doctrine. There was no choice if the
savings institutions were to manage at a time of fluctuating short-
term interest rates and free competition for funds. Similarly the
commercial banks have had no other option; their enthusiasm to

enter the capital markets has been a reflection not merely of vaulting ambition. Driven from their traditional reliance on corporate loans and straight deposits, they have seen that the only way to growth for many, if not most, is adaptation in order to benefit from the new forms of lending. If half the problems of both Continental Illinois and the FCA derived from their excessive dependence on the wholesale markets for funds, a major factor in this over-dependence was the traditional restriction on the financial institutions' development of a firm national base for retail deposits. To that extent the US has created problems for itself that would not apply in, for example, West Germany or the UK.

Banks claim, therefore, that to impose the additional burden of reserve requirements at this stage is to saddle them with extra financing costs that do not apply to their competitors among the securities houses, investment banks and non-bank financial groups such as Sears. It is a genuine difficulty. Financial supervision in the West has always been based on the view that it is the deposit-taking institutions that lie at the centre of the system and that they are most in need of supervision, for the sake of the system as much as of the depositor. Historically this has been correct. The banks had been the institutions that have turned the savings of those with money into the investment finance of the merchants and industrialists who have needed money for expansion. Supervision has always consisted of the imposition of some requirements regulating the balance between the capital of a bank (mainly in the form of equity, since this money is entirely at the bank's disposal) and its assets, or loans. There has always been some dispute about what precisely should be termed equity and what should be put on the asset and the liability (or deposit) sides of a bank's balance sheet. Different countries have followed different accounting principles and have imposed different reserve requirements.

In the first place, there are wide variations in the treatment of 'subordinated debt', long-term bonds issued by banks that, should the bank fail, give the bond holders more rights than equity holders but less than ordinary creditors. West Germany does not include subordinated debt in its capital–asset ratios for banks. Most other countries do include it as 'secondary capital' but limit its proportion of total capital to 10–50 per cent. The Bank of England allows banks to issue perpetual floating-rate bonds and to include these in their totals for primary capital. Most other supervisors do not.

There is even greater variety in different countries' definitions of a bank's assets for the purpose of calculating its capital–asset ratios. Japan, which has a relatively small number of commercial banks, has so far avoided specific formal ratios in favour of informal control of the banks, keeping as its ultimate weapon the power to refuse them permission to issue new equity or debt. The USA requires that a bank's loans can be no more than twenty times its capital, a capital–asset ratio of 5 per cent. Canada allows its domestic banks to lend thirty times their capital, but allows foreign-owned Canadian banks to lend only twenty times and the subsidiaries of foreign banks only 15. The Bank of England does not use this formula but employs instead a risk–asset ratio that tries to give different types of bank lending different weighting. Loans to the British government, for example, require less backing than loans to commercial companies or foreign governments.

Even the supervisory systems differ widely between countries. In Britain, Italy and the Netherlands supervision is carried out by central banks. West Germany, France, Canada and Belgium have all, in different ways, banking supervisors that are separate from their central banks. The USA, by accident as much as by design, has an extremely fragmented system of supervision. It divides control of the banks between local state agencies; the Comptroller of Currency, who supervises the 'national charter' banks; the Federal Home Loan Bank Board, which oversees the thrifts; the FDIC, which insures deposits and hence carries out some supervision; and the Federal Reserve, which is in charge of supervising the bank-holding companies that have been set up to get round regulation by states and by the Comptroller of Currency.

That is the difficulty, of course. The more regulation by supervisory authorities imposes extra costs on the commercial activities of banks, the more the banks will attempt to avoid them through the creation of new legal entities or the development of businesses that are at the margins of supervision and do not appear on the banks' own balance sheets. The changes in the world of finance of the last five or ten years have enormously increased the pressures on the banks to do this. Banks feel that they have to enter the world of capital markets if they are to survive. The spectre of problem loans to Latin America and the Third World has made supervisors ever more anxious to tie down the banks and limit their exposure; it has made the banks, in turn, ever keener to find new ways of gearing themselves up again to achieve growth.

Securitization has become a convenient means of reducing the regulatory pressure on the banks. By converting long-term loans into marketable securities the banks immediately reduce their assets for regulatory purposes and increase the money available to find new markets for growth. The principle is attractive. The practice, however, could result in the banks removing from their books their best assets, their loans to reliable customers with regular income through interest. The quality of the remaining assets, be they in the form of sovereign debt to Latin American countries or loans to industries in decline, becomes progressively worse, yet the formal capital–asset ratio for regulatory purposes is actually improved.

The situation could be all the more dangerous if the money released is ploughed into capital markets, where the risks are inherently much greater. It was for this reason, of course, that the Glass–Steagall rule was introduced into American law after the Depression. Its weakness now is that, in an age of securitized debt, it merely leaves the commercial banks with one hand tied behind their backs just when they need every weapon and every limb to keep abreast of the competition. The rule is also becoming increasingly redundant at a time when new instruments so easily bridge, or undermine, the traditional divisions between debt and equity.

In their search for fee income and for market activity outside the Glass–Steagall confines, the banks have become the principle investors and dealers in the new world of swaps, NIFs, RUFs, futures and options. The attractions for the banks are considerable. By providing the back-up loan facilities for NIFs and RUFs the banks become part of a note-issuing operation that would otherwise be prohibited by Glass–Steagall. And they earn a straight fee by providing the client with the facility for taking out a loan if need be.

'Writing', as the provision of options is called, has similarly become a major market for banks, particularly outside the USA, where the markets are more institutionalized. The risk lies in the future. The premium provides an immediate fee income. The biggest market for banks, however, has become swaps. The big commercial banks have a natural advantage in their international spread and in their relations with corporations in a wide variety of markets. They can thus more easily find partners for swaps either of currency or interest-rate obligations. And, in the traditional banking manner, they can use their name as the guarantor of a swap, earning a fee both for acting as marriage broker and for ensuring the honourable behaviour of the partners.

The worry for the supervisors, and for the health of the financial system, is that all these instruments ultimately pose risks for the banks. Yet no one is certain just how big the risk is. Indeed, none of the authorities is certain about the size of the market for them. In theory the risk of an NIF, for example, is a limited one, since in normal circumstances the client will issue notes rather than take out a loan. In the same way only 20 per cent or less of options are ever exercised. They are there for most corporations as a hedge, to be used if the markets move in a totally unexpected way. For swaps too the risk is limited theoretically to the continuing payment of interest by one of the parties. The loan itself is guaranteed by the original parties, not the bank. They swap interest payments, and that is where the bank's responsibility comes in.

Yet the nature of risks and markets is such that, individually and collectively, they make their mark when the whole financial world turns sour. Recent estimates suggest that, in the USA at least, the total amount of contingent risks could equal, and even exceed, the total amount of traditional loan risks. A joint study by the Comptroller of Currency and the FDIC in mid-1985 showed that, at the end of 1984, the fifteen largest banks had contingent liabilities of nearly $1 trillion as against assets of just over $850 billion. Under the regulatory rules, loans actually made were calculated as assets, but the promise to make a loan if required is calculated as a liability.

The study did not include the less easily definable risks involved in writing options or guaranteeing swaps, when the authorities have nothing to go on but rough estimates of the size of the market. According to OECD calculations the volume of NIFs, RUFs and other revolving-credit facilities jumped from some $4 billion in 1983 to $18 billion in 1984. Estimates by Salomon Brothers suggest that the total volume of swaps reached some $80 billion in interest-rate swaps and nearly $14 billion in currency swaps in 1984 – a quadrupling of the volume of the previous year. With borrowers with the respectability of the government of Sweden taking advantage of NIFs and corporations with the strength of General Motors swapping debt, the market is far from being a fly-by-night one, but it is becoming too big and too fast-moving to be left unrecognized.

Overhanging all this is the international debt crisis. The sums built up in the days of untrammelled syndicate lending in the 1970s and now at risk, are mind-boggling. By the end of 1985 more than thirty countries, with a total debt of nearly $300 billion, had been in arrears with payments or had had to ask for the fundamental rescheduling of their loans from the banks. Total bank claims on the developing

countries were over $400 billion. Even after the rescheduling of 1982–
4 the cost of servicing their debt absorbed about 20 per cent of the
total exports of the developing countries as a whole and nearly 30 per
cent of some oil producers' exports, while on average the ratio of debt
to total GNP of the developing countries was nearly one-third.

It is not only the scale of the Third World's debt problem that is so
staggering but also the way in which it falls. Certain banks and groups
of banks are especially exposed to particular countries. West German
banks have been deeply involved in Polish and East European debt
problems. The Japanese are major lenders to the Asian economies,
the Americans to Latin America. In the major lending countries
some banks are even more exposed. When Continental Illinois faced
crisis with some $8 billion worth of loans declared 'non-performing'
(defined in the USA as loans that have failed to yield interest after
ninety days), $1.6 billion was owed by just three countries – Mexico,
Brazil and Venezuela. Walter Wriston's oft-quoted statement, 'No
country ever went bust', may yet prove over-optimistic. But he may
well turn out to be right about the fact that no country will let a
major bank of its own go bust under the strain.

In the end anything that the bank supervisors do in these circumstances is bound to smack of locking the stable door after the horse
has bolted. Indeed, anything that is done to tighten commercial bank
lending may merely make matters worse by blocking off rescheduling.
It is a bigger problem than the banks can deal with and will be solved
only by government involvement, whether bilateral or international.
At the annual meeting of the IMF in October 1985 James Baker, US
Finance Secretary, at last formally recognized this fact in launching a
new initiative to increase World Bank and IMF resources. A revival
of commercial-bank lending may follow, but only under the protection of governments. If the Third World is not saved from the
debt crisis, the banks of the industrialized world will have to be. That
is the blunt choice facing the major creditor nations.

Apart from IMF initatives, the main efforts of the supervisors
have been applied to establishing systems that will give warning
signals of trouble ahead. Capital requirements and balance-sheet
supervision are being refined by rules limiting exposure to any one
country. The Swiss, the British and others are trying to develop
sophisticated risk measurements in an effort to pinpoint problem
areas and to assess how big an impact they could have on a bank's
balance sheet. Since 1975 a committee of supervisors from twelve
countries (the Group of Ten, plus Luxembourg and Switzerland)

have been meeting to try to co-ordinate information and agree on common standards of supervision.

The American authorities, following the recommendations of a task force headed by Vice-President George Bush, are considering the complete overhaul and simplification of their complex system of interlinked supervisory authorities by replacing the Comptroller of Currency with a Federal Banking Agency charged with overseeing all federally chartered banks, be they holding companies, thrifts or commercial banks. The Bank of England is moving towards a system of supervising markets and imposing capital requirements on all players in the market, whether they are subsidiaries of larger groups or not, rather than simply supervising the principals. The Japanese authorities are thinking both of imposing formal as well as informal operating rules on their banks and of setting up an International Banking Facility on American lines, requiring banks to set up distinct subsidiaries to operate in it.

The gaps in supervision remain alarming. The tradition of regulation is still that of supervising banks quite separately from securities houses and investment banks, although these are now just as important and potentially as vulnerable in the financial system of the world. The number of bank supervisors is actually declining in the USA, despite the increased workload. The JMB affair in Britain has shown up appalling lapses of practical supervision of bank accounts. The role of the auditor has been called in question by a number of recent failures. Are auditors there to protect their clients or to protect the depositor and the shareholder from mismanagement? The lack of real knowledge about options, swaps and other new instruments among bank supervisors is little short of frightening.

'None the less,' says one of Europe's leading central bank executives, 'when the Herstatt Bank crisis broke in 1974, we were all taken by complete surprise. Nobody had any idea then of the extent to which floating exchanges had induced interbank liabilities across national boundaries. This time at least we think we're running with the problem, not behind it.'

Maybe.

TEN

WHO BENEFITS?

'Under the banner of deregulation and total faith in the marketplace,' argued Felix Rohatyn, senior partner of Lazard Frères in New York, in an article in the *Wall Street Journal*, 'we're impairing our greatest assets: the credibility of our capital markets and the faith in our financial institutions . . . The growing feeling today is that the capital markets have become the property of insiders and speculators, of raiders and other professionals, to the detriment of the general public.' *

'It will all end in disaster,' declared Ian Fraser over on the other side of the Atlantic, on retiring as chairman of Lazard Brothers in the summer of 1985. 'It's an old, old story. Banks are getting into businesses they do not know: money-making, property . . . [Conglomerates] have bitten off a hell of a lot more risk at a time when everyone has to learn new rules of behaviour: how to make a market, how to deal. Meanwhile, there is great personal confusion, conflicting loyalties, stresses and strains of mergers. It is an entirely new way of living – all this trebles the risk.

'It was all very well,' he went on, discussing London's 'Big Bang', 'for the government to say, "Let's break up monopolies." But in finance they broke up a delicate mechanism with enormous knock-on effect, nationally and internationally.' 'Joe Public,' he concluded, 'will be worse off – he'll pay more and get less service.' †

It is easy enough to accuse Fraser and Rohatyn of special pleading. Lazard Frères of New York and Lazard Brothers of London have chosen the road of linking together, remaining small and continuing the old merchant-bank tradition of being advisers to clients, not dealers in the market. But their fears are shared by a large number of financiers, worried by the speed of change, appalled by the lowering of ethical standards and genuinely afraid of the chaos that these could bring in their wake when the markets go into reverse.

'We are drifting toward a financial system in which credit has no

* *Wall Street Journal*, March 1985.
† *Observer*, 4 August 1985.

guardian,' argues Henry Kaufman, Salomon Brothers' economic guru
and the man nicknamed 'Doctor Doom' by the London markets for
his gloomy, and accurate, forecasts on interest rates. And in a statement before the Committee on Energy and Commerce of the US
House of Representatives in June 1985, he propounded the view that
'Today the integrity of credit is being chipped away by a financial
revolution that is contributing to the lowering of credit standards and
muting the responsibilities of creditors and debots – few, if any,
developments are encouraging confidence in the credit structure. We
are failing to define correctly the role of financial institutions in our
society and how this role can best be performed. Instead, we have
responded in an ad hoc fashion whenever market pressures or strong
vested interests have prevailed; often, the far-reaching consequences
of market, regulatory and legislative changes have gone unnoticed.' *

'You Westerners,' says the vice-president of one of Japan's biggest
banks, staring across the grounds of the old Edo castle of Tokyo from
a plate-glass dining-room in modern Marunouchi, 'are always
obsessed with the Japanese way of consensus. You forget what it is
like to be opposed to that consensus. I say to the Ministry of Finance,
"What will you achieve from all this deregulation? I will tell you
what you will achieve; banks failing, companies finding it harder to
get funds, people doing things that they would never have had the
courage to try before this." They ignore me. I go to the finance
committee of the main party in the Diet and I say, "Why are you so
excited about liberalizing the yen and creating a euroyen market? Do
you know what will happen to it? Japanese companies will use it to
convert straight to dollars. That's all." They look at me, surprised.
But they say nothing. It is too late.'

Nor is it only the banks and financial institutions most affected by
change that are suspicious of it. Central bankers, who once encouraged deregulation as a spur to competition and a necessary means of
keeping their financial centres in the international stream of things,
are now beginning to voice increasing concern at the risks involved.
Fritz Leutweiler, the Swiss banker *par excellence*, former president of
the Swiss National Bank and head of the BIS in Basle, retired in
1985 openly voicing doubts about the state of international finance,
its ability to cope with the debt crisis and its relentless pursuit of new
markets. Even Paul Volcker, while broadly in favour of liberalizing

* 'The Integrity of Credit', a statement to the Committee's subcommittee on Telecommunications,
Consumer Protection and Finance, 5 June 1985. See also the speech by Paul Volcker to Harvard
University, 1985.

the US financial markets and opening them up to greater competition, was talking of the risks involved in what the banks were doing and calling for a substantial increase in banks' capital–asset ratios. One of the most scathing warnings of the dangers of the world of new instruments and new markets came from Kit McMahon, Deputy Governor of the Bank of England before he moved across to join the Midland Bank in 1986.

'Interest-rate and currency swaps, as well as options and futures, present banks with a whole new range of difficulties,' he told an audience of bankers in Switzerland. 'Complex techniques need to be employed to determine the extent of banks' exposure. It is important that managers themselves fully understand what it is involved and do not rely on others to assess what is involved. We already know of cases where not even those in daily contact with the new instruments have grasped fully what it is that they are taking on.

'As with all instruments, there is a honeymoon period when nobody has lost any money. That can, unfortunately, lead to complacency and eventually to hard lessons for those who do not take sufficient precautions against the risks which will inevitably materialize. Moreover, the honeymoon period of no losses may turn out to be surprisingly short. Instances are already known of experienced banks making sizeable losses on options business.'

The disquiet now being voiced – and felt far more widely than it is being voiced, it should be added – stems in part from a genuine concern that traditional values, as well as old loyalties, are being swept aside by the rush to new forms of trading. Most people in the senior ranks of financial institutions have been brought up in the old systems of rigidly separated markets and small, specialist firms. Even in the USA, where the changes have been occurring for longest, it is less than twenty years since Wall Street was run largely by broker partnerships, and investment banks were regarded as quite different from brokerage houses, never mind commercial banks. The average firm had perhaps a client list of a few dozen important investors, just as the average investment bank had relationships with a dozen or so major corporations. These brokers traded mainly in blocks of a few hundred shares, a few thousand at most. A broker would tend to put certain types of client into certain types of investment, depending on their needs. Brokers were there to sell stock to clients and live off the commission, not to deal in stock themselves. Investment banks were there to advise clients on the issue of stock or on debt, not to put these into the banks' own portfolios as items to be traded in diversified dealing-rooms. Equally, banks were there to lend money to customers, to take their deposits and to give them well understood rates of interest. They, unlike the brokerage houses, were not there to sell their clients a whole range of products.

That picture, idealized though it may be, is still the norm in most European countries and in Japan. Deregulation, competition and conglomeration are only just beginning to break up the old system of specialist market sectors and specialist institutions to serve them. The UK may be unique in the extent to which it has kept separate the functions of the broker, acting on the instructions of a client to buy and to sell shares ('a low wretch', as Dr Johnson defined him in his Dictionary), and the jobber, who earns his profit from holding the shares and trading them. But for most financial centres in Europe, stock exchanges remain clubs of individuals, and financial firms remain partnerships rather than conglomerates. The abiding spirit is that of the association or guild – a combination of members charged with special responsibilities because they are charged with handling other people's money.

It would be foolish to suggest that the system was without faults. One of the first problems of the London brokers who banded together in a club to ensure that scandals such as the South Sea Bubble would be avoided in future was that they brought down on themselves a lawsuit from a broker who had been excluded. He demanded right of entry. And he got it. 'People of the same trade,' Adam Smith wrote in *Wealth of Nations*, 'seldom meet together, even for merriment and diversion, but the conversation ends in a conspiracy against the public, or in some contrivance to raise prices.'

The imperative of clubs is as much the exclusion of competitors or outsiders as it is the provision of service, with standards, to the client. The series of bankruptcies, collapses and outright frauds that preceded and accompanied the Great Depression in virtually every major financial centre in the 1930s did not occur simply because of lack of regulation, although that was the lesson drawn from it, particularly in the USA. It was not so much the over-stretching of the major banks into securities activities that caused the problems as the myriad smaller banks that had started up as markets boomed.

Exactly the same was to occur in Britain during the secondary banking crisis of 1973–5. Eventually thirty banks had to be supported by the lifeboat launched by the Bank of England. They were all fringe, or secondary, outfits that had grown up on the back of buoyant wholesale markets and progressive relaxation of the rules governing

credit and control of the banking sector. But the tightening up of the
rules after this did not prevent the Bank of England from having to
be drawn in to support a bank yet again when JMB got into difficulties barely ten years later.

Money is a seductive object. However tight the controls, somebody
will see an opportunity to make money by evading regulations. In the
1960s quick profits lay in hire purchase, or instalment finance, and
consumer credit. In the 1970s their place was taken by foreign exchange. The failures of the Franklin National Bank in the USA and
the Herstatt Bank in West Germany in 1974 both resulted, in large
part, from excessive growth in a new area for the banks – currency
dealing. It also resulted from fraudulent trading, as did the downfall
in 1982 of Banco Ambrosiano, Italy's largest private bank and, it is
alleged, the insolvency of JMB in London. Even the Japanese, tight
though their controls have been, have seen their share of scandals.
Daichi-Kangyo, the biggest bank in Japan, lost well over $100 million
through the unauthorized dealings of one foreign-exchange manager
in the early 1980s. There is no evidence that the amount of fraud, or
even the amount of loss, is necessarily greater in an unregulated
market such as the eurobond market than in the regulated sectors of
commercial banking. If anything, the losses in the eurobond market
may actually have been rather less.* The greatest single step forward
after the Wall Street Crash and the bank failures of the early 1930s
was the development in the USA of Federal insurance for depositors.
The major lesson learned from the failures and collapses of the post-
war period would seem to be the need for central-bank action to
confine the damage through funding support after the event. In the
case of Herstatt the Bundesbank failed to prevent the ripples from
spreading throughout the interbank market. Indeed, the West German
authorities actually made matters worse by announcing Herstatt's
failure when the US markets were still open. The reforms to supervision afterwards did not prevent a crisis from developing over West
Germany's prestigious private bank, Schroder, Munchmeyer, Hengst
and Co., in 1983. But this time the bank was supported, its foreign
subsidiaries fully covered and the ripple effects reduced. The same
proved true of Continental Illinois in the following year and the
Overseas Trust Bank in Hong Kong in the year after that (1985).

* A survey, cited in Michael J. Comer's *Corporate Fraud*, 2nd edition (London, 1985), shows that
of fraud cases detected over half were found out by accident. Of those that were detected more (20
per cent of the total) were discovered as a result of information given by vengeful mistresses than
were revealed by the auditors, thus prompting the author to conclude that it would be better for
companies to fire their auditors and encourage their key managers to take up mistresses.

Today's world poses quite different problems, however. The sums are much larger; deregulation is providing far more exit routes; and communications allows funds to be transferred far faster. Hearings held in 1982 by the US House of Representatives' Committee on Energy and Commerce into dealings of Citibank through the 1970s unveiled numerous examples of what one executive called 'rinky-dink deals' to move money round the globe in order to avoid tax. The hearings, although they never led to a prosecution, were not that surprising. Corporations, like individuals, always wish to get around the rules when it comes to money and to tax.

Technology increases the risks of evasion and of fraud. No one knows just how much money is lost in the financial systems of the West through computer fraud. But no one doubts that the sum is considerable. Credit-card losses alone total $30 million each year in the UK, and there have been some notable cases of computer frauds totalling tens of millions of dollars in the USA. What has been even more worrying for the authorities in various countries, however, is the corporate use of electronic transfers to evade tax or regulations. A series of investigations launched by US investigators into the 'laundering' of criminal funds, starting with their first look into the books of the Bank of Boston, has uncovered billions of dollars in illegal accounts and covert transfers among some of the best-known names in the banking world. Government estimates in Washington indicate that as much as $60 billion a year of criminal funds may be laundered in the USA and a further $5 billion to $15 billion abroad. Try to pin it down at one point and it simply moves elsewhere – to Switzerland, with its constitutional right of secrecy, or to any number of off-shore centres, from the Cayman Islands to Liechtenstein.

An equally embarrassing and even more sophisticated abuse of the speed of financial communication was uncovered at E. F. Hutton, one of the USA's most prestigious investment houses. The firm finally pleaded guilty to 2,000 counts of wire and mail fraud after it was alleged that managers had obtained the use of more than $1 billion in interest-free funds by cleverly overdrawing checking accounts at several hundred banks. The scheme was imaginative and was the logical extension of what many corporations do as part of the new art of cash management – that is, to move their funds around to maximize interest rates and to minimize the time during which their cash rests idle in a non-interest deposit account. Hutton's managers took this a stage further by shuffling some $10 billion from one account to another, using the time between the presentation of a cheque and the moment when it was actually cleared by the bank to gain extra interest for themselves. The company would allow its account at a local bank branch in the middle of Illinois, for example, to go into temporary deficit while a deposit from its central account in New York was being cleared. The local bank would take several days to clear the cheque. The central bank would be funded by Hutton immediately and the sum set free for the period between central deposit and local clearance. Hutton was taking advantage of normal banking practice but on a scale that shocked the financial community.

It could be argued that this kind of abuse of the system is bound to arise, not from deregulation itself but as a consequence of the loopholes that will always characterize the intermediate stage between regulation and freedom from control. Once wire services are fully developed for local banking, presumably the time gap that Hutton exploited will no longer exist. The trouble, as Citicorp's evidence on fund shifting to tax-free financial havens suggests, occurs when, amid general regulation, particular avenues of decontrol open up (in this case, the removal of exchange controls). The difficulty with this view is that there will always be some regulation, if only a system of taxation, that decontrol will enable the greedy to exploit. The more general decontrol there is, the more each individual country will be forced to compete in dismantling its own regulations if it is to maintain any supervision at all. Competitive deregulation is already driving the nations of the West to move far faster than they wish.

There has always been a fundamental difference in approach to this question between the Americans and the non-Americans. The USA has always turned to the law as the arbiter of behaviour and believed criminal investigation by the authorities to be the way to combat abuse. The Wall Street Crash confirmed the view that a watchdog with real teeth was the only means of keeping order. The SEC was one result – a forceful semi-governmental agency with full legal powers, founded in 1934 to regulate all aspects of the securities business, to drive out insider trading and to prevent, by invoking the law, conflicts of interest within firms between their role as investment advisers to clients and their role as traders in securities on their own account.

The Europeans and the Japanese, on the other hand, have always tended to believe that the best safeguard against conflicts of interest is peer-group pressure, the code of conduct of the select community in which one works. Indeed, under almost universal pressure from the financial groups and contrary to the advice of Professor Jim Gower in his report on investor protection, the British government deliberately rejected the American post-Depression route, that of setting up a legal agency. Instead it has preferred to seek the formalization of self-regulating bodies on the grounds that self-regulation produces the highest professional standards. Given the fast-moving nature of the financial markets, the Bank of England and government ministers argued, efforts to impose legal constraints could only serve to impede progress and would tend merely to plug leaks in the system that would soon find cracks elsewhere.

Neither of these approaches is proving wholly satisfactory. The US system has been weakened by the fragmentation of the supervisory system and competition among supervisory authorities – the SEC, the FDIC, the Comptroller of the Currency and the Federal Reserve. The spate of scandals associated with repurchase agreements on Treasury bonds arose partly because the market, dominated by thrift buyers, fell between the two stools of SEC and banking supervision. Efforts by the Swiss to raise standards within their banking system through the introduction of new laws on insider trading, for example, have not been widely regarded as a success. Yet British efforts to form an alternative system of self-regulatory bodies have resulted, as the medieval guilds did, in a jostling for power between those bodies – between, for instance, the market-makers in eurobonds and the Stock Exchange over who should regulate foreign-stocks trade in London off the Stock Exchange floor. Self-regulation seemed a less obvious answer to the problem of controlling the financial conglomerates, whose business spreads throughout a number of different markets and whose headquarters may be thousands of miles from the City of London. Still less does it seem to assuage persistent concern over conflicts of interest now that, in London, the roles of broker and jobber are being merged.

The underlying problem, as many of the older members of the financial community see it, is the erosion not simply of regulation but also of standards. The market mentality and conglomerate structures, the 'unbundling' of services and the disappearance of the old bank–client relationship are all moving the financial world in a direction quite different from the traditional concept of finance as a service for the investor and the borrower, carried out with the client's interest in mind.

Hutton's cash-management scheme and the Bank of Boston's involvement in money laundering have been a considerable shock

to the financial establishment of the USA. Even more disturbing
have been the problems and scandals of the Lloyd's insurance market
in London. To the City of London Lloyd's has always been the
classic example of commercial success based on a discreet marriage
between wealth and opportunity. Attracted by tax advantages as well
as the returns, rich individuals, from pop stars to royalty, have long
put their money into Lloyd's market, pledging their personal wealth
as collateral. You apply to join. You put up so much in cash and
prove £100,000 in assets. If accepted, you become a 'name' or 'part-
name' in a syndicate of investors. Your money is then handled by a
broker or manager, who puts it out among underwriting agencies that
do the actual insurance.

For centuries there have been scandals over members walking off
with the petty cash. What has so shaken Lloyd's in the past few years
is a series of losses and legal cases. Some of its best-known figures
have been drummed out of the club after being accused of putting the
'names'' money into their own underwriting agencies and then laying
off the risk with outside companies in which they have had a holding,
using the reserves built up in good times for their own investments.
Large losses have been recorded for individual syndicates. Some of
the 'names', for the first time in Lloyd's history, have refused to pay
up. Allegations of fraud have been hurled about in an atmosphere
that would befit a boxing ring rather than the City of London's most
highly prized institution.

The response, in Lloyd's case, was the appointment of a chief
executive and an investigator in an attempt to clean up the market.
Lloyd's has also reacted by impelling brokers to sell their interests in
underwriting agencies on the grounds that conflicts of interest are
best prevented by removing the opportunity rather than by threatening punishment after the event. Yet the opposite is true in the case
of the securities markets. The ending of the broker/jobber separation
in Britain has increased companies' scope for using their clients to
increase their dealing profits, either by buying and selling un-
necessarily or by dumping unwanted stocks on them. The response
to this has been to accept the coming of dual capacity but to try to
insist, as the Americans, Swiss and others do, on a separation of
functions within an organization, backed by legal sanctions if
wrongdoing is discovered. The 'Chinese wall' system, in which various parts of the same firm are forbidden to talk to each other, is well
established in the USA but less well observed. 'I have never seen a
Chinese wall,' Professor Gower quips, 'that hasn't got a grapevine

growing over it.' It works only if those involved abide by the spirit of the system. What many in the financial world fear is that the spirit is no longer there and that governments are no longer attempting to give the lead, so enthusiastic is their rush to deregulate.

'Has the opening up of the markets,' an eminent British merchant banker was asked, 'induced a fall in standards, or has it merely revealed what was already going on in more restricted circles?' He paused for some time. 'I suppose,' he answered finally, 'it has given a wider circle of people an opportunity to practise what was once confined to a select few.' That is true. It was long considered reasonable practice – a mark of commitment, indeed – for senior partners to take a tranche of any underwriting and for partners to deal heavily on their own account in issues in which they were involved and to put their friends and contacts on to good deals.

But it is also true that the pressure to perform and the size of the rewards now being dangled before those in the capital markets are greatly increasing the temptation to push the limits of what is regarded as acceptable practice. The huge sums at which the partners of investment banks such as Lehman Brothers and Salomons sold out their inheritance of assets, of goodwill, of contacts and experience built up over generations, the capital gains made by the senior partners of British brokers and jobbers in disregard of the junior staff, the 'transfer fees' being paid to persuade star dealers or merger experts to change firms have all helped to create an atmosphere in which loyalty and restraint in public behaviour no longer prevail.

There is only a narrow dividing line between doing the best for one's firm by maximizing the profits from cash balances and the deliberate abuse of the cheque-clearing system practised by E. F. Hutton executives. Behind the collapse of Penn Square Bank, the problems of Continental Illinois and the difficulties of the Financial Corporation of America there were financial executives more eager to boost their figures and their returns than to pursue old-fashioned prudential lending and borrowing.

'Market participants cannot avoid being caught up in debt creation,' Henry Kaufman declared in his statement to the congressional committee in the summer of 1985. 'If they turn their backs on the world of securitized debt, proxy debt instruments and floating-rate financing, then they lose market share, they fail to maximize profits and they are unable to attract and hold talented people. The driving force is credit growth, and in the process the most conservative among institutions compromise standards and engage in practices that they would not have dared to pursue a decade or so ago. The heroes of credit markets without a guardian are the daring – those who are ready and willing to exploit financial leverage, risk the loss of credit standing, and revel in the present-day casino-like atmosphere of the markets.'

The emphasis on short-term results, which is now being applied as much to the investing institutions as to the financial intermediates, is bound to have its effect on ethical values. The sharp rise in share prices on Wall Street and in the City of London before a take-over bid is announced is indicative of what many in the stock exchanges believe is a spread of insider trading, especially as share schemes are becoming general practice in companies. Short of outright fraud or malpractice, it has become accepted, to a surprising extent, that brokers, investment advisers and agents will use clients' funds to generate interest income for their own use and that investment banks and securities houses will fail to reveal a conflict of interest in handling their clients' money.

Once firms move from gaining most of their income from com- missions to earning the major part of their profits from dealing on their own account, the temptation to cut ethical corners becomes even more overwhelming. The firm that advises an institution or an individual on where to invest money is also the firm that is earning a fee from a company by advising it how to get that money and is very probably making a turn on dealing on its own account at the same time. It is not only 'Chinese walls' that are required but the positive obligation for financial intermediaries to declare from the start where they may have a conflict of interests. That formal obligation is too rarely enforced in New York, in London, in Tokyo and in most other centres now that the informal contraint of censure by peers is breaking down. In all the incidents that have been revealed at Lloyd's of London the one fact that comes over with startling clarity is that none of the underwriting and managing agencies apparently ever felt any need to tell investors when they were putting their money into companies in which the agencies had a direct interest – even if they thought that they were acting perfectly legally in doing so.

Alongside the worries over ethics that are now bubbling up is concern about what *Business Week* dubbed the 'casino society', echoing the warning of John Maynard Keynes in 1936: 'Speculators may do no harm as bubbles on a steady stream of enterprise. But the position is serious when enterprise becomes the bubble on a whirlpool of speculation. When the capital development of a country becomes a by-product of the activities of a casino, the job is likely to be ill-done.' *

In the deregulated markets of today, so the argument goes, the rewards and the credit go increasingly to the speculator and the gambler – to investment in options and futures rather than in the underlying stocks, to commodities and 'repurchase' deals on government securities, to arbitrage between markets in anticipation of take-overs, above all to junk bonds and their use in 'everaged acquisitions' 'that is, bids based on bond-issuance facilities and borrowings set against the assets of the company to be taken over). In 1984 and 1985 the value of bids and buy-outs announced in the U S A amounted to a total amount of $300 billion (about $150 billion each year). An acquisition mania spread at the same time to London, to West Germany and even to the calm and controlled exchange of Oslo, where a sudden spurt of bids and speculation caused severe embarrassment to the Conservative government campaigning for re-election partly on a stated policy of financial liberalization.

The freeing of financial markets, the development of low-rated bonds and consortia of arbitrageurs and speculative financiers have enabled take-overs to be launched with far lower initial capital and with far more extended credit than would have been conceivable a generation ago. Quite apart from the revulsion aroused by the practice of companies that pay off raiders with their shareholders' cash ('greenmail', as it has been dubbed), the wave of bids, 'leveraged buy-outs' and mergers has led to a reduction in equity and an increase in American corporate debt on an unprecedented sale. In 1984 the total equity of U S corporations was actually reduced by $78 billion, while new debt was added at a record rate of $169 billion. Other financial centres have not been threatened in the same way so far. But the techniques of leveraged bids are now spreading to London and Europe, extending the indebtedness of purchasing companies, which are paying prices for assets that only the break-up of their acquisitions or rapid inflation would seem to justify.

In the same way, it is argued, the remorseless rise in institutional funds and the pressure to deal is resulting in more and more activity on the world's exchanges and secondary bond markets, in order both to keep earnings up while margins fall and to justify the role and bonuses of the dealers. Most of the major stock exchanges of the industrial countries have recorded in the mid-1980s levels of turnover not seen since before the energy crisis of 1973. Yet the volume of new

* *Business Week*, 16 September 1985.

equity issues has in most cases declined, falling far behind the volume of new debt, or bond, issues by corporations. Investors have sought increasingly to hedge, or simply to speculate, against uncertainty through the purchase of futures and options on stock indices and shares rather than on the underlying equities themselves, though they have helped to determine the value of those assets none the less. Because the initial payment for these futures and options is so much less than for the underlying equities, the result has again been stretching of debt. The technique and the gambling spirit of the commodity markets have moved across to the bond and equity markets with similar ill-discipline.

The string of collapses among US government securities dealers in the period 1982–5 (most notably Drysdale Government Securities, ESM Government Securities and Bevill, Bresler and Schulman) occurred largely because the low margin payment required in re-purchase deals on Treasury bonds encouraged firms to expand too fast and too far. The dealers were selling repurchase agreements to thrifts, using the money in the meantime and sometimes keeping the actual security for still further borrowing in order to build up positions on the market. Bevill Bresler's collapse alone threatened US thrifts with losses of $200 million. The fear is that the explosion of options and futures trading in the financial markets will lead to a similar series of disasters once the market turns.

What the critics of deregulation often miss, however, is the simple point that market changes have developed not because of the whim of governments or the greed of practitioners but because events have forced change and consumers have wanted it. The explosion of in-flationary pressures in the 1970s obliged lenders to seek new ways to adjust the cost of credit to keep pace. American thrifts and banks went into adjustable-rate mortgages; investors moved their spare cash into money-market funds; corporate borrowers and investors took the FRNs to the eurobond market; and banks, thrifts, British building societies and Japanese savings institutions started inevitably to push at the walls of interest control and institutional demarcation. Ex-change rates were freed in the 1970s because technology, the rise of private financial flows and the disparate rates of inflation made main-tenance of rigid controls impossible. Once exchange rates were free to float, the markets were bound to seek ways of lessening the risks of swaps and futures trading, all the more so when inflation rates began to fall again in the early to mid-1980s. The rise and rise of the pension funds and insurance companies, and their dominance of savings, has inexorably altered the balance of power between investor, borrower and intermediary in the financial markets. They account now for well over two-thirds of the trading of London, New York, Tokyo and most other stock exchanges. The old structures, based on professional associations of investment banks and brokers and supported by fixed commission, could not survive. Even if they had tried, technology would, and still threatens to, bypass them.

The average depositor is far better off as a result of money-market funds, the development of interest-bearing accounts and competition for his custom between banks, building societies or thrifts and retail stores than ever he was in the days of controlled interest rates and protected institutions. The development of new industries and international competition in electronics, cars and consumer goods have required a global system of financing to fuel them. The search for new points of growth demands a financial system that can redirect investment funds to the ideas and opportunities that are part of a search to break out of stagnation. Management buy-outs, venture capitalism, efforts to extend share ownership to a wider section of the community are all aspects of a post-energy-crisis world that needs the flexibility of money as well as entrepreneurial skills if it is to find a way to sustained growth. The hope that the small stockholder will reassert his pre-eminence in the capitalist system is probably illusory. But the accompanying belief that in an era of industrial change the management of corporations has become stultified and self-seeking may well be justified. Freer markets have become the goal of corporate managements besieged by take-over bids. They are also the spurs to necessary restructuring and the encouragement of competition.

Indeed, it could be argued that what is happening to the world of finance today is the only means by which the economies of the industrialized world could have adapted to an era of first high and then diminishing inflation, fluctuating interest rates and explosive exchange rates. Most of the instruments that have appeared in the 1980s – the N I Fs, the futures and options, the swaps and the hybrid notes – have been developed to spread risk and to create a flexible response to an uncertain market. Most of the strategies adopted by financial institutions in order to securitize their loan portfolios and to develop commercial-paper markets and secondary-bond trading have been evolved to give them a robust means of coping with volatility.

These new developments do not necessarily predict disaster. Indeed, in some ways it is remarkable how well the system has adjusted so far. 'When I was woken up at 4.30 in the morning to be told that the new Iranian government of Khomeini had seized our hostages and that we were seizing their assets,' recalls John Heimann, then Comptroller of the Currency and now with Merrill Lynch, 'I thought, oh Christ, this is it. A payment of several hundred million dollars was due to Germany and if they had kicked up, who knows where it would have ended. They didn't. And ever since then I've been an optimist about the system.' 'When you consider what we have coped with,' argues Walter Wriston, 'the debt crisis, the recycling of OPEC money, Continental Illinois, we should be optimistic, not the other way round.'

Some of this resilience can be attributed to greater international co-operation of the authorities. Over the Iranian hostage crisis, the run on Continental Illinois and the present moves for co-ordinated supervision of new instruments the central banks of the world have displayed far greater cohesion than would have been thought possible in the last decade. Government co-operation over debt and currencies has been rather slower in coming. But the Plaza agreement and the statements of James Baker, US Finance Secretary, at the IMF meeting of October 1985 show a shift in mood that may well presage greater co-ordination to come.

Much of this resilience must also come from that of the financial system itself. Internationalization and deregulation have made the financial sector far more able to cope with structural shocks than much of manufacturing industry, for example. Even if they had not, the trend cannot be reversed now. The main problem associated with the regulation of the financial markets in the last decade is that it became impossible to sustain once funds could move abroad and investors began to demand flexible instruments. In the end many of the remaining controls will go the same way, including the Glass–Steagall provisions separating commercial banking from underwriting, in Japan as much as the USA. The answer is not to turn the clock back: this could not be accomplished without reinstating trade and investment controls as well.

But then neither is the answer to let all loose and hope that diversity and freedom alone will cope. Sir Seigmund Warburg used to warn his staff constantly against worrying too much about the short-term results. There was, he said, 'no natural law that stipulated that every year had to be better than the last one'.* He, like so many others in the financial world, belonged to a generation and a race that knew better. In the last few years the system has coped against a background

* See Eric Roll, *Crowded Hours* (London, Faber & Faber, 1985).

of a rapidly expanding U S economy and rising stock-market indices in most of the major financial centres. It has wrought a turnabout in a world where larger and larger institutional savings are chasing fewer and fewer investment outlets. The major manufacturing industries are contracting. The Third World has been shut off from new funds. The funds within the system are moving in ever faster circles, chasing the marginal profit that they can glean from their own movement. It is not just a sense of declining ethics in financial firms that causes critics to be concerned about the revolution now taking place; it is also the more fundamental feeling that, in pursuing their own returns so energetically, institutions are losing sight of the idea of service to their customers and the community. They may also be in danger of losing contact with the real world beyond the screens of the trading-rooms. The huge salaries being earned and the frequent performance reviews of fund managers are forcing an emphasis on short-term trading profit at the expense of long-term investment judgement.

To a certain extent, the accidents and the strains are part of the growing pains of a system that has suddenly been forced to leave the protected environment of regulated interest rates and market segmentation and to fend for itself all at once. You cannot make an omelette without breaking eggs, even in the financial world. And it may be too constricting to over-protect the investor. Sir Jeremy Morse, chairman of Lloyds Bank of the U K, put it thus in a lecture at the start of the I M F meeting in South Korea in October 1985: 'In a time, like the present, of vigorous innovation, not all of it understood, occasional accidents and failures are a necessary part of the process by which the market learns . . . The small depositor, investor or policy-holder is entitled to some protection against the mistakes of financial companies or practitioners, but that is all.'

That would be all right if finance were the same as an electrical appliance and the job of protector one merely of ensuring that the product met certain minimum safety standards. But the ramifications of a serious failure in the financial system not just on investor confidence but on market stability, exchange rates, money supply and interest rates as well are too great for financial supervision to be regarded merely as a matter of consumer protection. The Continental Illinois crisis was felt first of all on the interbank market and then, within minutes, on the gold market and in the downgrading of the dollar on Asian and then European markets – and all while Americans were still asleep. The debt crisis presents the same threat writ large. It is not solved, merely contained. Any lurch – a collapse in oil prices, a dramatic downturn in US imports, a rise in US interest rates – could set if off again, causing a run on currencies, sudden shifts in wholesale funds and a rapid domino effect from one market to another across the globe.

The task of coping with such a crisis has been made immeasurably more difficult, and the chance of its happening considerably more likely, by the development of new instruments, the increase in competition and the breakdown of old barriers in the financial markets. In the old days the front-line guardian of the system was the loan officer, or bank manager, the man who assessed the credit risk, the borrower and his ability to pay. The newer forms of credit – swaps, futures, note-issuance facilities, commercial paper – are there to spread the risk. But they are also there, quite deliberately, to remove that initial risk assessment and to dissipate it between partners. 'Innovation,' argues John Heimann, 'doesn't improve the underlying credit. It transfers it. But it transfers it to people, like other companies in a swap arrangement, who are not used to making credit judgements in the financial field.' The 'loosening of the link between borrower and creditor' (Henry Kaufman's description) was initiated by government deposit guarantees, which removed some of the responsibility of the creditor in assessing risk, and has been greatly accelerated by FRNs, which allow creditors to avoid the disciplines of interest rates. New market structures are not only a response to market volatility and economic uncertainty; they are a direct contributor to it.

So far most of the reaction to these concerns has concentrated on the institutional framework of the markets – whether it is right to end broker/jobber separation in Britain, whether it is time to allow banks to underwrite securities in the USA and Japan. In the 'level playing field' debate banks have protested that they would have to get into underwriting to have a fair chance of continuing to fund their customers. Investment banks have retorted that this would give banks an unjust advantage, as they have the implicit assurance of a government bail-out if things go wrong. The trouble with this argument is that it comes too late. The growth of institutional power in the market and the force of electronic trading means that the distinctions will break down whatever legislators decree.

Governments will have to adopt a fresh approach to the problems of supervision in today's world. So far, the authorities (as they are called in financial circles) have concentrated on imposing tighter and higher capital ratios on banks, on co-ordinating information internationally and on making it clear – in the case of Continental Illinois, the JMB crisis in the UK and the Overseas Trust Bank collapse in Hong Kong – that they are ready to stand as lenders of last resort when major financial institutions are threatened.

But this is essentially a banking approach. What is needed now is the recognition that all financial institutions – securities houses, insurance companies and banks – are one and need to be supervised as one. The US division of responsibilities between the Federal Reserve, the Comptroller, the SEC and the FDIC should give way to a broader authority with the right to impose capital provisions on all institutions and with the skills to understand new markets. International co-operation, which has so far tended to concern itself mainly with monitoring, should now be directed towards developing common accounting systems to define risks and to give early warning signs of danger. If money is to recognize no national boundaries, then neither should its supervision.

The question of ethics in the financial world is just as pressing. Formerly the investor had some right to assume that general standards would be high, even if there were occasional lapses. That assumption can no longer be made. The conflicts of interest inherent in deregulated markets are intense, not least among the auditors, who are supposed to catch any sign of fraud. Yet the traditional means of policing the market, through associations of practitioners imposing professional codes, is breaking down. The UK experiment in self-regulation based on these associations, and backed by law, was being widely dismissed in London even before it was introduced. Of all countries perhaps only Japan has sufficient cohesion to exercise restraint through an implicit acceptance of codes of behaviour. And even in Japan those codes are being quite openly breached at times. Other centres will find it more and more difficult to rely on accepted standards of conduct.

The central question, however, remains what the new world of finance will do for the general economic health of the industrial world. Its effect to date has been, in many ways, beneficial. Finance is more flexible; it is channelled more efficiently and transacted more cheaply than in the era of regulated markets. But it has also tended to take on a life of its own, independent of the economies that it is supposed to serve. 'We have freed the capital side of the balance-of-payments equation at the expense of doing the opposite on the current account of goods and services, points out David Walker, an executive director of the Bank of England and one of the key figures in London's financial revolution. Money has been liberated. However, the cost in terms of lost jobs and growing import penetration has caused a rising tide of trade protectionism that may yet do far more damage to the consumer than would the restricted movement of capital. The markets have assisted the process of the restructuring of industries but only at the cost of forcing companies to increase their debts and managements to lower their horizons in order to achieve short-term results that have little to do with the rational distribution of resources in an economy.

The sobriquet 'casino society' has force. There is something inevitable and necessary about the changes going on in the financial world. But there is also something lopsided about it. Much of the heat of activity and the volatility of the markets has arisen from an excessive rebalancing of power between investor and borrower. For most of the last century it has been the borrower's needs (the investment requirements of railroads, factories and refineries) that have driven the market. Now it is the investor's needs that predominate and the investment institutions that rule. The size of the institutions, the short-term pressure on their managers to perform and the lack of obvious and profitable long-term investment opportunities have helped produce a financial market that is geared to high short-term returns and a constant 'churning' of funds.

The volatility of the markets owes at least something to the contraction of the traditional borrowing ability of the developing world. Without a widening market the funds of the industrialized world will continue to move around within their own arena with ever-increasing volatility. For the last few years they have found outlets in the breakdown of international barriers. At the end of this process they will still have to find a purpose in new industry and new activity in growth in the Third World as well as the industrialized nations.

Finance is not, of its own accord, going to produce the means to sustain growth and low inflation. But its practitioners should never be allowed to forget that it is a servant in this cause, not an end in its own right, or that the effectiveness of a financial system is seen not in expansion but in contraction.

'You know what's really different about this lot?' says the manager of one of New York's largest trading floors, gazing around a battery of screens manned by ranks of young dealers. 'Not one of them knows what it is like to go through a recession.'

GLOSSARY:
THE LANGUAGE OF NEW FINANCE

The following definitions are drawn from publications of the Chicago Mercantile Exchange and Board of Trade and the New York and London Stock Exchanges, *Euromoney Year Book, International Capital Markets 1984* and *Reuters Glossary of International Economic and Financial Terms* (1982).

AAA Top rating for bonds given by the U S rating agencies Standard and Poor's and Moody's

ACCEPTING HOUSE COMMITTEE The group of seventeen leading London merchant groups, with strictly controlled membership approved by the Bank of England

ACCRUED INTEREST Interest earned on loan or bond since last payment date

ACH Automated Clearing House: U S term for computer clearing and settlement system, often under the aegis of the Federal Reserve Bank

ACTUALS The physical commodity in a commodities market

ADR American depository receipts: the form in which foreign shares, held physically by the U S banks, can be traded in the American markets without local listing

ADVISORY FUNDS Funds placed with a bank or other financial institution to invest at its own discretion on behalf of a client

AFTERMARKET Trading of bonds immediately after issue

AIBD Association of International Bond Dealers: formed in 1969 with headquarters in Zurich, as the self-regulatory organization of dealers in eurobonds

ALLOTMENT Amount of a new issue 'allotted' by the lead manager to the syndicate members, normally after the terms have been fixed

ARBITRAGE Broadly used term meaning to take advantage of differences in prices or rates between one market and another. Usually effected by buying and selling simultaneously in two markets to profit from a gap, often in the futures market

ARBITRAGEURS A group of financiers in the U S A specializing in 'arbitrage', particularly in bids, when they buy or sell forward in anticipation of the eventual outcome

ARMS Adjustable-rate mortgages: a term used in the U S A

ASIAN DOLLARS Dollar deposits held in Asia and traded off-shore like the eurodollar. The market in Asian dollars, a relatively small one, is based in Singapore

AT BEST Instruction to broker to carry out a buy or sell order at the best available price

ATM Automated teller machine: unmanned terminal, usually activated by a magnetically coded card, which can be used to dispense cash, take instructions on fund transfers and summarize information on the state of the account, etc.

BACK-TO-BACK LOAN Loan made in one currency that is set against an equivalent loan in another currency

BACKWARDATION Foreign-exchange term. The immediate price is at a premium to the forward delivery price

BALLOON MATURITY OR REPAYMENT The final payment on a bond or loan is much larger than the earlier payments

BANK HOLDING COMPANY US term for a holding company that owns one or more banks and comes within the supervisory ambit of the Federal Reserve Board

BANKER'S ACCEPTANCE Note, draft or letter of credit backed by a bank. A market that developed out of letters of credit for traders

BANQUE D'AFFAIRES French equivalent to a US investment bank or UK merchant bank

BASIS POINT Usually one-hundredth of 1 per cent, used in expressing interest rates (e.g. so many basis points above LIBOR) or movements in rates or yields (rates moved so many basis points)

BEAR Term for a falling market. A bear is an investor who sells an equity, bond or commodity short in the belief that the market will fall

BEAR RAID Active short-selling by a trader trying to depress prices to buy at low rates

BEAR SQUEEZE Action taken by central banks or market authorities to catch out traders selling short by buying heavily to force the price up and thus catch the trader short of stock, commodity, currency, etc.

BEARER BOND A bond held by whoever is in possession. With no registration of ownership, it has the advantage of anonymity

BEST EFFORTS A bond or equity issue that is not fully underwritten. The security is sold on the basis of what the market will stand

BID The price at which a potential buyer offers to purchase a security

BLOCK TRADING Buying or selling of securities in large lots (usually blocks of over 10,000 equity shares) by institutions

BLOCKED CURRENCY Currency whose use is tightly controlled by the responsible government

BOND Certificate issued by a borrower giving the holder the right to receive a specified sum on the due date of maturity and interest payments in the meantime, usually paid annually or semi-annually. Can be fixed or floating rate. Maturity is generally for ten years. It is called short-term if less than five years, medium-term if between six and fifteen years

BONUS ISSUE Issue of new equity shares given free to the existing shareholders. Sometimes called 'scrip' or 'capitalization' issue

BOOK LOSS/GAIN The notional profit or loss arising from the difference between the cost of a security and its market value at any one time

BOOK VALUE The value given to a security in the accounting books of the holder

BOUGHT DEAL A bond issue that is completely bought up by a bank or syndicate on fixed terms

BREAK A sharp fall in prices; the opposite of a bulge

BROKER Recognized agent in securities, currencies and commodities who acts as middleman between buyer and seller. In UK, as distinct from jobber he only acts as retailer for a client and does not quote prices himself. In the money markets, he matches bids and offers but does not operate on his own account

BROKERAGE Fee or commission charged by broker

BUILDING SOCIETY UK equivalent of US savings and loans. Developed to collect deposits and lend on housing

BULGE A sharp rise in prices; the opposite of a break

BULL A rising market. A bull is one trading on the expectation of a price rise

BULLDOG BOND Bond denominated in sterling issued by non-UK resident in the UK market

BULLET A borrowing in which the repayment of all the principal is made at maturity

BUSTED CONVERTIBLE US term for a convertible issue made worthless by the fall in the value of the underlying equity

BUY-IN When a security is purchased at market price to complete a deal when the seller has failed to deliver. The buyer then goes elsewhere in the market to 'buy in' the agreed quantity of securities. Also, in futures markets, to close (cover) a short position

BUY ON CLOSE To purchase at the end of the trading session at a price within the closing range

BUY ON OPENING To purchase at the beginning of the session within the opening range. Used mostly in commodity futures markets

CALL The right of an issuer of bonds to repay before maturity, at a given price and on any given day

CALL OPTION An options contract giving the holder the right to buy equity or commodity future at a certain sum by, or at, a specified date

CAPITAL MARKETS The market for securities, usually used when referring to medium- or long-term instruments in contrast to the money markets for short-term debt

CASH AND CARRY Simultaneous purchase of a commodity for physical delivery and the sale of the same commodity for delivery at a future date

CASH COMMODITY The physical commodity or actual share on which futures or options are written

CASH MARKET Used to refer to the market in the underlying currency or money instrument on which futures and options are traded

CATS Certificates of Accrual on Treasury Securities. Securities representing the principle of a US Treasury Bond, stripped of its interest payments (coupons), to make it a vehicle for capital appreciation only. Similar instruments are TIGRs in the USA and STAGs and ZEBRAs in the UK

CD Certificate of deposit: a negotiable, interest-bearing certificate issued by a bank usually for up to ninety days' maturity, though sometimes longer

CEDEL One of the two eurobond clearing houses, based in Luxembourg and owned by a group of banks

CFTC Commodity Futures Trading Commission: an independent Federal agency established in 1975

CHIPS The New York-based Clearing House Interbank Payment System, founded in 1970. Payments made through the system are now settled at the end of the same day

CLEARING HOUSE An organization on a commodity exchange that arranges for the settlement of trades made on the floor

CLEARING MEMBER Member firm of a clearing house. Has to be a member of the relevant commodities exchange, although not all exchange members are clearing members

CLEARING SYSTEM A organization that accepts securities for safe-keeping and handles transactions

CLOSE The end of a trading session

CLOSING DAY Used in the bond markets to indicate the day when the bond or securities in a new issue are handed over to syndicate members in exchange for the payment

CLOSING RANGE Prices recorded during the official CLOSE

CLUB DEAL A syndicated loan in which each participant has an equal commitment

CO-MANAGER One of a group of managers in a syndicated loan or bond issue, normally with a higher level of commitment than an ordinary syndicate member

COMMERCIAL PAPER Short-term paper (up to 270 days in USA) unsecured against any of the assets of the issuer. Developed in America and now starting up in the euromarkets

COMMITMENT Amount that a bank has agreed to lend as its part of a syndicated loan

COMMON STOCK US term for ordinary shares

CONTRACT Term used in financial markets to describe a unit of trading for a financial future; also the actual agreement between two parties in a futures transaction

CONTRACT MONTH The month in which a futures contract comes to fruition; also known as delivery month

CONVERSION Usually applied in bond markets to the offer of shares or new bonds for old ones when the original bond issue matures

CONVERSION ISSUE When a new issue is timed to coincide with the maturing of an older issue

CONVERSION PREMIUM/DISCOUNT The additional cost (premium) or gain (discount), expressed as a percentage, of buying the shares on conversion compared with their market price at the time

CONVERSION PRICE The price at which the bond is convertible into shares

CONVERSION RATIO The ratio of shares that may be obtained on converting a bond (see next entry)

CONVERTIBLE BOND A bond that can be converted, on the holder's option, into the shares of the issuing company, or its parent company, usually within a specified time

COUPON The annual rate of interest on a security

COVER In futures trading, the purchase of futures to offset a previous transaction, most commonly used for short covering. In equity markets cover is used to describe the extent to which a company's dividend is matched by its earnings

COVERED-INTEREST ARBITRAGE Borrowing in one currency, converting it to another currency, then selling the second currency for future delivery against the first

CROSS-CURRENCY EXPOSURE A company's position when its debt-service obligations in a currency are inadequately covered by its income in that currency

CURRENCY-LINKED BOND A bond expressed in terms of one currency although fixed by reference to another

CURRENCY SWAP Transfer of equivalent debt obligations in different currencies between two counterpart companies

CURRENT OPTION The current rate of interest on a floating-rate security

CURRENT YIELD The return to a holder of a security expressed as the percentage interest rate, or coupon, on the market price (e.g. 'The current yield is 11.3 per cent')

DAYLIGHT EXPOSURE LIMIT Foreign-exchange market term for the limits set by a bank on its dealings in a specified currency during any one working day

DAY ORDER An order in the commodities markets placed for execution during a trading day; it automatically lapses if it is not executed by the end of that day

DAY TRADING Establishing and liquidating a position within the same day

DEBENTURE Strictly, any evidence of indebtedness. In international markets bonds secured only against the unpledged assets and general standing of a company; in the UK nearly the opposite – a bond that is secured against the assets of the issuing company

DEFERRED FUTURES The most distant months of a futures contract, as opposed to 'near-bys'

DELAYED DELIVERY A clause in a new issue allowing certain investors to take up part of the issue after the official closing date

DELIVERY The physical delivery of a commodity or financial instrument in futures trading

DELIVERY MONTH The month in which this takes place

DELIVERY PRICE The price, fixed by the clearing house, at which the deliveries are invoiced

DEPOSIT The initial outlay required to open a futures position, returnable after the position is closed

DIRECT PLACEMENT The direct placing of an issue of securities with financial institutions without using underwriters

DISCRETIONARY ACCOUNT An account for which buying and selling can be carried out without the prior consent of the client

DISINTERMEDIATION Direct investment or market borrowing by companies without going through a bank or other financial intermediary

DIVIDEND YIELD Dividend per share, calculated as a percentage of the market price of the share

DOCUMENTATION The details of the issuer and the securities being offered in a new offer; also the underwriting agreements

DOUBLE OPTION An option to buy or sell a commodity, financial future or security

DROP-LOCK A floating-rate bond that automatically switches to fixed-rate interest if rates fall below a predetermined point

ECU European currency unit, a composite currency made up of the currencies of the members of the EEC

EFTPOS Electronic Funds Transfer at Point of Sale. Systems which allow the funds to be switched automatically as goods are bought in a store

EFTS Electronic Funds Transfer System. System that allows funds to be switched by electronic communication rather than paper

ELIGIBLE LIABILITIES UK term for the liabilities that may be allowed in calculating the reserve–asset ratio of British banks

EQUITY Shares in a company; also, in futures trading, used to describe the residual value of a futures trading account assuming its liquidation at the prevailing market price

EUROBOND Internationally traded bond denominated in a *eurocurrency*, a currency held by a non-resident of the currency's country

EUROCLEAR One of the two main clearing organizations for the eurobond market based in Brussels and operated under contract by Morgan Guaranty

EURODOLLAR US dollar held by a non-resident of the US, usually in the form of a deposit with a bank outside the US or the foreign branch of an American bank

EURONOTE Short-term notes issued on a three- to six-month basis in the syndicated loan market, usually structured as a medium-term loan in which the underwriters agree to issue notes on request

EVENING UP In futures markets, buying or selling to offset an existing position

EVERGREEN CREDIT A credit without fixed maturity that a bank can, usually annually, opt to convert to a term credit

EX COUPON Security excluding the right to the coupon, or interest rate, on the bond

EX DIVIDEND Excluding the right to the dividend on a share

EXTENDABLE A bond that gives the holder the right to extend the initial maturity by set periods at specified moments

FACE VALUE The amount, excluding interest, due to a bondholder on maturity of bond, or security; also called par, or nominal value

FED FUNDS Deposits by banks in the US Federal Reserve System

FEDERAL FUNDS RATE The rate at which the funds are trading among US banks and financial institutions, taken as the key rate in US interest rates

FIRM ORDER An order to buy or sell a security that can be executed without further confirmation within the time allotted.

FIRST NOTICE DAY The first date on which notices of intention to deliver financial instruments or commodities against futures are authorized within the delivery month

FISCAL AGENT A bank appointed by the issuer of a bond to act as its agent

FLAT INCOME BOND US term for bond quoted at a price that includes accrued interest

FLOATING-RATE INTEREST Interest rate changed regularly, on a set formula, to reflect changes in market rates. Usually calculated at so many points above interbank rate; hence floating-rate CDs, floating-rate bonds, floating-rate notes (FRNs), etc.

FLOOR BROKER On commodity exchanges, a broker who is paid a fee for executing orders for clearing members

FLOOR TRADER A commodity-exchange member who generally trades on his own account or for an account controlled by him; also called a 'local'

FRA Forward-rate agreement: custom-made hedge, usually drawn up by a bank, enabling a client to fix an interest rate for up to three years

FOREIGN BOND A bond issued by a foreign borrower in the domestic market of a particular country and denominated in that country's currency

FORWARD CONTRACT A contract for a financial instrument or commodity to be settled on a mutually agreed future date. Contrasts with futures contract in that it is not standardized

FRN See FLOATING-RATE INTEREST

FRONT-END FEE The fee paid by a borrower to the lead manager at the start of a syndicated loan or issue

FUNGIBLE Interchangeable

FUNGIBLE SECURITIES Identical securities, without specific serial numbers and assignations, that are allotted as needed by a clearing house

FUTURES CONTRACT A standardized contract covering the sale or purchase at a future date of a set quantity of commodity, financial instruments, cash, etc.

FCM Futures Commission Merchant: a US term indicating a firm or individual licensed to engage in futures trading for others in return for a commission fee

GENSAKI Japanese term for the sale or purchase of a bond for a set temporary period

GILTS UK government securities, described as 'gilt-edged' because such low risk is attached to them

GOVERNMENT NATIONAL MORTGAGE ASSOCIATION Popularly known as 'Ginnie Mae': US government agency that approves and guarantees issue of mortgage-backed securities

GRACE PERIOD Period between issue and first repayment of principal in a syndicated loan

GREY MARKET Euromarket term for the market in a new issue before the formal offering of the issue

GROSS SPREAD The total fees and commission on a new issue, normally expressed as a percentage of the face value of the securities

GROSS-UP The provision of extra payments by the borrower to compensate for withholding or other taxes on the investor

HEDGING The technique of limiting risk, usually through the purchase of futures or options on a commodities or financial position giving the opposite result. A 'hedge' is the sale or purchase of the futures position to effect this counterbalance

INFO RATE Money-market rates quoted by dealers for 'information only', not as a firm quote

INSTITUTIONAL POT US term for portion of an issue reserved for institutions

INTERBANK RATES The rates at which international banks place deposits with each other

IRC Interest-rate cap (collar or guarantee): agreement, written by bank or institution, that puts a ceiling on a floating-rate loan for up to twelve years.

INTEREST-RATE DIFFERENTIAL The difference between interest rates among currencies on a security with the same maturity

INTEREST-RATE SWAP Exchange between two counterparties of interest-rate obligations on their debt, usually to transfer fixed- and floating-rate interest between the two

'IN THE MONEY' When a security to be bought at a fixed price under a warrant option or conversion clause is less than the market price, the holder is said to be 'in the money'. If the opposite is the case, he is 'out of the money'

INVERTED MARKET A futures market in which the nearer months are selling at a higher premium than the more distant months

INVITATION TELEX Telex sent by a lead manager of a syndicated loan to prospective syndicate members asking them to join

ISSUE DATE Date from which accrued interest on a security is calculated

ISSUE PRICE The gross price, before the deduction of commissions, etc., placed on an issue of securities, expressed as a percentage of principal amount

JUNK BONDS High-risk bonds issued for low- or unrated companies in the US

KERB TRADING Trading after close of the official market

LAST NOTICE DAY The final day on which notice can be give of intention to deliver against a futures contract

LAST TRADING DAY The last day, under an exchange's rules, for trading a particular delivery in the futures market

LEAD MANAGER The managing bank in a new issue or loan, responsible for the co-ordination of the issue, selecting co-managers, 'running the book' and dealing with the borrower

LEVERAGE US term for extent of indebtedness. Used for margin–capital ratio in commodities and futures trading

LIMIT PRICE On commodity exchanges, the maximum amount that a price can move up or down during a trading session

LIMIT ORDER Instruction to execute a trade at a set price or better

LIBID The London Interbank Bid Rate: the rate at which banks buy deposits

LIBOR The London Interbank Offered Rate: the rate of interest offered by banks in the London eurodollar market. Used as the benchmark for a large proportion of international loans and floating-rate issues

LOCK-UP Period between the closing date of an issue and the issue of actual securities, used as a procedure to prevent sale to US residents during initial distribution when the issue has not yet been registered with the Securities and Exchange Commission

LONG In futures trading, someone who has bought contracts in expectation of a price rise but has yet to close out his position with an offsetting sale

LONG HEDGE Purchase of a futures contract in anticipation of physical purchases in the cash market, to guard against changes in the cash price

MANDATE Borrower's authorization to proceed with loan or bond issue on terms agreed with lead manager

MARGIN In bond markets, used to express the difference between bid and asked price. On loans, the rate of interest over and above reference price, e.g. LIBOR, expressed as a percentage. In commodity markets, a cash deposit with the broker for each contract as a guarantee of fulfilment of the futures contract. Also called the 'spread' in bond and loan markets and the 'security deposit' in futures markets

MARGIN CALL, OR MAINTENANCE MARGIN A demand for additional cash funds to ensure that a customer's margin does not fall below a certain percentage in the event of a price fall in his position

MARKET-MAKER Securities house, trader or other financial institution that is consistently ready to quote a firm price on a security

MARKET ORDER Order for immediate execution given to a broker or agent to buy or sell at the best obtainable price

MATURITY Date on which a loan or bond becomes due

MAXIMUM PRICE FLUCTUATION In commodity markets, the highest amount that a price can change up or down in a trading session under the rules of the exchange. As limit price

MINIMUM PRICE FLUCTUATION Smallest allowable price movement on a futures contract

MIT Market if touched: in commodities trading, a price order that automatically becomes a market order if the price is reached

MONEY MARKET Broad term normally applying to the market for interbank deposits and certificates of deposit, but also used more generally for the market in money instruments of short-term maturity (i.e. less than a year)

MULTI-CURRENCY Loan or bond repayable in more than one currency

NAKED POSITION Unhedged position in the futures and options markets

NEARBYS The nearest active trading month in the financial futures market

NEGATIVE PLEDGE Promise by a bond issuer that he will not offer better terms on a similar bond during the lifetime of the issue and that, if he does, the same terms will then be applied to the original issue

NET WORTH Total assets of a company minus its liabilities

NEW TIME On the London Stock Exchange, trading for the next account period in the last two days of the old one

NIF Note-issuance facility: arrangement under which a manager, or group of managers, agrees to underwrite an issue of short-term paper as and when required and to back the facility with medium-term bank credit should the notes not find a market

NOMINAL PRICE Estimated price for a security during a trading session in which no deals were done

NOMINAL YIELD The interest on the face value of a bond. Same as interest coupon

NOMINEE Person or company holding a security on behalf of another to protect his anonymity

NON-CALLABLE Bonds that cannot be redeemed by a borrower within a specified time from issue

NOTE A certificate of indebtedness like a bond but used most frequently of short-term issues

NUMERAIRE A money unit, such as the ECU, that is not in itself tradeable but is made up of tradeable units

OBF Off-shore banking facility: bank subsidiary allowed to transact business, such as eurocurrency dealing, that is normally prohibited to domestic banks

OBU Off-shore banking unit. See OBF

ODD LOT A block of securities smaller than the usual lot in which they are traded

OFFER Willingness to sell a security or futures contract

OFFSET As evening up and liquidation in a futures market, the complete cover on a futures position by the equivalent sale or purchase of a futures contract in the same month

OPEN CONTRACTS Futures contracts that have been bought or sold without the transaction being covered by the physical purchase or sale or commodity or financial instrument

OPEN INTEREST The number of open futures contracts

OPENING Period at the beginning of a trading session officially designated as the opening and in which an opening price is recorded

OPTION Contract giving the purchaser the right to buy ('call' option) or sell ('put' option) an underlying security or futures contract within or at a specified time

OTC Over-the-counter: Trading in securities or shares outside the formal stock exchanges

OVERBOUGHT/OVERSOLD Market thought to be in danger of going down or up as a correction to excessive buying or selling of securities

PAR Price of principal at which an issuer of bonds agrees to redeem them at maturity

PARTICIPANT Bank taking part in a lending syndicate

PARTICIPATION The amount that a bank contributes to a syndicated loan

PARTLY PAID Security on which part of the issue price has been paid but the remainder is still to be paid at a specified future date

PERPETUAL Floating-rate without a time limit. A recent alternative to equity

PHYSICALS Actual commodities rather than futures contracts

PLACING POWER Ability of an institution to place a new issue with investors

POINT In bond markets, 1 per cent of the value of the principal. In US stock markets, $1. In futures markets, a minimum price fluctuation

POSITION The number of securities or futures contracts held by a dealer (long position) or the number of securities or contracts that he has agreed to deliver but has not yet purchased (short position)

PRE-EMPTIVE RIGHT The right of equity holders to maintain their relative share in a company in the event of a new issue of equity holdings

PREFERRED OR PREFERENCE SHARES Fixed-dividend shares ranked above ordinary or common shares

PREMIUM Amount by which the price of a security exceeds its face value. In the futures market, the excess of one futures contract price over that of another

PRIMARY MARKET The new market for a new issue of securities in which payment is made to the issuer. Once dealing starts between traders, the market is a secondary one

PRIME RATE US term for interest rate charged by banks to their most creditworthy customers

PRINCIPAL Face value of a security excluding premium or interest payments. Interest is calculated on the principal

PRIVATE PLACEMENT An issue placed with one or a limited number of investors, not normally listed in Europe or registered with the SEC in the US

PROSPECTUS Document setting out details of the issue and borrower in a new issue of securities

PUBLIC OFFERING A registered or listed offering of securities to the public

PURCHASE FUND Sum set aside by the issuer of a bond to buy back a set amount of the issue if the price falls below a specified level, usually par

PUT OPTION An option to sell securities, commodities or financial instruments at an agreed price within or at a predetermined time

RALLY Rise in a market after a decline

RATING Rating agencies' grading, by letter, of the creditworthiness of borrowers in the USA

REACTION Decline in market prices following an upward movement

REDEMPTION Extinguishing of a bond or security through payment to the holders

REGISTRATION Requirement in the USA for a company to be registered under the Securities Exchange Act of 1934 before it can issue securities on the exchanges

REPURCHASE AGREEMENT (REPO) Agreement to sell a security at one price and to buy it back at another price in the future (the difference between the prices being partly in lieu of interest), thus providing the seller with cash for the intervening period

RETRACTABLE Euromarket term for security issued by a borrower with the right of early redemption

REVOLVING CREDIT A loan that allows the borrower to use the facility and to repay it at his discretion during a specified period

ROUND LOT Minimum unit of a security that can be normally traded

ROUNDTRIPPING When a company takes advantage of a short-term rise in market rates to a level higher than its own borrowing rates, thus enabling the company to borrow and lend on the market at a profit

RUF Revolving underwriting facility: like N I Fs, a line of credit underwritten by a syndicate in which the borrower can issue short-term notes if market conditions permit, with a legal guarantee that underwriters will provide the funds whatever the success of the note issue

RUNNING THE BOOKS The lead manager's role in organizing a new issue of securities, keeping both borrower and underwriters informed

SAMURAI BOND Japanese term for bond issued by a foreign entity in Japan, denominated in yen and purchasable by non-residents of Japan

SCALP To trade for small gains, normally establishing and liquidating positions continuously within a short time

SCRIP ISSUE A free share issue to existing shareholders

SEASONED SECURITIES Securities that have traded in the secondary markets for at least ninety days. The majority of eurobonds cannot be sold in the USA, unless registered, until seasoned

SECONDARY MARKET Market for bonds after initial issue

SECURITIES General term for bonds, shares or stock and other financial instruments

SELLING CONCESSION A deduction, expressed as percentage of face value, made to underwriters and selling group members as remuneration for their support of an issue

SELLING GROUP Institutions invited by an issue's lead manager to place an issue. They do not have management or underwriting obligations

SENIOR SECURITIES Securities with a prior claim for payment in the event of insolvency

SETTLEMENT DATE Day when a transaction is formally completed

SETTLEMENT PRICE In commodity markets the daily price at which the clearing house clears all trades, based on the closing range of the day's trading

SHORT Sale of a security or a futures contract without the cover of actual purchase, in expectation of a decline in price, as in 'short selling' and 'short hedge'

SINKING FUND A fund set aside for the repurchase by a borrower, at regular intervals, of part of a debt issue. The borrower has a legal obligation to use the fund fully, unlike a purchase fund

SNIF Short-term note-issuance facility: a variation on NIF

SNOW WHITE Warrants for debt issued separately, without a bond issue

SPECIAL BRACKET A group of participating banks in an issue or syndicated loan who appear in the advertisements, just below the managers, because of the large size of their commitment

SPLIT SPREAD A euromarket term for the provision of different interest rates during different periods of the life of a loan

SPREAD The same as margin. The rate of interest over the reference point in loans, the difference between bid and ask prices in the bond markets. In the futures markets, the simultaneous sale and purchase of the same instrument for delivery in different months or the sale and purchase of different contracts in the same month

STABILIZATION Action by managers of an issue to settle price through purchases in the secondary market

STAG UK term for a dealer or investor who buys a new issue with the intention of selling it immediately at a profit on the issue price

STOP-LOSS ORDER Order to buy or sell when a certain price is reached, either above or below the market price when the order was given

STRADDLE Technique of purchasing in one market, while simultaneously selling in another, the same futures contract

STRAIGHT BOND Fixed-rate bond without conversion

STREAKER Zero-coupon bond issued at a deep discount to give, by the time of redemption, a computed interest rate at face value on maturity

SUBORDINATED DEBT Debt that can claim, in the event of liquidation, only after the claims of other debts have been met

SWAP The exchange of debt obligations between two counter-parties to take advantage of differing interest rates or currency opportunities that each can obtain

SWITCHING In the futures market, liquidating an existing position and simultaneously re-establishing that position in another future on the same commodity or financial instrument

SYNDICATE Term for managers, underwriters and selling agents of a bond

TAP STOCK British government bond issued through the government broker at a stated price. Its supply to the market can be adjusted, like a tap, in order to influence the gilts market

TENDER Delivery against futures

TICK Commodities-market expression for change in price, either up or down

TIGRS Treasury Investment Growth Receipts: securities based on US Treasury bonds, stripped of coupons

TOMBSTONE An advertisement giving, as a matter of record, the details of a new issue or loan and listing terms, the name of the issuer, the amount and the names of the managers and underwriters or syndicate members

UNDERWRITING An agreement in which a group of securities houses, banks or other financial concerns guarantee to subscribe to a set proportion of a new issue, at a specified price, to ensure the issue's full subscription

UNSECURED LOANS AND NOTES Securities issued by a company, without charge, to its assets in the event of default

VALUE DATE Used in the foreign-currency and eurocurrency markets to signify the delivery date of funds to settle a transaction (usually seven days after the deal is agreed)

VANILLA ISSUE A straight fixed-rate bond issued according to the usual practice of that market

WARRANT A certificate attached to a bond or security giving the holder the right to buy shares in the issuer's company at a set price or to subscribe to future bond issues by the same issuer. Warrantable bonds are the bonds acquired by exercise of the certificate

WINGS Warrant into Negotiable Government Securities: an option giving the holder the right to buy U S Treasury bonds within a certain period at a set price

WITHHOLDING TAX Tax deducted at source on interest and dividend payments

YANKEE BOND Bond issued by non-U S entities in the U S market registered with the Securities and Exchange Commission

YEARLING British stock issued by municipal authorities, maturing within a year

YIELD Annualized return on an investment. Yield curve is the relationship between the return and maturity for a given number of securities

ZERO COUPON BOND A bond issued without interest coupon but at a discounted price on issue that will give a computed interest by the time it is redeemed at face value. Same as streaker

BIBLIOGRAPHY

General

The best source of information for the changes as they are now developing in
the financial world is the specialist press, notably the monthlies: the London-
based *Euromoney* and *The Banker* and the U S A-based *Institutional Investor*.
Detailed daily coverage is provided by the *Wall Street Journal* and the
Financial Times. Themes and institutions are the subject of frequent articles
in *Business Week*, *Fortune* and other business journals, while the *Economist*
publishes exceptionally well researched surveys of financial topics.

Among general books covering particular aspects of the financial scene are
Anthony Sampson's *The Money Lenders* (London, Hodder & Stoughton,
1981) on international banking, Martin Mayer's *The Money Bazaars* (New
York, New American Library, 1985) on US banking and Paul Ferris's
Gentlemen of Fortune (London, Weidenfeld & Nicolson, 1984) on investment
and merchant bankers.

Changes in themes and arguments have also been covered in speeches and
presentations at a number of recent conferences, including the 'Financial
Services Industry Forum', sponsored by Arthur Anderson and the *Institutional Investor* in Washington, D C, June 1984; the colloquium 'Shifting
Frontiers in Financial Markets', held by the Société Universitaire Euro-
péenne de Recherches Financières in Cambridge, England, March 1985;
and the regular conferences held in London on 'World Banking' and 'The
Euromarkets' by the *Financial Times* Business Conference and on developments in the City of London by Westminster and City Programmes.

The Scene

Aside from the above, the broad sweep of financial developments of the last
decade are summarized in the quarterly reports of the Bank of International
Settlements in Basle; the annual Financial Statistics of the OECD and its
occasional papers, especially R. M. Pecchioli's *The Internationalization of
Banking* (Paris, OECD, 1973); the regular papers on *International Capital
Markets* published by the International Monetary Fund, and the IMF Research Department's occasional papers on exchange rates and debt; the quarterly publications of the US Federal Reserve Banks, the *Bank of England
Bulletin*, and the regular publications of the Bank of Japan and the Bundesbank; and a series of publications by the Group of Thirty, particularly on the
foreign exchanges.

Most of the issues are tackled in depth, at least from an American viewpoint, in the *Handbook for Banking Strategy*, edited by Richard Aspinwall and Robert Eisenbeis (New York/Chichester, John Wiley, 1985) and, more popularly, in Michael Moffitt's *The World's Money: International Banking from Bretton Woods to the Brink of Insolvency* (London, Michael Joseph, 1983). See also the papers from the Global Interdependence Center conferences, published in *The Global Financial Structure in Transition*, edited by Joel McClellan (Lexington, M A, Lexington Books, 1985).

Technology

For general summaries of the state of the art, see the report of the Office of Technology Assessment, U S Congress, *Effects of Information Technology on Financial Services Systems* (Washington, D C, 1984), Peter Gallant's *Electronic Treasury Management* (Cambridge, Woodhead Faulkner, 1985) and a number of studies carried out by the Economist Intelligence Unit, consultants McKinsey and Co. and accountants Touche Ross.

The subject also receives regular covarage in the *American Banker*, the U K Institute of Bankers' *Banking World* and the London-based monthly *Banking Technology*.

For a history of Reuters, see John Lawrenson's and Lionel Barber's *The Price of Truth* (Edinburgh, Mainstream, 1985).

The Markets

Ian M. Kerr's *A History of the Eurobond Market: The First 21 Years* (London Euromoney Publications, 1984) gives the myth and facts on the rise of the eurobond market; the Group of Thirty's *The Foreign Exchange Market of the 1980s* (New York, 1985) gives the most authoritative snapshot of this field. For the bond and loan markets internationally the publications of the Research Department of Salomon Brothers and Morgan Guaranty's monthly *World Capital Markets* give the most up-to-date estimates of developments. Futures and options are explained in the publications of the Chicago Mercantile Exchange, the Chicago Board of Trade, the Philadelphia Exchange and others. Equity-market statistics are published annually by most of the major stock exchanges.

The Players

Aside from Paul Ferris's *Gentlemen of Fortune* (above), specific developments in Wall Street are covered in Tim Carrington's *The Year They Sold Wall Street* (Boston, Houghton Mifflin, 1985), an account of the Shearson/American Express merger, and in the financial press.

New York

Recent summaries of the changes in the regulatory regime for banks, thrifts and others include Alan Gart's *Banks, Thrifts and Insurance Companies: Surviving the 1980s* (Lexington, MA, Lexington Books, 1985), Thomas F. Cargill's and Gillian G. Garcia's *Financial Reform in the 1980s* (Stanford, Hoover Institution Press, 1985) and the hearings of the U S Senate Banking Committee.

The argument over the U S contribution to innovation is put forcibly in an article by Dimitri Vittas in *The Banker*, May 1985.

London

The most recent book on the developments in London is John Plender's and Paul Wallace's *The Square Mile* (London, Century, 1985). Other general surveys of the workings of the City of London are Hamish McRae's and Frances Cairncross's *Capital City*, rev. edn (London, Methuen, 1984), Kevin W. Wilson, *British Financial Institutions* (London, Pitman, 1983) and William M. Clarke's *Inside the City* (London, Allen & Unwin, 1979). Older books are Paul Ferris's *The City* (London, Gollancz, 1960) and Richard Spiegelberg's *The City* (London, Blond & Briggs, 1973). The position and problems of the Lloyd's insurance market are dealt with in Godfrey Hodgson's *In Utmost Good Faith* (London, Allen Lane, 1984). The early history of merchant banking is described in Stanley Chapman's *The Rise of Merchant Banking* (London, Allen & Unwin, 1984) and the modern practice in C. J. J. Clay's and B. S. Wheble's *Modern Merchant Banking* (Cambridge, Woodhead Faulkner, 1983).

Tokyo and Other Centres

The general background to the structure of Japanese finance is described in Andreas Prindle's *Japanese Finance* (New York/Chichester, John Wiley, 1985). The latest changes are dealt with comprehensively in the two-part study by the Japan Center for International Finance, *Study on the Internationalization of Tokyo's Money Markets* (Tokyo, 1984, 1985), in the annual *Japan Economic Almanac*, published in Tokyo by Nihon Keizai Shimbun, in Hamish McRae's study for the Group of Thirty, *Japan's Role in the Emerging Global Securities Market* (New York, 1985), and in the publications of the Ministry of Finance, the Federation of Bankers' Associations of Japan and the Association of Securities Houses.

Other Asian financial developments are reported in the *Far East Economic Review* and the *Asian Wall Street Journal*. Developments in the Middle East and other European centres are the subject of regular surveys by the *Financial Times*, the *International Herald Tribune* and the financial magazines. For Swiss banking traditions see Nicholas Faith's *Safety in Numbers* (London, Hamish Hamilton, 1982).

Regulation

The best general survey is *The Regulation of International Banking* by Richard Dale (Cambridge, Woodhead Faulkner, 1984). Occasional studies are published by the Bank of International Settlements and by the Group of Thirty (by Otmar Emminger, Henry Wallich and Michael Mussa); see also articles in the bulletins of the Federal Reserve Banks of the U S A and the European central banks. The Penn Square Bank collapse is dealt with in Philip Zweig's *Belly Up* (New York, Crown, 1985).

INDEX

INDEX